NEW EVANGELIZATION EDITION

W9-BEV-835

Christ Our Life

4

God Guides Us

Authors

Sisters of Notre Dame
Chardon, Ohio

Reviewers

Sister Mary Judith Bucco, S.N.D.

Sister Mary Grace Corbett, S.N.D.

Sister Margaret Mary Friel, S.N.D.

Sister Mary Jean Hoelke, S.N.D.

Sister Mary Cordell Kopec, S.N.D.

Sister Mary Carol Marek, S.N.D.

Sister Mary Donnalee Resar, S.N.D.

Sister Eileen Marie Skutt, S.N.D.

Sister Mary Jane Vovk, S.N.D.

LOYOLAPRESS.
A JESUIT MINISTRY
Chicago

Imprimatur

In accordance with c. 827, permission to publish is granted on April 16, 2014, by Most Reverend Francis J. Kane, Vicar General of the Archdiocese of Chicago. Permission to publish is an official declaration of ecclesiastical authority that the material is free from doctrinal and moral error. No legal responsibility is assumed by the grant of this permission.

Christ Our Life **found to be in conformity**

The Subcommittee on the Catechism, United States Conference of Catholic Bishops, has found this catechetical series, copyright 2016, to be in conformity with the *Catechism of the Catholic Church.*

Acknowledgments

Excerpts from the *New American Bible with Revised New Testament and Psalms* Copyright © 1991, 1986, 1970 Confraternity of Christian Doctrine, Inc., Washington, DC. All rights reserved. No portion of the *New American Bible* may be reprinted without permission in writing from the copyright holder.

Excerpts from the English translation of *The Roman Missal* © 2010, International Commission on English in the Liturgy Corporation (ICEL). All rights reserved.

Excerpts from the *Compendium of the Catechism of the Catholic Church* © 2005, Libreria Editrice Vaticana. Used with permission. All rights reserved. No portion of this text may be reproduced by any means without written permission from the copyright holder.

Excerpts from the *United States Catholic Catechism for Adults* © 2006 United States Conference of Catholic Bishops (USCCB). Used with permission. All rights reserved. No portion of this text may be reproduced by any means without written permission from the copyright holder.

Loyola Press has made every effort to locate the copyright holders for the cited works used in this publication and to make full acknowledgment for their use. In the case of any omissions, the publisher will be pleased to make suitable acknowledgments in future editions.

Cover art: Lori Lohstoeter
Cover design: Loyola Press and Jill Arena
Interior design: Think Design Group and Kathryn Seckman Kirsch, Loyola Press

ISBN-13: 978-0-8294-3962-5, ISBN-10: 0-8294-3962-5

© 2016 Loyola Press and
Sisters of Notre Dame, Chardon, Ohio

For more information related to the English translation of the *Roman Missal, Third Edition,* see www.loyolapress.com/romanmissal.

Dedicated to St. Julie Billiart, foundress of the Sisters of Notre Dame, in gratitude for her inspiration and example

LOYOLAPRESS.
A JESUIT MINISTRY

3441 N. Ashland Avenue
Chicago, Illinois 60657
(800) 621-1008
www.loyolapress.com

20 21 22 23 Web 10 9 8 7 6

Contents

(continued next page)

Especially for Families

A Note to Families begins on page v. There is a Letter Home at the beginning of each unit. At the end of each unit, you will find a Family Feature that explores ways to nurture faith at home.

(continued from previous page)

The New Evangelization

Gather and Go Forth pages at the end of each chapter support faith, knowledge, and the goals of discipleship.

Note to Families

Goals of This Year's Program

This year your child will be learning how God calls us to live with him forever. The commandments are taught as signs of God's love, and the Beatitudes are introduced as Jesus' way to happiness. Your child is led to a greater appreciation of the sacraments and is encouraged to respond joyfully to God's call to live in the spirit of his love.

A Family Program

Because your faith makes a profound impact on your child, the *Christ Our Life* series provides a Building Family Faith feature at the end of chapters. Usually one chapter is presented in class each week. The activities in the Building Family Faith encourage you to nurture your child's faith by sharing your own response to God. Building Family Faith begins by stating the goals of the chapter. Family activities that promote these aims are listed under four topics:

Reflect
suggests a Scripture reference related to the topic of the chapter.

Discuss as a Family
provides questions to help you apply the Scripture reading to daily life.

Pray
sums up the message for the week in a short prayer that everyone can pray daily. This prayer can be copied and posted on the refrigerator or a mirror. You may add it to meal prayers or other family prayer times.

Do
provides ideas for sharing at meals and for other family activities related to the message of the chapter. You may wish to read all the suggestions to the family and then decide which to do that week. You may also wish to choose other activities that family members suggest.

You are urged to help your child evaluate his or her growth at the end of each unit by discussing with your child the goals on the Looking Back page at the end of each unit.

Each of the units in this book ends with four Family Feature pages that suggest ways to engage the entire family through fun projects, discussion, and review activities.

You can also help your child refer to What Every Catholic Should Know on pages 233–256 and the We Remember sections at the end of chapters.

Note to Families

Ten Principles to Nurture Your Child's Faith

1. Listen with your heart as well as with your head.

2. Encourage wonder and curiosity in your child.

3. Coach your child in empathy early. It's a building block for morality.

4. Display religious artwork in your home. This will serve as a steady witness that faith is an important part of life.

5. Gently guide your child to a life of honesty.

6. Whenever appropriate, model for your child how to say "I'm sorry."

7. Eat meals together regularly as a family. It will be an anchor for your child in days to come.

8. Pray together in good times and bad. Worship together regularly as a family.

9. Be generous to those who need help. Make helping others an important focus of your life as a family.

10. See your child for the wonder that God made. Communicate your conviction that your child was created for a noble purpose—to serve God and others in this life and to be happy with God forever in the next.

Visit **www.christourlife.com** for more family resources.

We Come to Know God

See what love the Father has bestowed on us that we may be called the children of God.

1 John 3:1

A Letter Home

Dear Parents and Family,

Welcome! You have an exciting role ahead in supporting your child's learning about the faith. Your interest, participation, and discussion will expand your fourth grader's understanding of these lessons and convey their importance.

In Unit One, the children will discover the many ways God is reaching out to us. They first learn how God reveals himself in creation and especially in his Son, Jesus. Not only does God speak through Jesus, but Jesus is God, speaking and acting. The children will grow to see God's hand in creation and to respond to his call with a real desire to learn more about him. You can help them identify God's handiwork in the world around them.

The children will learn that the key message of the Bible is that God loves us. A better understanding of Scripture will help them develop a devotion to and a new respect for the Word of God. You, too, can gain insight into the readings at Mass with the Sunday Connection found in the Resources section at www.christourlife.com.

This first unit also describes how God continues to reach out to us through the Church. The authority that Jesus gave to the Apostles is the same authority handed down to today's pope and bishops. The children will be encouraged to show their appreciation for Church leaders as well as to use their own talents to help spread the good news of Jesus' Resurrection through prayer; through their efforts at school, at home, and in the community; and through their example. This is a worthy goal for your whole family.

At the end of each chapter in this unit, the children will bring home a review of the chapter along with either the Building Family Faith page or the Family Feature section. These features give you a quick review of what your child learned and offer practical ways to reinforce the lesson at home so that the whole family may benefit.

Visit **www.christourlife.com** for more family resources.

God Reveals Himself to Us Through His Son

God Calls Us to Be His Friends

"Jack, come over here," Matthew called excitedly as Jack walked into the classroom the first day back to school after vacation. "Wait till you hear what I did this summer!"

- What may Matthew have wanted to tell Jack?

- Why are we so eager to tell our friends about our summer?

God calls us friends. He reveals himself to us because he loves us. God reveals himself as three Persons—Father, Son, and Holy Spirit. We call this the Trinity. God wants us to come to know him better so that we will love him more. You will come to know God in many ways, but especially through Jesus.

Jesus calls each of us to share God's friendship. This year you will learn how to live the way a friend of God does. You will study the commandments he gave, which guide us to happiness here and to perfect happiness with God forever.

God Reveals Himself in Creation

None of us has seen God. How can we know him? We listen to God as he reveals, or tells us about, himself. God reveals himself to us in many ways.

All the things God has created tell us something about him. They tell us that God is great and good and loving!

God created everything for us to use and to enjoy. How good God is!

O Lord, How Great and Good You Are!

O Lord, my God, how great you are! You put springs of cool water in the valleys, where the wild animals come to drink. The birds make their nests in the trees.

You make fresh grass grow for the cattle and bring forth crops from the soil so that people may have food to eat. How many are your works, O Lord God!

adapted from Psalm 104:1, 10–12, 14, 24

Write a postcard to a friend describing a nice place to play outdoors near your home.

Postcard

postage

To:_____

What does your description of creation tell you about God?

God Reveals Himself Through Jesus

God reveals himself in the words he speaks to us and in the deeds he does for us. God reveals himself perfectly through Jesus.

Two thousand years ago the Son of God became man. This mystery is called the Incarnation. Jesus is both God and man. Why did God become man? The Bible tells us:

> "For God so loved the world that he gave his only Son, so that everyone who believes in him might not perish but might have eternal life."
>
> John 3:16

> At the Last Supper, Philip said to Jesus, "Master, show us the Father, and that will be enough for us!" Jesus answered, "Have I been with you for so long a time and you still do not know me, Philip? Whoever has seen me has seen the Father. . . . The words that I speak to you I do not speak on my own. The Father who dwells in me is doing his works. Believe me that I am in the Father and the Father is in me."
>
> adapted from John 14:8–11

In many ways, Jesus reveals how much God our Father loves us. Jesus' words and deeds tell us how great and good God is. He shows us God's kindness, forgiveness, and love for the poor. God wants us to show loving concern and care for those who are poor too.

5

Jesus Invites Us to Believe

On the first Easter evening, when Jesus came to the apostles, Thomas was not with them. Thomas did not believe the apostles when they told him that Jesus was risen from the dead. Thomas said, "Unless I see the mark of the nails in his hands and put my finger into the nailmarks and put my hand into his side, I will not believe."

A week later Jesus came to the apostles again, and Thomas was with them. Then Jesus said to Thomas, "Put your finger here and see my hands, and bring your hand and put it into my side, and do not be unbelieving, but believe."

Thomas answered, "My Lord and my God!"

Jesus said,

> "Have you come to believe because you have seen me? Blessed are those who have not seen and have believed."
>
> adapted from John 20:24–29

We believe without seeing because we have faith. Faith is a precious gift from God that helps us to believe in him. It makes us able to trust in him. God is always truthful; he cannot deceive us.

When we were baptized, God gave us the gift of faith and a share in his own life. Faith leads us to enjoy eternal life with God. Through his Church, Jesus helps our faith to deepen. Our faith becomes stronger when we pray and celebrate the sacraments, when we listen to God's Word and study the Church's teachings, and when we do what God tells us to do.

A Moment with Jesus

Think about the postcard you wrote earlier in the chapter. Invite Jesus to join you in that special place you described. Thank him for his awesome gifts of creation. Ask him to help you deepen your faith. Tell him how much you love him, and enjoy knowing how much he loves you.

How We Come to Know Jesus Today

Draw lines to the words that complete the sentences.

We meet Jesus in the   •   • Scripture.

We read about Jesus in   •   • people.

Jesus teaches us through the •   • sacraments.

We see Jesus in other   •   • Church.

Think of how you and your family do things together in your home that help you know Jesus better, such as reading, praying, or helping someone. In the house, draw yourself and your family doing that activity.

A Faith Puzzle

Fill in the puzzle with the missing words.

1. Faith leads us to eternal l _____ .

2. In Baptism we s _____ God's life.

3. Faith is the power to b _____ .

4. When we believe, we t _____ in God.

5. God tells only the t _____ , not lies.

We Remember

How does God reveal himself?
God reveals himself through creation, Scripture, and perfectly through Jesus.

How can we help God's gift of faith to grow?
We can help our faith to grow by praying, celebrating the sacraments, listening to God's Word, studying the Church's teachings, and doing what God tells us.

We Respond

Act of Faith (adapted)
O my God, I firmly believe that you are one God in three divine Persons: Father, Son, and Holy Spirit. I believe that your divine Son became man and died for our sins, and that he will come to judge the living and the dead. I believe these and all the truths which the holy Catholic Church teaches, because you have revealed them, who can neither deceive nor be deceived.
Amen.

Building Family Faith

CHAPTER SUMMARY We believe God created us out of love, and we come to know God through creation, his words and deeds, and his Son, Jesus. We respond to God's love with faith.

REFLECT
For God so loved the world that he gave his only Son, so that everyone who believes in him might not perish but might have eternal life.
John 3:16–17

DISCUSS AS A FAMILY
• how God reveals himself through nature, other people, the Church, and Jesus.
• some ways your family can grow in faith.

PRAY
Lord, help me grow strong in my faith.

DO
• Notice what amazes or delights you at a park, a nature conservatory, or even in your own backyard and realize that these are signs of God.
• At mealtime name one person, place, thing, or experience that helped you realize God's love.
• Read a story or watch a family movie about believing, such as *Field of Dreams*.

Visit **www.christourlife.com** for more family resources.

Gather and Go Forth

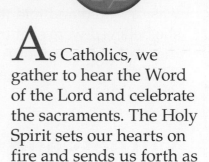

CHAPTER 1

Know and Proclaim

We share God's loving care with all those we come to know.

We Know Our Faith	We Proclaim Our Faith
We know that God is good and loves us because he created everything in the world for us to use and enjoy.	As Catholics, we show God gratitude for all the wonderful things he has given us. We show gratitude by praying simple prayers of thanks and by treating the gifts God gives us with reverence.
God reveals himself to us perfectly through Jesus. We know how great and good God is by knowing the Person of Jesus.	We come to know God better when we follow Jesus' example. We come to know God's love and compassion when we serve those who are poor and others in need.
God gives us the gift of faith when we are baptized. Jesus gave us his Church and the sacraments to deepen our faith.	During Mass, Catholics celebrate the Sacrament of the Eucharist. When we receive Christ's Body and Blood, our faith is nourished.

As Catholics, we gather to hear the Word of the Lord and celebrate the sacraments. The Holy Spirit sets our hearts on fire and sends us forth as disciples to live our faith.

"Go into the whole world and proclaim the gospel to every creature."

Mark 16:15

Test Your Catholic Knowledge

Fill in the circle that best completes the sentence.

Jesus, the Son of God, became incarnate of the Virgin Mary through the power of the Holy Spirit. In assuming a human nature, Jesus did not lose his divine nature. This mystery is called the:

○ Ascension ○ Incarnation

○ Assumption ○ Immaculate Conception

A Catholic to Know

Joan of Arc lived in France during a time of war when the country had no leader to inspire justice. Joan believed Saint Michael and other saints visited her with messages from God telling her to lead the French army. While Joan seemed an unlikely person for the job, she had great faith. She led the French army to victory over the English army in 1429 but was captured and told to deny hearing the voices she believed were sent by God. Joan did not deny the truth. Like Joan of Arc, we are called to show our faith by example even when it is difficult.

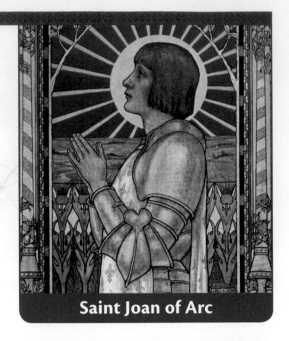
Saint Joan of Arc

Witness and Share

These sentences describe what Catholics believe. Listen carefully as they are read. Ask yourself, "How strong are my Catholic beliefs?"

My Way to Faith

- I pray so I can know Jesus better.

- I know God created the world for me to use, care for, share justly with others, and enjoy.

- I experience God's love when I help those in need.

- I celebrate the sacraments to deepen my faith.

- I believe God reveals himself as three Persons—Father, Son, and Holy Spirit.

Share Your Faith

Think of one way you followed Jesus' example this week. Write your ideas on the lines. Invite a friend to share a way he or she was inspired by Jesus' life. Pray that your example inspires others.

_____

_____

_____

_____

God Speaks to Us in Scripture

God Reveals Himself in Scripture

At every celebration of the Eucharist, the Scripture is read aloud. At the end of the first reading, the reader says, "The Word of the Lord." We answer, "Thanks be to God." A deacon or priest reads from the Gospels. He ends with the words, "The Gospel of the Lord," and we answer, "Praise to you, Lord Jesus Christ!"

The Bible is a very special book. The Church tells us that God reveals himself to us in Scripture. We call the Bible *Sacred Scripture*, which means "holy writing."

Sacred Scripture is made up of many books written over hundreds of years. The Church teaches us that God **inspired,** or worked within the minds of, the Scripture writers. That is why we believe Scripture is the Word of God.

The Bible is separated into two parts. The Old Testament is about what God did for his people during the time before Jesus came. The New Testament is about the words and deeds of Jesus and the early Church.

> In Scripture God comes to meet his children with great love and speaks with them.
>
> adapted from *Dogmatic Constitution on Divine Revelation*, Chapter VI, Article 2

Scripture Tells God's Message of Love

Both parts of the Bible tell us about God's love for us.

The Old Testament

The Old Testament is full of stories about God's love for his chosen people. Some of the books show how God revealed himself to the **Hebrews**, led them out of Egypt, and gave them his laws of love, making them his own people.

Parts of the Old Testament tell how God wanted his people to live. Many books record the messages God gave his people through the **prophets**, who were sent by God to teach his people.

In the Book of Psalms, God shows his people how to pray. The psalms are prayers of praise, thanksgiving, petition, and sorrow. God's people sang the psalms. So did Jesus. We say them or sing them at Mass.

The New Testament

The New Testament tells how Jesus showed us God's love. There are four Gospels, according to Matthew, Mark, Luke, and John, whom we call the **Evangelists**. The Gospels have a central place in the New Testament because they have Jesus Christ at their center. The Gospel is the "Good News" of Jesus, our Savior, who offers us eternal life. We hear the Gospel read every time we go to Mass.

In addition to the Gospels, the New Testament contains the Acts of the Apostles. The Acts of the Apostles tells how the Holy Spirit guided the early Church. It has stories that show how the first Christians loved and followed Jesus Christ. The writer of the Gospel of Luke is also the author of the Acts of the Apostles.

The New Testament also has letters that were meant to teach the early Christians about Jesus. Now the letters teach us, telling us how to live as Christians. Peter, Paul, James, and John wrote some of these letters.

As the last book of the New Testament, the Book of Revelation tells of a prophet named John who talks about the glories of God's kingdom. This book was written to encourage Christians who were suffering from persecution.

The Message of the Bible

Use the secret code to write the important message from the Bible on the lines.

Code

D E G L O S U V

Ø Σ □ ⅃ Γ ∧ ⊥ Δ

Message

___ ___ ___   ___ ___ ___   ___ ___ ___ ___ .

Ø Σ □ ⅃ ∧ Γ Ø ⊥ Δ   □ Γ Ø   Δ ⅃ ∧ Σ Ø ⊥ Ø

More Messages from the Bible

Read these four messages that were taken from Scripture. Choose one and circle it. Using your own words, write what you think that message is saying and how you can use it in your life.

> God is love, and whoever remains in love remains in God and God in him.
>
> 1 John 4:16

> But you, our God, are good and true, slow to anger, and governing all with mercy.
>
> Wisdom 15:1

> Your kindness should be known to all.
>
> Philippians 4:5

> Call on me in time of distress, and I will rescue you.
>
> adapted from Psalm 50:15

_____

_____

_____

_____

_____

A Moment with Jesus

God speaks to us through the Bible and through his Son, Jesus. Let's take some time to thank Jesus for showing us the way to his Father and for giving us the Holy Spirit as our helper.

We Enthrone the Bible

Song and Procession

Enthronement

> **Leader:** Your Word, O Lord, is the joy of my heart!
>
> *(Readings from the Bible; see page 12, opposite)*
>
> **All:** *(After each reading)* Thanks be to God.

Silent Prayer

Intercessions

> **All:** *(Response after each petition)* I will love your Word with all my heart!

> **Leader:** Help us to listen with open hearts to your Word, Lord God. . . . ℞.
> Fill our hearts with love for your Word, Lord God. . . . ℞.
> Guide us to live according to your Word, Lord God. . . . ℞.
> Use us to spread your Word, Lord God. . . . ℞.

> **All:** Your written Word, heavenly Father, has a place of honor in our classroom. May your Word always have first place in our hearts and lives. This we ask through your Son, Jesus, and the Holy Spirit. Amen.

Knowing the Bible

Circle the correct word to complete each sentence.

1. Another name for the Bible is

   Acts of the Apostles   Sacred Scripture

2. The part of the Bible that tells what God did for his people before Jesus came is the

   Old Testament   New Testament

3. The part of the Bible that tells about Jesus and the early Church is the

   Old Testament   New Testament

4. The books that contain the life and teachings of Jesus are the

   Gospels   Acts of the Apostles

We Remember

What is the Bible?
The Bible is the written Word of God. It is Sacred Scripture.

What is the message of Scripture?
The message of Scripture is that God loves us.

Words to Know
Hebrews   inspired
prophet   Evangelists

We Respond

Whenever I listen to or read the Bible, I remember that God is speaking to me because he loves me.

Building Family Faith

CHAPTER SUMMARY Sacred Scripture is the written Word of God. Its most important message is love. Christians who grow in love and respect for the Bible reverently listen to and proclaim God's Word.

REFLECT
All scripture is inspired by God and is useful for teaching, for refutation, for correction, and for training in righteousness, so that one who belongs to God may be competent, equipped for every good work.

2 Timothy 3:16–17

DISCUSS AS A FAMILY
• your favorite story in the Bible or a favorite Bible passage.
• how remembering the stories of the Bible can help you during the day.
• how you can best use the Bible.

PRAY
Your Word is spirit and life, O Lord.

DO
• Offer your child the gift of a Bible specific to his or her age range. Inscribe it with a message of encouragement and love.
• After Sunday Mass discuss the readings and ways you can apply them during the week.
• Memorize one passage from the Old Testament and one from the New Testament. Recite one passage as your morning prayer and one as your evening prayer for several weeks. Continue this practice throughout the year.

Visit **www.christourlife.com** for more family resources.

Gather and Go Forth

Know and Proclaim

As we learn more about our faith, we see that our actions and words can help others know God better.

We Know Our Faith	We Proclaim Our Faith
The Bible is Sacred Scripture, which means that it is "holy writing."	As Christians, we read the Old Testament to learn what God did for his people before Jesus came. We read the New Testament to learn about Jesus and the early Church.
God made the Hebrews his own people when he gave them his laws of love.	Catholics continue to live the values of God's kingdom on earth by living the Beatitudes.
God shows us one way to pray in the Book of Psalms.	Catholics pray and sing the psalms at Mass and other celebrations of the Church.

Test Your Catholic Knowledge

Fill in the circle that best answers the question.

Where would you find stories about God's love for the Chosen People, the children of Israel?

- ○ the New Testament
- ○ the Old Testament
- ○ the Ten Commandments
- ○ the Beatitudes

Scripture helps us know God. The Word fills us with the desire to share our faith.

So shall my word be
that goes forth from my
mouth;
It shall not return to me
empty
but shall do what pleases
me,
achieving the end for
which I sent it.

Isaiah 55:11

A Catholic to Know

John Bosco spent his life in the 1800s and helped troubled boys who were poor and orphaned. He saw the good in these boys and cared for them like a father. John gave them many responsibilities and helped train them for work. He also taught them about their faith, encouraging them to live Christian lives. Like Saint John Bosco, we are called to share our faith. By our words and actions, we can teach others that Jesus loves them.

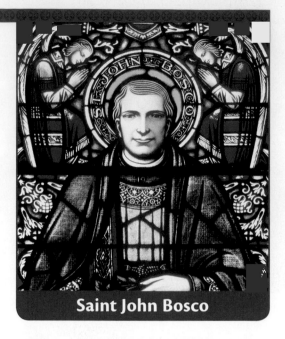

Saint John Bosco

Witness and Share

These sentences describe what Catholics believe. Listen carefully as they are read. Ask yourself, "How strong are my Catholic beliefs?"

My Way to Faith

- I talk to God by praying the psalms.

- I read the Old Testament to learn about God's love and care for his people.

- I read the New Testament to learn about Jesus and his disciples.

- I study the words and deeds of Jesus in the Gospels.

- I thank Jesus for showing me the way to his Father.

Share Your Faith

Look through the New Testament. Choose a story about Jesus and write a summary below. Then tell your family what you learned. Invite family members to share their favorite Bible passages. Discuss what lessons you learned.

_____

_____

_____

_____

God Speaks to Us Through the Church

The Church Spreads the Good News

The Church is the people of God. The baptized members who believe in Jesus and follow the leadership of the pope and the bishops are called Catholics. God speaks to us through the Church, and he sent the Holy Spirit to be with it and to guide it. When we listen to the Catholic Church, we follow Jesus.

The Holy Spirit calls Christians to work together to spread the Good News: *God loves us so much he sent Jesus to be our Savior.*

Everyone in the Church helps to do this. The pope and the bishops teach and govern the Church. They are shepherds who care for God's people and lead them to a holy way of life. Priests celebrate the sacraments with the people. They preach about Jesus' message and about how he died and rose to make us God's children. Deacons preach, baptize, and share in Jesus' work in other ways.

God's People Love and Serve

God's people are united in the celebration of the Eucharist. They receive strength through the sacraments and the presence of the Holy Spirit to spread the Good News and to serve God's kingdom. By loving each other, married men and women show us how Jesus loves the Church. Parents and teachers show children what it means to be a Christian by teaching them to love and help others as Jesus did. Men and women religious show Jesus' love and the holiness of the Church through their special way of life. Single people also serve the Church in many different ways.

Look closely at the photographs on the page. Choose one and explain how it shows someone serving God's kingdom.

_____

_____

_____

_____

_____

Jesus Gave Special Authority to Peter

Narrator: Jesus gave special teaching authority to Peter. One day Jesus asked his apostles a question.

Jesus: Who do people say I am?

Apostles: Some say that you are John the Baptist. Others say you are Elijah or Jeremiah or one of the prophets.

Jesus: But who do you say that I am?

Narrator: Simon Peter answered:

Peter: You are the Messiah, the Son of the living God!

Narrator: Jesus was pleased with Peter's answer.

Jesus: Blessed are you, Simon! No human being has revealed this truth to you. My Father in heaven has made it known to you. And so I say to you, you are Peter, the rock, and on this rock I will build my Church. Nothing, not even the powers of hell, will be able to overcome it. I will give you the keys to the kingdom of heaven. Whatever you bind on earth shall be bound in heaven. Whatever you free on earth shall be freed in heaven.

adapted from Matthew 16:13–19

A Moment with Jesus

Imagine that Jesus asked you the same question he asked Peter, Who do you say that I am? How would you answer him? Ask Jesus to help you learn more and more about him. Then spend a little time thinking about how much you love Jesus.

Francis appears to the public for the first time as pope, at the balcony of St. Peter's Basilica, March 13, 2013.

The Pope Speaks in Jesus' Name

Peter believed that Jesus was truly the Messiah, the Savior that God had promised. Jesus praised Peter's faith. Then Jesus promised to build a Church, to form a new people of God. Jesus is the head of the Church. He chose Peter to be the visible head. Peter would teach and lead the Church in the name of Jesus.

The power to speak in Jesus' name was not given just to Peter, the first pope. Every pope receives the same authority. When the Holy Father, the pope, speaks as the head of the Church, Jesus speaks through him. The Holy Spirit guides the pope and the other bishops who teach and lead.

We love, honor, and obey our Holy Father because he represents Christ on earth. We pray for our Holy Father and our bishops, the shepherds of Christ's Church.

Our pope's name is

_____ .

My bishop's name is

_____ .

Messages from the Popes

Without prayer, your faith and love will die.

Saint John Paul II

Love is the light—and in the end, the only light—that can always illuminate a world grown dim and give us the courage needed to keep living and working.

Pope Emeritus Benedict XVI

Every believer in this world of ours must be a spark of light, a center of love.

Saint John XXIII

No more war; war never again.

Blessed Paul VI

Another Gospel Story About Peter

One day after Jesus rose from the dead, Peter said, "I'm going fishing." Some of the other apostles went with him. They fished all night but caught nothing.

At dawn Jesus stood on the shore, but the apostles didn't recognize him. Jesus called, "Cast your net over the right side of the boat, and you will find something." When the apostles did so, it was so heavy that they could not pull in the huge catch.

Then one apostle said, "It is the Lord." With that, Peter jumped off the boat and swam ashore. The others came by boat, dragging the net with 153 large fish in it.

Jesus had a charcoal fire going. He served the disciples bread and fish. After breakfast Jesus said to Simon Peter, "Simon, son of John, do you love me more than these?" Peter answered, "Yes, Lord, you know that I love you." Then Jesus said, "Feed my lambs."

Jesus asked a second time, "Simon, son of John, do you love me?" Peter replied, "Yes, Lord, you know that I love you." Jesus said, "Tend my sheep."

He said to Peter a third time, "Simon, son of John, do you love me?" Peter answered, "Lord, you know everything. You know that I love you." Jesus said to him again, "Feed my sheep."

adapted from John 21:1–17

The Church is like an ark, with Peter at the helm. How are all disciples to be fishers of men?

_____

In the story, how did Jesus first help the apostles?

_____

How do the popes "feed" the flock of Jesus just as Peter did?

_____

How do you know from the story that Peter loved Jesus?

_____

_____

How can you tell that Jesus loved Peter?

_____

_____

Check It Out

Complete the following sentences with words from pages 21, 22, and 23.

1. Peter believed that Jesus was the

   _____ .

2. Jesus calls Peter his _____ , on which he will build his Church.

3. Peter and all popes have the power

   to teach and to _____ God's people.

4. When the pope speaks as the visible head of the Church,

   _____ speaks.

5. The Church is always guided by the

   _____ .

6. Everyone in the Church must spread

   the _____ .

We Remember

Why do we believe what the Church teaches?

Jesus gave the leaders of his Church the authority to teach in his name. The Holy Spirit guides the leaders and all the people of the Church

We Respond

O my God, I believe in the Catholic Church and all that it teaches.

Building Family Faith

CHAPTER SUMMARY The Church teaches in Jesus' name, guided by the Holy Spirit. We must pray for and respect the Church and its leaders.

REFLECT

Whoever listens to you listens to me. Whoever rejects you rejects me. And whoever rejects me rejects the one who sent me.

Luke 10:16

DISCUSS AS A FAMILY

- what Jesus wants the Church and its leaders to teach about his life and mission.
- the ways you can help the Church to continue its mission to teach.
- why it is important to belong to the Church.

PRAY

Holy Spirit, inspire and guide our leaders.

DO

- Explore the Vatican Web site, www.vatican.va.
- At mealtime discuss examples of current issues on which the Church has served as a teacher.
- Read Matthew 28:18–20 and then say a prayer for our Church leaders.

Visit **www.christourlife.com** for more family resources.

Gather and Go Forth

CHAPTER 3

Know and Proclaim

We explore the many ways Christ shows his love for us. Then we tell others the Good News.

We Know Our Faith	We Proclaim Our Faith
The Holy Spirit calls Christians to work together to spread the Good News.	As Catholics, we receive the grace of the Holy Spirit in the Sacrament of Baptism. The Holy Spirit give us the strength to spread the Gospel.
Jesus gave Peter special teaching authority. Peter was the first pope.	As Catholics, we honor the pope's teaching in areas of faith and morals as being guided by the Holy Spirit.
Jesus speaks through the pope when the pope speaks as the head of the Church.	The pope celebrates a special Mass on feast days, such as Easter and Christmas. Many Catholics gather as a community to watch the Holy Father celebrate Mass on television.

In the Gospels, we hear Jesus call his apostles. He calls us too. Filled with the Holy Spirit, we joyfully share his Word.

He appointed twelve [whom he also named apostles] that they might be with him and he might send them forth to preach.

Mark 3:14

Test Your Catholic Knowledge

Fill in the circle that best answers the question.

Who is the visible head of the Church on earth?

○ priests

○ laity

○ deacons

○ the pope

A Catholic to Know

According to the Gospel of John, Andrew was the first apostle Jesus called to follow him. After spending an afternoon with Jesus, Andrew was filled with excitement. He immediately went to his brother Simon Peter and shared his experience. "We have found the Messiah," he proclaimed. Both men gave up their work as fishermen to become apostles of Jesus. Like Andrew, we are called to know Christ and then tell others about our exciting discovery of his love and friendship.

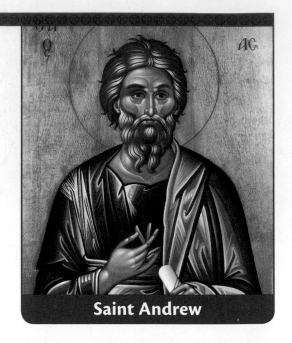
Saint Andrew

Witness and Share

These sentences describe what Catholics believe. Listen carefully as they are read. Ask yourself, "How strong are my Catholic beliefs?"

My Way to Faith

- I obey God the Father when I obey Jesus.

- I receive God's strength when I celebrate the sacraments.

- I pray for the leaders of our Church.

- I look to the teachings of the pope, bishops, and other Church leaders to guide me in my life.

- I help build a better world by serving God's kingdom.

Share Your Faith

Think of one act of service you can do this week. Write your idea on the lines. Share your idea with a classmate. Invite the classmate to join you in this service. Work together to serve God's kingdom!

_____

_____

_____

_____

God Offers Us Eternal Life

Knowing God Brings Us to Heaven

God made us for happiness. He knows we can be perfectly happy only when we are with him in heaven. At the Last Supper, Jesus said to his apostles:

> "In my Father's house there are many dwelling places. If there were not, would I have told you that I am going to prepare a place for you? . . . I will come back again and take you to myself, so that where I am you also may be."

John 14:2–3

Heaven is our true home. It is more beautiful and wonderful than we can imagine. It is seeing God face to face in all his beauty. It is living in love with God forever. In heaven we will have joy that never ends. Glorified in body and soul, we will reign with Christ forever.

In a parable Jesus told us how precious heaven is. He said:

> "The kingdom of heaven is like a treasure buried in a field, which a person finds and hides again, and out of joy goes and sells all that he has and buys that field."

Matthew 13:44

What did the person give up to get the treasure?

_____

Once we know God, we love him. We long to be with him always.

Missing-Letter Game

Look at the pictures that show us ways we come to know God. Use them to help you fill in the missing letters in the puzzle.

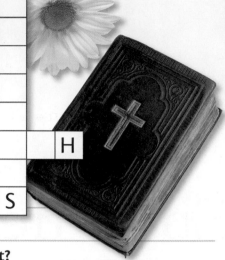

S ☐ ☐ ☐ ☐ ☐ ☐ N

C ☐ ☐ ☐ H

J ☐ ☐ S

Ideas to Remember

How well do you remember the important ideas in this unit? Complete each sentence in the first column with the letter of the ending in the second column. Sentence 1 is done.

1. We celebrate the gift of faith __C__ .

2. Faith is the power to believe _____ .

3. Scripture is _____ .

4. The Old Testament tells what _____ .

5. The New Testament tells about _____ .

6. Jesus gave his Church the authority _____ .

7. Those who believe in Jesus will _____ .

8. All members of the Church are to _____ .

9. Jesus said, "Whoever has seen me _____ ."

10. When the pope speaks as the visible head of the Church, _____ .

A. God did for his people before Jesus came

B. the written Word of God

C. in Baptism

D. in God

E. have eternal life

F. to teach in his name

G. Jesus and the early Church

H. Jesus speaks through him

I. has seen the Father

J. spread the Good News

Names to Remember

Choose a word from the Word Bank to match the descriptions.
Not all choices will be used.

WORD BANK

A. Thomas
B. Peter
C. bishops
D. Jesus
E. Holy Spirit
F. John
G. Philip

_____ **1.** The apostle who asked Jesus to show him the Father

_____ **2.** The one who reveals the Father perfectly

_____ **3.** The apostle who believed only after he had seen Jesus

_____ **4.** The men who teach and govern the Church

_____ **5.** The apostle Jesus gave special authority to teach

_____ **6.** The one sent by Jesus to guide the Church

My Gifts to God

We can work with God to help our life of faith grow. Write in the gift tags
things you can do that will help you grow in your faith. The titles will help
you think of ideas.

1. Praying

I will _____

_____

_____

2. Serving

I will _____

_____

3. Learning

I will _____

_____

We Celebrate Our Faith

Opening Song

> **Leader:** Let us begin our prayer today with the Sign of the Cross.
>
> **All:** In the name of the Father, and of the Son, and of the Holy Spirit. Amen.

Prayer

> **Leader:** God our Father, we listen to your words of eternal life. Help us be your faithful children forever. We ask this through Jesus Christ our Lord.
>
> **All:** Amen.

First Reading
Ephesians 1:17–19 adapted

> **Reader:** May the God of our Lord Jesus Christ, the Father of glory, give you a spirit to know and love him. May the eyes of your hearts be enlightened that you may know the rich glories he has promised the holy ones. May you see the greatness of his power in the things he does for us who believe.

> The Word of the Lord
>
> **All:** Thanks be to God.

Intercessions

> **Leader:** Jesus is truly with us. Let us ask him to grant our needs. Our response is "Lord, hear our prayer."
>
> **Child 1:** That the Holy Father, bishops, priests, deacons, and missionaries may speak God's Word to many people, we pray to the Lord . . . ℟
>
> **Child 2:** That our parents, brothers, sisters, and all who listen to God's Word may live it in their lives, we pray to the Lord . . . ℟
>
> **Child 3:** That we may be mindful of God's presence and obey God, we pray to the Lord . . . ℟
>
> **Child 4:** That we may bring others to God by professing our faith, we pray to the Lord . . . ℟

Child 5: That the sick, the lonely, and the suffering peoples may hear God's words of comfort, we pray to the Lord . . . ℟

Leader: Father in heaven, hear the prayers of your children and help us to come to know you better. We ask this through Jesus Christ our Lord.

All: Amen.

Second Reading
John 17:3, 7, 8, 11 adapted

Reader: A reading from the holy Gospel according to John.

Jesus said to his Father: This is eternal life: to know you, the only true God, and the one whom you have sent, Jesus Christ. Your people know that everything you gave me is from you. They have believed that it was you who sent me. My Father, keep them true to your name so that they may be one just as we are.

The Gospel of the Lord

All: Praise to you, Lord Jesus Christ.

Prayer

Leader: Jesus, you have given us a share in your life. You promise eternal life to those who believe!

All: Lord, I believe! You have the words of eternal life!

Leader: Jesus, you gave us yourself in the Eucharist so we can have new life.

All: Lord, I believe! I come to you for life.

Leader: Jesus, you promised that you would live in us and we would live in you.

All: Lord, I believe! Live in me and let me live in you.

Leader: Jesus, you promised that we would live forever and be raised up on the last day.

All: Lord, I believe! I hope for eternal life! Amen.

Closing Song

Looking Back at Unit 1

In this unit you have learned that God calls us to faith and eternal life. To help us follow his call, God reveals himself. God shows his might and power in creation and speaks to us in his Word. In the Old Testament God reveals his loving care of his people. In the New Testament God reveals himself through his Son.

Jesus revealed his Father through his words and deeds. He sent his apostles out to spread the Good News. He gave special authority for teaching to Peter and to each pope. He sent the Holy Spirit to guide his Church.

We grow in faith when we pray (especially the Act of Faith), celebrate the sacraments, and do what God tells us. At Mass, we profess our faith in the Nicene Creed, a prayer that lists the chief mysteries of our

faith. With Jesus' help, faith can help us live like true children of God. Then after death, we will live happily with God forever.

Living the Message

Check (✓) each sentence that describes you.

❑ **1.** I can explain what faith is and how to help it grow.

❑ **2.** I can pray the Act of Faith.

❑ **3.** I show respect for Scripture, the Word of God.

❑ **4.** I pray for the leaders of the Church.

❑ **5.** I know what I believe as a Catholic Christian.

Planning to Grow

Calendars help us plan our days by marking events, such as birthdays, dental appointments, or soccer matches. Use the calendar below to plan something to do each day of the week to help your faith grow.

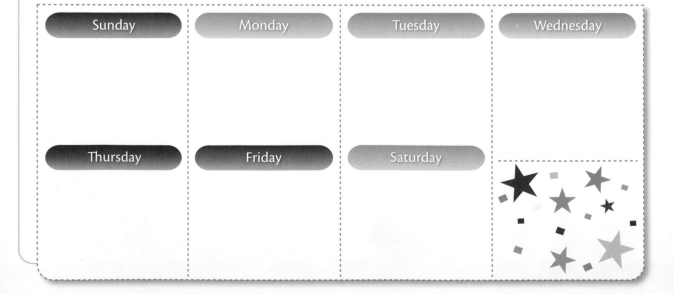

Sunday	Monday	Tuesday	Wednesday
Thursday	Friday	Saturday	

Gather and Go Forth

Know and Proclaim

The more we know Christ, the more we want to be with him. We tell others so that they can know and love him too.

We Know Our Faith	We Proclaim Our Faith
God calls us to faith and eternal life. God reveals himself to help us follow his call.	As Catholics, we pray the Litany of Saints, calling upon those who have gone before us in faith.
Jesus gave his apostles the Holy Spirit and sent them out to spread the Good News.	Catholics pray for the bishops and other Church leaders during the Eucharistic Prayer at Mass.
God shows his might and power in creation.	We show humility and honor the Lord when we care for his creation.

Test Your Catholic Knowledge

Fill in the circle that best completes the sentence.

Catholics believe that knowing God:

○ leads us to Heaven.

○ keeps us from true happiness.

○ leads us to pursue earthly possessions.

○ is too hard to try.

We grow closer to Jesus by praying and celebrating the sacraments. With God's grace, we are filled with the desire to share our story of faith with others.

And this is the promise that he made us: eternal life.

1 John 2:25

A Catholic to Know

In the 1300s, Catherine of Siena brought Jesus' love to the world through her vocation to religious life. She had a vision of Saint Dominic inviting her to join the religious order he had founded. As a Tertiary Sister of Saint Dominic, she prayed for and served those who were sick, poor, or in prison. Her actions and example brought many people who had fallen away from the Church back to prayer and the sacraments. Our lives can also lead others to Christ, whether they know the faith or have not yet learned how much God loves them.

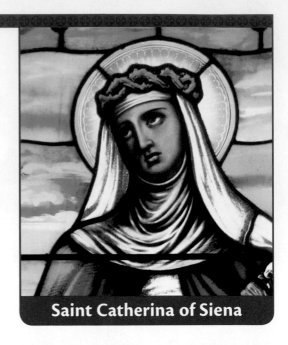

Saint Catherina of Siena

Witness and Share

These sentences describe what Catholics believe. Listen carefully as they are read. Ask yourself, "How strong are my Catholic beliefs?"

My Way to Faith

- I pay attention to what I am praying when I proclaim the Nicene Creed.

- I pray the Act of Faith to strengthen my belief.

- I ask the Holy Spirit to help me live like a true child of God.

- I honor God by practicing stewardship and caring for his creation.

- I look forward to living a faithful life and living happily with God forever after death.

Share Your Faith

Think of ways you can show appreciation for God's creation. Choose one idea and invite a friend to join you in putting it into action. Say a prayer of thanks for this gift from God.

_____

_____

_____

_____

God's Goodness Reflected in Others

God longs to reveal himself to us, and so we are blessed with many ways, large and small, to encounter God in our world and in our daily living. We can meet God through Scripture, the teachings of the Church, and the beauty of creation. For many people, another way to see God more clearly is through the goodness of other people.

We get glimpses of God's saving grace in the compassionate and loving deeds of people who cross our paths each day. Some of these holy people may eventually be recognized and honored by the Church as saints, but most will be remembered by a much smaller circle of family and friends. All who follow the way of Jesus are to be honored for living out the gospel in the times and circumstances of their own lives.

Canonized Saints

The saints are ordinary people who lived extraordinary lives. Some are famous. Some changed the course of history. Many lived quiet lives of humble service. But all the saints are men and women we can learn from. They teach us how to live good lives as we do our work, love our family and friends, and meet life's challenges. The saints prove that God is with us, even when life is most challenging.

Because the saints live with God, all who love God can get to know them. They can be our friends, companions, and teachers. We can ask Saint Jude to pray to God for us in difficult times.

We can learn courage from Saint Joan of Arc and patience from Saint Joseph. Saint Thérèse of Lisieux can teach us how to turn our small and ordinary actions into a prayer.

St. Jude ❯

Family Feature

Some countries are devoted to certain saints and observe their feast days with special rituals.

The Sanchez family's ancestors are from Mexico. Every December 12 this family celebrates the feast of Our Lady of Guadalupe by rising before dawn, joining fellow parishioners to sing hymns to Our Lady, and processing through the neighborhood carrying a banner displaying her image.

The Walshes celebrate the feast of Saint Patrick, patron of Ireland, on March 17 in grand style. They often wear green, attend Mass, and march in a parade.

The Serios from Italy celebrate the feast of Saint Joseph on March 19 by inviting friends and relatives to a feast of specially prepared foods that are also shared with people who are poor.

The Samuelsson family from Sweden observes the feast of Saint Lucy on December 13, eight days before the shortest day of the year. The day is celebrated with bonfires and candles.

The oldest daughter traditionally wears a white dress with a red sash; on her head is a crown of evergreen branches with lit candles. As she brings morning coffee and saffron rolls to her parents, she sings the song "Santa Lucia" and the Christmas season in Sweden officially begins.

St. Lucy Saffron Rolls

2 packages of dry yeast	1 ½ teaspoons salt
½ cup warm water	½ cup butter
1 cup warm milk	2 eggs
¼ cup honey	6–7 cups unbleached
1 teaspoon ground cardamom	white flour
pinch of saffron or drop	raisins
of yellow food coloring	1 slightly beaten egg white

Combine the yeast and water. In another bowl combine milk, honey, spices, and salt. Then add butter, eggs, and the yeast mixture. Beat in enough flour to make a stiff dough. Put it onto a lightly floured surface and knead until smooth, about 10 minutes. Place in a greased bowl, cover lightly, and allow to rise for an hour. The dough will double. Knead it for 3 minutes. Return it to the bowl, cover it, and allow to rise for 45 minutes. Punch it down and knead it for 3 more minutes. Cover the dough and let it rest for 15 minutes. Divide the dough into 24 pieces and roll each into a foot-long rope. Form the ropes into an S shape on a greased baking sheet. Coil each end of the S until it looks like a double snail shell. Put a raisin in the eye of each coil. Brush the buns with egg white and bake at 350° F for 15 to 20 minutes. They will be brown on top. Serve warm.

One Family's Example

Many of us think about our parents when we think of generous and giving people who have helped us know God through their acts of love. But for the Inserra family, the person who also helped them know God was their Aunt Chris. Chris spent several years in a Catholic Worker house, living among the poor and actively promoting peace and justice. She joined thousands of other Catholics and people of faith in an annual request for the closure of the School of the Americas, which has been condemned by U.S. and Latin American Catholic Bishops for training soldiers responsible for atrocities, such as the murder of Archbishop Oscar Romero of El Salvador. She sings in the church choir, sits on the local school board, and puts pressure on local politicians to live up to their campaign promises to serve the community. People who know her have gained insight into what it means to live the faith. When Chris hears the words of Christ we say at Mass: "Peace I leave with you; my peace I give to you" (John 14:27), she feels compelled to share that peace with others.

Faith Word Search

Find and circle words in the puzzle that are related to saints and our own journey in faith.

```
A C O N E Y R R M T E
G S G A N X U M H O T
A U S R S E A S N G S
N O I S S A P M O C E
P R A Y E R I Y P Y E
E E O G N N T N T L S
S N P I I I D I T S E
T E E G L C R O N S O
R G E I O A P O O H R
U U M P H D S H A G E
T U R C O U R A G E H
H T I A F H S T T E N
```

WORD BANK

Heroes	Holiness
Example	Faith
Hope	Charity
God	Prayer
Saints	Courage
Compassion	Truth
Goodness	Humility
Generous	

Family Feature

Activities with Your Family

Read through the suggested family activities below and pick one or more that appeal to you as ways to use the ordinary opportunities of family life to nurture your child's faith.

At dinner some evening soon, tell which saint is your favorite and why. What are the traits that most appeal to you about this saint? Ask everyone gathered around the table to share their favorite saints.

Pick a family saint to inspire, support, and pray for your family. Invite your child to help you research saints online at http://www.catholic.org/saints/ or purchase a book on saints, such as *Loyola Kids Book of Saints* by Amy Welborn (Loyola Press). On your family saint's feast day each year, plan a special meal, light a candle, and say a prayer asking for that saint's guidance. Include that saint in your prayers throughout the year.

Tell about one extended family member, coworker, or friend who exemplified a Christian virtue (for example, honesty, courage, wisdom, holiness, faith, hope, or charity). Ask the children in the family if they can tell about someone who inspires them in the same way.

Impress upon your children the importance of being a good example to others. Because our behavior reflects on God who created us, guide your children in learning to be more like him— kind, inclusive, forgiving, trustworthy, faithful, just, and compassionate.

Visit **www.christourlife.com** for more family resources.

God Strengthens Us to Be Holy

Whoever acknowledges that Jesus is the Son of God, God remains in him and he in God.

1 John 4:15

A Letter Home

Dear Parents and Family,

Unit Two of *Christ Our Life* presents children with the ultimate road map to good living: the teachings of Jesus.

At the beginning of this unit, the children are reminded of their responsibility as Christians to live as Jesus did, loving God and others. They are encouraged to follow the path Jesus left for us, making prayer and good works part of their daily lives. The children's study of prayer provides a great opportunity for you to make prayer a bigger part of your family life.

Of course, everyone gets a little lost now and then. In Unit Two, the children will pause and reflect on their need for mercy, as well as on God's readiness to grant it. The children will deepen their understanding of conscience and how to form it in accord with Jesus' teaching. Acknowledging the times when they are lost will foster a greater appreciation for the Sacrament of Reconciliation. You can share your own appreciation of this opportunity for forgiveness by participating in the sacrament in your parish.

Finally in Unit Two, the children will learn the importance of worshiping God. In fact, it's one of the Ten Commandments, a clear set of guidelines to living right, a gift demonstrating God's love for us and his desire to bring us close to him.

At the end of each chapter in this unit, the children will bring home a review of the chapter along with either the Building Family Faith page or the Family Feature section. These features give you a quick review of what your child learned and offer practical ways to reinforce the lesson at home so that the whole family may benefit.

Visit **www.christourlife.com** for more family resources.

CHAPTER 5

We Are Called to Follow Jesus

Jesus Teaches Us How to Live

During his lifetime in Palestine, Jesus showed us how to be the best persons we can be. By his words and actions he taught us how to live holy and happy lives. Baptized Christians try to live like Jesus and follow his teachings. We are called to bring his life and love into the world. Jesus said,

> "I came that you might have life—and have it to the full."
>
> adapted from John 10:10

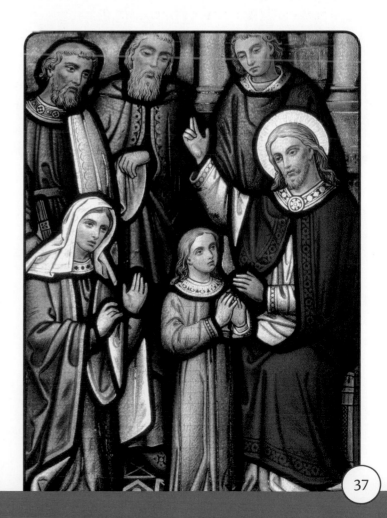

Jesus Showed Love and Concern

A man named Jairus rushed through the crowd to reach Jesus. He knelt before Jesus and said, "My daughter has just died. But come, lay your hand on her, and she will live."

Jesus went with Jairus to his house. He took the little girl by the hand, and she got up. Jesus gave life back to her. Jairus and the girl's mother were filled with joy.

adapted from Matthew 9:18–19,23–2

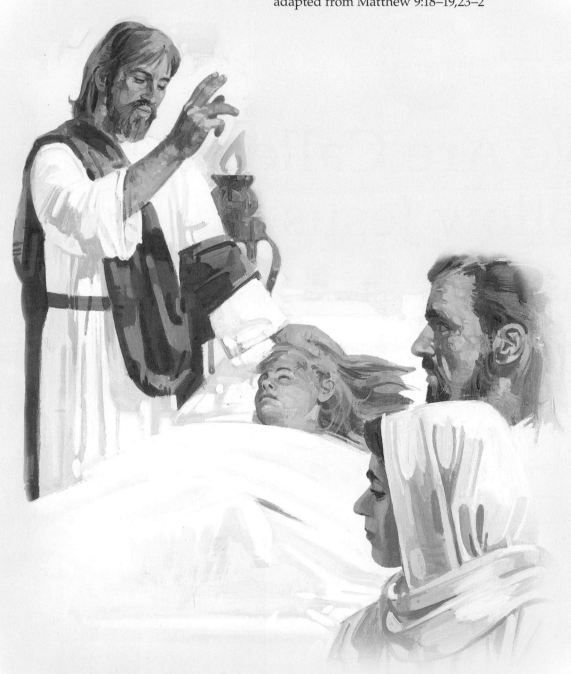

Jesus' Forgiving Love Healed People

One day Jesus was teaching in a house. Many people gathered to hear him speak. They crowded into the house and around the door.

In the crowd was a paralyzed man who wanted to see Jesus. Because the man couldn't get into the house, his friends carried him to the roof. They lifted up part of the roof until they had a large opening. Then they lowered the sick man on his mat.

Jesus stopped teaching. He looked at the sick man and said, "Child, your sins are forgiven."

Then he cured the man's body. The man got up, picked up his mat, and walked out in front of everyone.

adapted from Mark 2:1–5,11–12

Jesus Prayed to His Father

The apostles watched Jesus when he was at prayer. They could see that he knew how to speak to God our Father. Afterward they came to him and said, "Lord, teach us to pray."

Then Jesus taught them the prayer we call the Lord's Prayer. We should try to pray it every day. In this prayer we praise God and ask for all our needs. We ask to be forgiven as we forgive others. We also ask to be saved from evil.

Lord's Prayer

Print the phrase from the Lord's Prayer that matches each sentence. The prayer on the inside cover of your book can help.

God, everyone's loving Father, has given us life.

_____

Heaven is where God lives.

_____

We pray that all people will respect God and God's holy name.

_____

We pray that all people on earth will belong to God's kingdom and do God's will.

_____

_____

We ask for food and for the living bread, the Eucharist. We ask for the things we need every day.

_____

We ask God to forgive us our sins as we forgive others.

_____

_____

We ask God to help us in time of temptation.

_____

We ask God to keep us from all evil, especially sin.

_____

People Who Act Like Jesus

Here are three examples of people who have done what Jesus taught. Read each story and then write the word that matches the deeds described in the story: *pray, serve,* or *forgive*.

A young driver made a serious mistake. She drank too much and then drove. This caused an accident that took the lives of a young man and a young woman. While in prison, the driver became very ill. Mrs. Reyes, the mother of the young woman who had been killed, wrote a letter to the state. In it she asked for the release of the driver, who was responsible for the death of her daughter.

Mrs. Reyes knows how to

_____ .

While troops were being sent to the Middle East before the war with Iraq, the fourth graders at Ascension School set aside a special corner in their classroom. There they took turns asking God for peace.

These children know how to

_____ .

When Sister Emmanuelle visited Egypt, she found that thousands of people lived in the garbage dumps. This is where they made their homes. They were bare, with dirt floors and roofs made from palm leaves. Both parents and children survived by collecting garbage, sorting it, and reselling it. Most of these people didn't know how to read or write. Sister moved in with them to give them hope and to teach them that God is love. She has built a school, a clinic, a vocational center, and soccer fields. She says, "I wouldn't want to be anywhere else because here I feel I am giving the life of Jesus Christ to the children."

Sister Emmanuelle knows how to

_____ .

A Moment with Jesus

Is there someone in your family who needs your prayers? Pray to Jesus now for that person, telling him about this family member's needs. Trust that Jesus will bring peace and comfort to him or her. Thank Jesus for his loving care.

Add a Happy Ending

- Tyrone bumped into Carlos in the hall. Carlos' lunchbox opened, and food spilled onto the floor.

- All of Danica's friends brought money to buy a treat, but Danica was unable to bring any money.

- Miguel and Connor were good friends. Both boys tried out for a part in a play. Miguel got a part, but Connor did not.

- Marisol laughed and teased her brother about his new haircut.

- Sophia's friend Molly will not talk to her because Sophia went skating with other friends without inviting Molly.

Can you think of a time when you received kindness? Share this with a partner.

We Remember

What does Jesus say about forgiving others?
Jesus says,

"If you forgive others . . . , your heavenly Father will forgive you."

Matthew 6:14

We Respond

I will forgive those who hurt me.

Building Family Faith

CHAPTER SUMMARY The Gospel shows Jesus curing sick people, forgiving sins, and teaching all how to live in his love. As Jesus' followers, we share his concern for others and forgive those who have hurt us.

REFLECT
When Jesus returned to Capernaum after some days, it became known that he was at home. . . . They came bringing to him a paralytic carried by four men.

Mark 2:1,3

DISCUSS AS A FAMILY
- how loving acceptance and forgiveness are the greatest gifts we have to share with friends and family.
- times that you have forgiven someone who hurt you and how you worked through your anger, sadness, and pain.

PRAY
Jesus, open my eyes to the needs of others.

DO
- Plan a family help day: Volunteer for a parish outreach effort; clean out closets, bookshelves, and toy boxes, and donate these items to a charity.

- Make a pact with your family that together you will work through any arguments or hurt feelings, not simply sweep them under the rug.

- Think globally, act locally by studying as a family the problems of poverty and hunger in the world and learning what you can do in your community to help a family in need.

Visit **www.christourlife.com** for more family resources.

Gather and Go Forth

Know and Proclaim

We learn more about Jesus by reading the Gospels. Then we proclaim his words and work in our daily lives.

We Know Our Faith	We Proclaim Our Faith
In his public ministry, Jesus taught us how to be holy and happy by his words and actions.	As Catholics, we live by Jesus' Great Commandment—by loving God with our whole heart and loving others as we love ourselves.
Jesus teaches us that whatever we do for the neediest people, we do for him.	We praise and honor Jesus when we sacrifice something of ours for other people, such as giving our time in service to others or donating clothing.
The Bible shows us Jesus' power and goodness. The story about the daughter of Jairus teaches us that nothing is greater than God's love, not even death.	Catholics share Jesus' power and goodness by caring for those who are sick, elderly, or infirm.

We look to Jesus for examples of how to live holy and happy lives. Filled with the Holy Spirit, we share his message of love with all those we meet.

"Do to others whatever you would have them do to you."

Matthew 7:12

Test Your Catholic Knowledge

Fill in the circle that best answers the question.

What prayer did Jesus teach his apostles?

○ Hail Mary

○ Lord's Prayer

○ Act of Faith

○ Act of Contrition

A Catholic to Know

Jesus appeared in a vision to Margaret Mary Alacoque, a French nun who lived about 300 years ago. Jesus showed her his wounded heart and said, "See this Heart that has loved so much and received so little love in return. Tell everyone to love my Sacred Heart and make up for those people who do not love me." Jesus told her to show devotion to him by making the first Friday of each month a day of special love and to pray for those who did not love him. We can invite others to know and love Jesus by following Saint Margaret Mary's example.

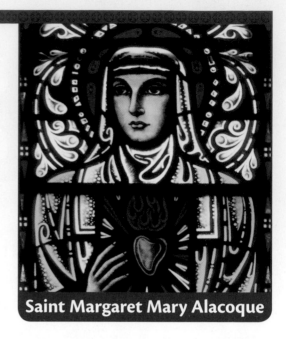

Saint Margaret Mary Alacoque

Witness and Share

These sentences describe what Catholics believe. Listen carefully as they are read. Ask yourself, "How strong are my Catholic beliefs?"

My Way to Faith

- I read the Bible to learn how to be more like Jesus.

- I follow Jesus' example when I help those in need.

- I make personal sacrifices as a way to follow Jesus' example.

- I pray to be led away from temptation and to avoid evil.

- I celebrate God's forgiveness by forgiving others.

Share Your Faith

Jesus taught his disciples the Lord's Prayer. Choose one of your favorite prayers or write your own prayer and record it below. Share your prayer with family members and invite them to pray it with you as a family.

_____

_____

_____

_____

Jesus Invites Us to Receive God's Mercy

Our God Is a God of Mercy

The people brought to Jesus a woman who had committed a serious sin. The law said to stone her to death. The people asked Jesus what he thought about that law. Jesus stooped down and began writing on the ground. Then he said, "Let the one among you who has not sinned throw the first stone." He bent down and wrote again.

The people in the crowd were surprised by Jesus' answer, but all of them knew in their hearts that Jesus was right. They too had sinned. Each person walked away. Jesus looked up at the woman and said, "Woman, where are they? Has no one condemned you? Neither will I. Go and from now on do not sin anymore."

adapted from John 8:3–11

The woman had done wrong. She expected a terrible punishment. How surprised she was when Jesus forgave her. Her heart was full of joy!

Jesus loved the other people too. He also wanted to forgive them for their sins, but they had walked away.

Jesus offers forgiveness to all of us. He forgives us in the Sacrament of Penance and Reconciliation.

I Plan My Journey to Jesus in the Sacrament of Reconciliation

Number the stepping stones along Reconciliation Road in the order we do them when we celebrate the Sacrament of Reconciliation.

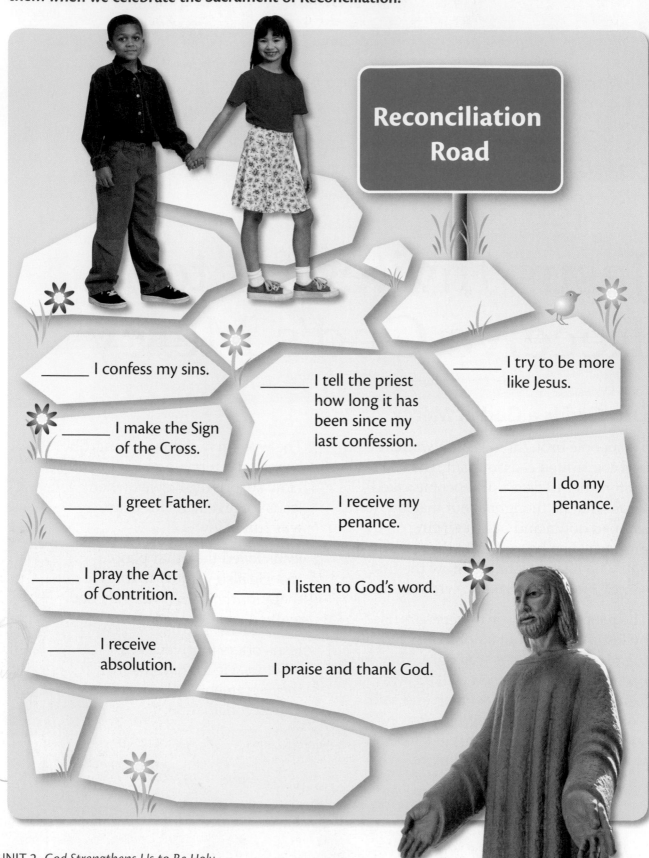

Reconciliation Road

_____ I confess my sins.

_____ I tell the priest how long it has been since my last confession.

_____ I try to be more like Jesus.

_____ I make the Sign of the Cross.

_____ I greet Father.

_____ I receive my penance.

_____ I do my penance.

_____ I pray the Act of Contrition.

_____ I listen to God's word.

_____ I receive absolution.

_____ I praise and thank God.

We Seek Forgiveness

Jesus is waiting for us to come to him in the Sacrament of Reconciliation. He wants to tell us of his love, to forgive our sins, and to make us stronger by following his way. We meet with Jesus through the priest, who acts in Jesus' name and in the name of the Church.

Use the words in the Word Bank to complete the sentences.

1. I pray to the _____ to help me.

2. I read what Jesus said of _____ .

3. I examine my _____ .

4. I tell God I am _____ for my sins.

5. I think about how to be more loving and _____ God to try.

6. I _____ my sins to a priest.

7. I receive _____ forgiveness.

8. I do my _____ .

We Use Guides to Make Decisions

We are God's children, and we try to follow his way. We know God is always with us to help us. He has given us the commandments and Beatitudes to guide us. He has also given each of us a conscience that helps us know what is right. From deep in our hearts, our consciences act like judges, deciding what is good and what is evil. Conscience calls us to love and to choose the good, which will take us to God our Father. It calls us to avoid sin and to hate what turns us away from God.

We form good consciences by studying what Christ and his Church teach us. Each of us should always obey his or her conscience. When we do not obey our consciences, we do wrong and sometimes sin.

An important step in preparing to celebrate the Sacrament of Reconciliation is the **examination of conscience.** We examine our consciences by prayerfully thinking about whether our actions have hurt our relationship with God or others.

When we sin, we turn away from God. **Mortal sin** is a very serious wrong. It cuts us off from God's life. **Venial sin** is less serious, but it too should be avoided. All sin hurts our relationship with God, the Church, and others.

Fortunately, even after we have sinned, our consciences help us. Through our consciences, Jesus calls us to his mercy and forgiveness in the Sacrament of Reconciliation.

A Moment with Jesus

Think for a moment about the choices you made today. Were they good choices or could you have made better ones? Thank Jesus for the gift of conscience that helped you make good decisions. Ask for forgiveness for the poor choices you may have made. Now rest quietly in Jesus' love for you.

My Conscience Helps Me Every Day

Read the sentences below and decide whether the actions described are good or bad. Put the numbers of the sentences in the correct box below.

1. I shared my chocolate chip cookies with my friends.

2. I got a good grade by cheating on my test.

3. I earned money to get Gabrielle a birthday present.

4. I lied when the teacher asked whether I had finished my work.

5. I gave my snack money to the missions.

6. I watched a good television program after I had finished my homework.

7. I didn't go to Sunday Mass because I wanted to ride my new skateboard.

8. I read a good book to learn about people in China.

9. I used Kwan's pencil and kept it because I needed one.

10. I did not do my homework last night because I watched television.

These actions are good.

They follow God's law of love.

— — — — —

These actions are wrong.

They do not follow God's law of love.

— — — — —

A. absolution
B. Contrition
C. conscience
D. priest
E. forgiveness

Riddles—What Am I?

Write on the lines the letters of the answer choices for these riddles.

1. I help you recognize right from wrong. I am your _____ .

2. Jesus wants to give me to sinners. I am _____ .

3. Your sins are forgiven when I happen in the Sacrament of Reconciliation. I am _____ .

4. God knows you are sorry for your sins when you say me. I am the Act of _____ .

5. I act in Jesus' name when you confess your sins. I am the _____ .

We Remember

How does your conscience help you?

1. It helps me know right from wrong.

2. It leads me to choose what is right.

3. It tells me to be sorry for my sins and ask for forgiveness.

Words to Know

examination of conscience
mortal sin   venial sin

We Respond

Jesus, help me to follow my conscience and make good choices.

Building Family Faith

CHAPTER SUMMARY Our consciences help us make good choices. Celebrating the Sacrament of Reconciliation regularly helps us form our consciences and grow strong in God's love.

REFLECT
He straightened up and said to them, "Let the one among you who is without sin be the first to throw a stone at her."
Adapted from John 8:7–11

DISCUSS AS A FAMILY
• why Jesus said that the one without sin could throw the first stone.

• what the woman might have been thinking when she was brought to Jesus.

• how you think she may have felt when Jesus said, "Go and . . . do not sin anymore"?
John 8:11

PRAY
Help us, O God, to know and do your will.

DO
• Tell your child about a time you chose to do the right thing in a difficult situation and were glad you did.

• Discuss the choices a character makes in a children's story or television program. Consider the options and reasons for the choices.

• Talk about the great gift God gave us in the Sacrament of Reconciliation. Have the family celebrate the sacrament at church, then afterward share a family treat.

Visit **www.christourlife.com** for more family resources.

Gather and Go Forth

Know and Proclaim

Learning about our faith helps us know how God wants us to live. Then we can spread this message to others through our words and deeds.

We Know Our Faith	We Proclaim Our Faith
All people sin, even good people. Jesus loves all of us and forgives our sins.	As Catholics, we acknowledge the sins we have committed and ask for Jesus' forgiveness in the Sacrament of Penance and Reconciliation.
Our conscience calls us to love and to choose to do good so that we can follow God's will.	We examine our consciences by prayerfully thinking of ways that we have failed to live up to God's law of love because of sin.
We are God's children. He created us to know, love, and serve him.	Catholics study and pray the Ten Commandments to learn how God wants us to follow him.

Test Your Catholic Knowledge

Fill in the circle that best answers the question.

Who acts in Jesus' name and the name of the Church in the Sacrament of Penance and Reconciliation?

- ○ a teacher
- ○ your parents
- ○ a priest
- ○ your friends

God loves us completely even when we choose to do wrong. His great mercy is a gift we are excited to tell others about.

Lord, you are good and forgiving,
most merciful to all who call on you.

Psalm 86:5

A Catholic to Know

Peter Claver was a Jesuit missionary born in Spain in 1581. When he was 29 years old, Peter traveled to South America and spent the next 40 years there caring for African slaves who were wounded in body and in spirit. These slaves were not treated as human beings by their captors, but Peter saw them as his brothers and sisters. He acted as a visible sign that they were children of God, bringing them food, water, and clothing and caring for those who were sick or dying. Peter taught the slaves about Christ and baptized many of them. Peter's work to bring the love of Jesus to these slaves built a foundation of justice and charity in society for the future.

Saint Peter Claver

Witness and Share

These sentences describe what Catholics believe. Listen carefully as they are read. Ask yourself, "How strong are my Catholic beliefs?"

My Way to Faith

- I believe Jesus loves everyone.

- I listen to my conscience when choosing right from wrong.

- I receive forgiveness of my sins by God through the Sacrament of Penance and Reconciliation.

- I live the Beatitudes to follow God's law of love.

Share Your Faith

Think of choices you make every day. Write a prayer asking the Holy Spirit to help you make good choices. Invite a family member to pray the prayer with you every day this week. Pay attention to the Spirit working in your life.

_____

_____

_____

_____

We Worship God

We Worship God with Love

We see God's greatness and love in the things he has made and in the wonderful things he does for us. We read about God's love for us in the Bible.

Once we know how great and holy God is, we know that he alone deserves all our love. We want to give God the greatest praise and serve him with all our strength.

Our loving response to God is called worship. We worship God by praying and serving him.

Prayer Is Worship

When we pray, we **adore** God as our Creator and Lord. We love God because he is good. We thank God for all his goodness to us, and we tell God we are sorry for sometimes turning away from his love. With trust in God's goodness, we ask him for what we need. When we do these things, we are worshiping God in prayer. The Eucharist is our highest form of worship.

Service Is Worship

We also worship God when we serve him. Serving God is doing the things he wants us to do. It is obeying God's commandments that tell us how to love him and others. Doing good to others is an important part of our worship of God.

Real Worship Comes from the Heart

Our worship is not real unless it comes from our hearts. God had to remind his Chosen People again and again to worship him with love. Many times the people forgot this. They offered prayers and sacrifices in the Temple, but their hearts were far from God. Through the prophets God told them that this empty worship did not please him because it was not worship at all. Worship can only be true when it is offered in love.

> "It is love that I desire, not sacrifice. It is not your offerings I want, but that you should know me, your God."
>
> adapted from Hosea 6:6
>
> "These people honor me with their lips alone. Their hearts are far from me."
>
> adapted from Isaiah 29:13

We build upon the love in our hearts when we offer our own sacrifices to God. Fill in the building blocks with your own ideas of ways to offer your love to God.

We Unite Ourselves with Jesus' Sacrifice

You shall make an altar and upon it shall sacrifice your offerings.

adapted from Exodus 20:24

The Israelites worshiped God by offering him gifts. A gift to God is called a sacrifice. God's people brought their best animals, fruit, and grain to the temple priest. The priest placed these gifts on the altar, offering them to God.

The people offered these sacrifices to acknowledge that all the good things they had were gifts from God. Offering some of them in sacrifice to God was a way of saying "You alone, Lord, created these gifts. We offer them back to you in praise."

Write the sacrifices that the Israelites offered to God.

1. _____

2. _____

3. _____

A Moment with Jesus

Share with Jesus one happy thing and one sad thing that happened to you recently. Offer both of them to Jesus. Thank Jesus for the gift of each day and offer all that you do and say to him.

We Offer Ourselves to God

Jesus' whole life was an act of worship. He offered everything he said and did to God his Father. He showed the greatness of his love when he suffered and died on the Cross. The sacrifice of Jesus on the Cross was the perfect love offering of God's own Son.

In the Mass we gather as God's people to worship him. Jesus has given us his sacrifice to offer to God. Each time we celebrate the Eucharist, we offer Jesus to God under the forms of bread and wine.

We offer all that we think, say, and do to Jesus. We ask him to unite our gift with his own and to give it to our heavenly Father. Then Jesus Christ gives us himself as food and drink to unite and to strengthen us as a holy people.

Our Daily Gift

Although we may not celebrate the Eucharist daily, we can still offer ourselves to God each day. There is a prayer that tells Jesus we offer all our *prayers, works, joys,* and *sufferings* with his holy sacrifice.

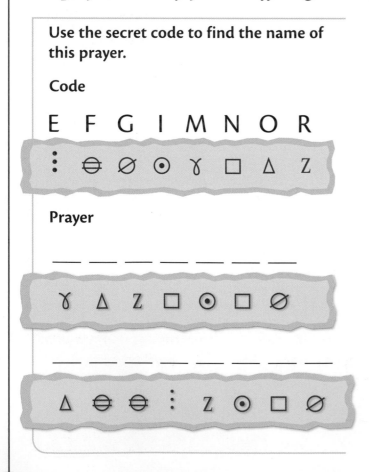

Use the secret code to find the name of this prayer.

Code

E F G I M N O R

Prayer

Fill in the puzzle with four things you offer to God in the Morning Offering.

O F F E R I N G

Something to Think About

How are the people in the pictures worshiping God? Find the definition in the Worship Box that fits each picture, and put the number on the line. In the last space draw a way that you will try to worship God a little better and with more love. Write the number for your picture and finish the sentence.

A. The Johnson family celebrates the Sunday Eucharist, taking part in all the prayers and songs.

_____

B. The Janski family rests and enjoys one another's company on Sundays.

_____

C. Olivia's mother asks for help with the cleaning. Olivia helps gladly.

_____

D. Mrs. Cho is old and lives alone. Orlando cares for her yard.

_____

E. Rosa prays each night before going to bed.

_____

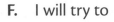

F. I will try to

_____

_____

We Remember

What is worship?
Worship is our loving response to God's greatness and holiness.

Word to Know
adore

We Respond

O Jesus, through the Immaculate Heart
    of Mary,
I offer you my prayers, works, joys, and
    sufferings of this day
for all the intentions of your Sacred Heart,
in union with the Holy Sacrifice of the
    Mass throughout the world,
for the salvation of souls, the reparation
    for sins, the reunion of all Christians,
    and in particular for the intentions of
    the Holy Father this month.
Amen.

Make all your life something beautiful for God.

Blessed Teresa of Calcutta

Building Family Faith

CHAPTER SUMMARY Worship of God includes prayer and service. We can worship God in all our actions throughout the day.

REFLECT
Oh, that today you would hear his voice: Do not harden your hearts.

adapted from Psalm 95

DISCUSS AS A FAMILY
• some of the ways your family loves and serves God.

• whether we recognize that when we help others or others help us, God is pleased and present in our lives.

PRAY
God, help us love you in all that we do.

DO
• Put a copy of the Morning Offering prayer on the bathroom mirror or the breakfast table so everyone can pray it at the start of each day.

• Have your child tell you the story of Saint Elizabeth Ann Seton or Saint John Bosco at dinner this week.

• Put an empty bowl on the kitchen table with a cup of small candies, such as jelly beans or mints, next to it. Every time a family member makes a sacrifice for another family member, classmate, coworker, or friend, he or she puts a candy in the bowl. At the end of the week, the family can enjoy the treats.

Visit **www.christourlife.com** for more family resources.

Gather and Go Forth

Know and Proclaim

As we grow in faith, our hearts are filled with love. We proclaim God's goodness when we share that love with others.

We Know Our Faith	We Proclaim Our Faith
God's greatness and love shine through all the things he has made and done for the world.	As Catholics, we worship with a heart-felt response to God's greatness. If our hearts are far from God, our prayers can be empty.
Worship is our response to God's love and goodness.	Catholics' highest form of worship is the Sacrament of the Eucharist. Through the Eucharist, we praise God for the gift of eternal life in him.
Jesus' whole life was an act of worship. He offered everything he said and did to God the Father.	We pray the Morning Offering daily to dedicate our prayers, works, joys, and sufferings to God.

E ach time we gather to worship and celebrate the sacraments, Jesus is with us. Filled with grace, we invite others to know him too.

"For where two or three are gathered together in my name, there am I in the midst of them."

Matthew 18:20

Test Your Catholic Knowledge

Fill in the circle that best completes the sentence.

The highest form of worship for Catholics is the:

○ Lord's Prayer.

○ Sign of the Cross.

○ Rosary.

○ Eucharist.

A Catholic to Know

Matthew was one of the twelve apostles and a Gospel writer. Before meeting Jesus, Matthew worked as a tax collector. His job was unpopular with Jews because their taxes went to the Roman conquerors. Matthew probably felt a little lonely; however, Jesus saw the good in Matthew and called him to be one of his followers. Matthew listened to Jesus' call and changed both his life and his heart. Matthew's Gospel teaches us about God's love and mercy.

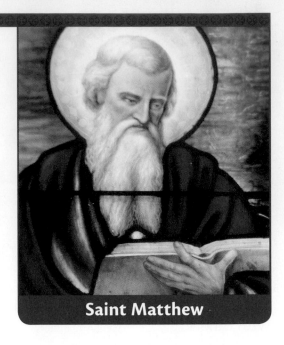

Saint Matthew

Witness and Share

These sentences describe what Catholics believe. Listen carefully as they are read. Ask yourself, "How strong are my Catholic beliefs?"

My Way to Faith

- I praise God for all he has made and has done for me.

- I worship God with all of my heart and mind.

- I worship God by serving others.

- In prayer, I offer God the gift of my thoughts, words, and deeds.

- I unite myself with Jesus through the celebration of the Eucharist.

Share Your Faith

What are some ways you worship God? Write your ideas below. Share your ideas with a friend. Invite friends to tell how they worship God in their lives. Put at least one idea into practice this week.

_____

_____

_____

_____

God Gave Us Laws for Living

God Tells Us How to Live

Narrator: One night Michael dreamed that he was going on a wilderness expedition in the Rocky Mountains. The expedition leader knew that Michael didn't have much hiking experience, so he gave him the book *How to Hike in the Rocky Mountains* to take along on the trip.

Leader: Michael, if you follow the rules in this book, you'll be able to explore the mountains and return safely. Here at base camp we've helped you all we can, but now you're on your own. Follow the directions and you'll enjoy the mountain wilderness.

Michael: Thank you, sir. I'll do everything it says.

Narrator: Then Michael put on his backpack, grabbed the book and a compass, and set off for his hike.

Leader: Have fun on your expedition!

Narrator: The screeching of an eagle startled Michael and woke him up. He realized he had only been dreaming.

God made us and knows what is best for us. God told us how to live well. He gave us laws that tell us how to relate to God, ourselves, other people, and our world. The Church teaches us what God's laws mean.

Moses Receives the Commandments

God led his people out of slavery in Egypt, with Moses as their guide. As they marched through the desert, God protected and cared for them. He made them his special people.

Mount Sinai

One day God told Moses that he would come down on Mount Sinai in three days. The people prepared for the event. On the third day a heavy cloud came down upon the mountain. The people heard thunder and trumpet blasts. They saw lightning. God came down in fire, and Mount Sinai was wrapped in smoke. God called Moses to the top of the mountain and gave him the Ten Commandments. Moses went back to the people and told them God's law. They agreed to do everything God commanded.

The next day Moses sealed the covenant between God and the people, offering a sacrifice to God. Moses sprinkled the blood of the animals he had offered on the altar and on the people. Then God called Moses up to him on the mountain. There God wrote his laws on stone tablets and gave them to Moses.

adapted from Exodus chapters 19 and 24

Complete the sentences with words from the Word Bank.

> **WORD BANK**
>
> Egypt   people
> everything   sacrifice
> Moses   stone

1. God gave the Ten Commandments to

   _____ long ago.

2. God led his people out of _____ and made them his special

   _____ .

3. After the people heard God's laws, they said, "We will do _____ that the Lord has told us."

4. Moses sealed the covenant by offering a _____ to God.

5. God wrote the commandments on _____ tablets.

God Has a Covenant with His People

God had been faithful to the people. He freed them from slavery, protected and fed them in the desert, and gave them a guide for living— the Ten Commandments. These commandments are our **moral law**. They show us how to live lives that are pleasing to God and respectful of others.

When the people accepted the commandments and agreed to live according to them, they made a choice to belong to God. They made an agreement, a covenant with God. God was their God and they were God's people in a special way.

We too are God's people. We have a special covenant relationship with him. We follow the Ten Commandments and Jesus' example of loving and caring for others, especially those who are in special need of our help.

God's People Love His Commandments

God's people praise and thank him for his laws.

How can a young person be good?
　　By keeping to your words.
With all my heart I seek you;
　　help me to obey your commands.

Within my heart I treasure your promise,
　　that I may not sin against you.
Blessed are you, O LORD;
　　teach me your commandments.

With my lips I declare
　　the commands of your mouth.
In the way of your laws I rejoice,
　　as much as in all riches.

I will think of your teachings
　　and study your ways.
In your laws I will delight;
　　I will not forget your words.

adapted from Psalm 119:9–16

A Moment with Jesus

Imagine this! When Jesus was a boy, he learned about Moses and God's people. He was expected to obey the commandments. He went to the Temple to worship. His life was very much like yours is now. Share with Jesus whatever is on your mind or in your heart. Jesus listens and understands.

The Commandments Are Laws of Love

God gave us his laws with love to show us how to love him and others. They help us live so that we can be happy on earth and with God in heaven. There we will be forever with Jesus, Mary, the angels, the saints, and those we love.

Finish the Ten Commandments below by writing the missing words from the Word Bank.

WORD BANK

adultery	gods
name	covet
goods	steal
false	holy
father	kill

Love God

1. I am the Lord your God:

   you shall not have strange _____ before me.

2. You shall not take the _____ of the Lord your God in vain.

3. Remember to keep _____ the Lord's Day.

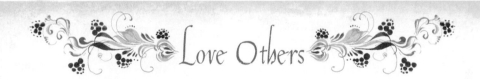
Love Others

4. Honor your _____ and your mother.

5. You shall not _____ .

6. You shall not commit _____ .

7. You shall not _____ .

8. You shall not bear _____ witness against your neighbor.

9. You shall not _____ your neighbor's wife.

10. You shall not covet your neighbor's _____ .

Decoding God's Message

Use the code to find another name for the Ten Commandments. Print the code letter above each number on the stone tablet.

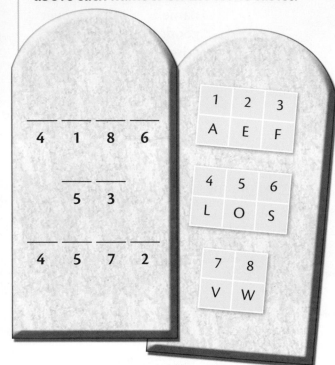

1	2	3
A	E	F

4	5	6
L	O	S

7	8
V	W

Tablet:
__ __ __ __
4 1 8 6

__ __
5 3

__ __ __ __
4 5 7 2

We Remember

Why did God give us the Ten Commandments?

God gave us the Ten Commandments to show us how to live lives that are pleasing to him and respectful of others.

Word to Know
moral law

We Respond

I will keep all the commands that the Lord has given me.

adapted from Exodus 24:3

Building Family Faith

CHAPTER SUMMARY Because he loves us, God gave the Ten Commandments as a pattern of living that leads to eternal life. The commandments call us to love God and love our neighbor.

REFLECT

I, the LORD, am your God, who brought you out of the land of Egypt, that place of slavery.

Deuteronomy 5:6

DISCUSS AS A FAMILY

• how living according to the commandments is choosing to belong to God.

• the commandments that call us to love God.

• the commandments that tell us how to love our neighbor and ourselves.

PRAY

You have placed your law in our hearts, O God.

DO

• Take turns as a family listing one of the commandments until you have all 10 listed. This is a way to reinforce learning the commandments by heart.

• Rent the movie *The Ten Commandments* and watch it as a family. Discuss any questions you or your child may have after viewing it.

• Make a replica of the two tablets given to Moses and work with your child to decorate them, either with the words of the commandments or with images depicting the ways we love God and others.

Visit **www.christourlife.com** for more family resources.

Gather and Go Forth

Know and Proclaim

We study our faith to learn what God desires for us. Then we can proclaim our beliefs in what we say and do.

We Know Our Faith	We Proclaim Our Faith
The Old Testament teaches us how God gave the Israelites his law, the Ten Commandments.	As Catholics, we pray and sing the psalms to give God praise. We praise God for giving us his laws to live by when we pray Psalm 119.
God made a covenant with the Israelites to be his special people if they followed his laws. God makes the same covenant with us.	Catholics attend Mass and study the teachings of the Church to learn how to live by God's laws.
The Ten Commandments are our moral laws. They show us how to live holy lives and be respectful of others.	Catholics prayerfully reflect on the Ten Commandments to prepare for the Sacrament of Penance and Reconciliation.

Following God's laws shows the world our love for him.

Moses summoned all Israel and said to them, Hear, O Israel, the statutes and ordinances which I proclaim in your hearing this day, that you may learn them and take care to observe them.

Deuteronomy 5:1

Test Your Catholic Knowledge

Fill in the circle that best completes the sentence.

When God's people accepted his covenant, they agreed to:

○ belong to God and follow his laws.

○ eat only manna in the desert.

○ remain slaves in Egypt.

○ write their own set of laws.

A Catholic to Know

In the 1800s, Thérèse was nurtured from birth in her faith by her devout parents. Thérèse wanted to dedicate herself to the contemplative life, but she was prevented from joining the Carmelite Sisters because of her young age. However, on a pilgrimage to Rome with her father, she pleaded with Pope Leo XIII for permission to join the Carmel of Lisieux. Thérèse was soon granted entry, where she was inspired by the Gospel to dedicate her every act and suffering to Christ. Through quiet prayer and sacrifice, she turned common everyday activities into acts of love.

Saint Thérèse of Lisieux

Witness and Share

These sentences describe what Catholics believe. Listen carefully as they are read. Ask yourself, "How strong are my Catholic beliefs?"

My Way to Faith

- I recognize myself as a member of the People of God, the Church.

- I obey the Ten Commandments because they are God's laws of love.

- I pray or sing the psalms at Mass to praise God.

- I study the teachings of the Church to learn the meaning of God's law.

Share Your Faith

Write a short prayer thanking God for giving you the Ten Commandments as a guide for living. Share the prayer with your family. Invite family members to say the prayer with you.

_____

_____

_____

_____

We Honor Mary

Mary Is the Best Disciple

When we pray the Hail Mary, we call God's Mother "holy Mary." After Jesus, the Virgin Mary is the holiest person who ever lived. She loved God and was filled with his life. She did whatever God asked, even when it was puzzling and would bring her much suffering. She always loved and helped others.

Our heavenly mother, Mary, prays for us. She is always ready to help us follow her Son as she did. She wants us to bring Jesus and his love into the world too.

The Annunciation

Narrator: The angel Gabriel was sent by God to a town called Nazareth. He came to a virgin whose name was Mary. The angel said to her:

Angel: Hail, favored one! The Lord is with you.

Narrator: Mary was greatly troubled by these words. She wondered what this greeting could mean. The angel said:

Angel: Do not be afraid, Mary. Behold, you will have a son, and you shall name him Jesus. He will be great and will be called Son of the Most High.

Mary: But how can this come about?

Angel: The Holy Spirit will come upon you, and God's power will overshadow you. And so the Child to be born will be called holy, the Son of God.

Mary: I am the handmaid of the Lord. May it be done to me according to your word.

Narrator: Mary became the Mother of God. Jesus, the Son of God, became Mary's son.

adapted from Luke 1:26–38

We Pray to Mary

Mary's willingness to be the mother of Jesus made her the first and most important follower of Jesus. Through the ages, Catholics have recognized her closeness to Jesus and have prayed to her as Mother of the Church, Queen of all Saints, and Help of Christians. Mary has become the person we most often ask to pray for us. We especially come to her when we are in need.

There are many prayers honoring Mary. The most important is the Hail Mary, which repeats the words of the angel Gabriel. In this prayer we ask Mary to help us, especially at the hour of our death. We pray the Hail Mary 10 times with each decade of the Rosary. We can also pray the Hail Mary morning, noon, and evening when we pray the *Angelus*.

Mary is the Mother of God and our mother. She is the Queen of Heaven because she was taken into heaven when her life on earth was over. From her place next to her Son Jesus, Mary shows her loving concern for our needs and for the needs of the world. Remember her often and never hesitate to ask her to pray for you.

Mary

Comforter of the Afflicted

Queen of Heaven

Cause of Our Joy

Mirror of Justice

House of Gold

Vessel of Honor

Seat of Wisdom

Refuge of Sinners

We Honor Mary in Prayer

When we pray the *Angelus*, we recall the great mystery of the Incarnation. In this prayer we repeat the words said by the angel and Mary's reply. We honor Mary and give glory to God, who made her and filled her with grace. The *Angelus* is prayed morning, noon, and evening. In the past church bells rang to remind the people that it was time to pray this prayer. At the ringing of the bells, people would stop whatever they were doing to join together in praying the *Angelus*.

Jean Francois Millet, *The Angelus*, 1857.

Mary, Full of Grace

Design and color a stained-glass window honoring Mary.

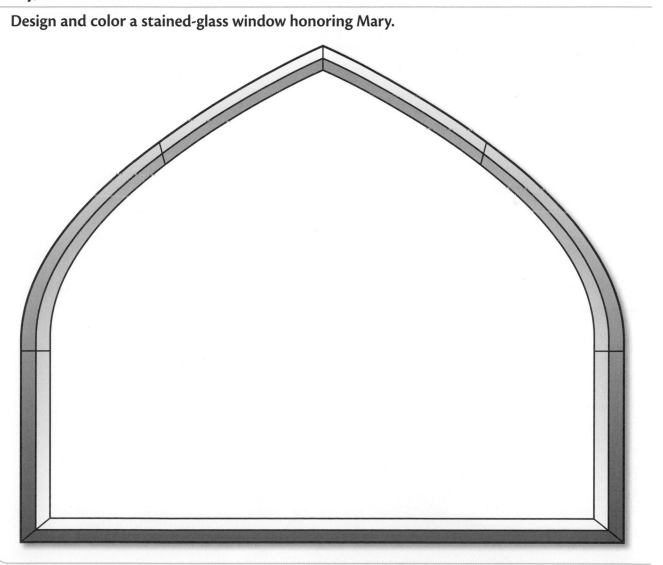

A Puzzle for Experts

Use the clues and the words in the Word Bank to solve the crossword puzzle.

WORD BANK

absolution	hearts
Angelus	Jesus
bread	life
commandments	love
conscience	Reconciliation
contrition	sacrifice
Eucharist	serve

WORD BANK

absolution	hearts
Angelus	Jesus
bread	life
commandments	love
conscience	Reconciliation
contrition	sacrifice
Eucharist	serve

Across

3. What we do if we follow Jesus
7. Sacrament in which God forgives us
11. Sorrow for sin
12. What God's laws show us how to do
13. Our highest form of worship
14. Rules God gave us to be happy

Down

1. What we ask for in the Lord's Prayer
2. Something that helps us know right from wrong
4. Person who taught us the Lord's Prayer
5. What Jesus came to bring us
6. Prayer in which we remember the Incarnation
8. An offering to God
9. Forgiveness of sin
10. What God wants more than sacrifices

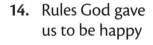

Meet the Needs of Others

We cannot perform miracles to help people as Jesus did, but we can do many thoughtful things for others.

Read each situation below and fill in the box if you can say a prayer asking God to help, if you can make a sacrifice for others, or if you can help by doing something loving. You can fill in one, two, or all three boxes for each situation.

say a prayer · make a sacrifice · offer help

☐ ☐ ☐ Your mother has a bad headache.

☐ ☐ ☐ Your neighbor's home burned down.

☐ ☐ ☐ A flood destroyed a town.

☐ ☐ ☐ A classmate has the flu.

☐ ☐ ☐ Hospitals in India need medicine.

☐ ☐ ☐ Your father has lost his job.

☐ ☐ ☐ A new student joins your class.

☐ ☐ ☐ Your friend did not make the soccer team.

☐ ☐ ☐ Your younger sister cannot read very well yet.

1. Pray

2. Sacrifice

3. Help

We Pray the *Angelus*

Song

Prayer

Leader: We begin our prayer with the words the angel Gabriel used, "Hail Mary." What joy to speak directly to the Mother of God.

Reader 1: She is full of grace, full of God's life because Jesus has come to dwell in her.

Reader 2: She is blessed among women and shares with us God's greatest blessing, Jesus.

Reader 3: Holy Mary, Mother of God, thank you for being our mother too and for praying for us.

Intercessions

Leader: Mary is the mother of Jesus. She is our mother too. Let us bring our needs and hopes to her. She will bring them to her Son for us.

Our response is "Holy Mary, pray for us.

Child 1: So that we worship God with loving hearts, we ask . . . ℟

Child 2 So that we may be faithful followers of your son Jesus, we ask . . . ℟

Child 3: So that we may be unselfish in serving others, we ask . . . ℟

Child 4: So that we are not afraid to speak to others about God's love and goodness, we ask . . . ℟

Child 5: So that God's will is our will, we ask . . . ℞.

Leader: Loving God, hear the requests of your children and give them what they need to live loving and holy lives. We ask this in the name of Mary and through Jesus Christ, her son and our Lord. Amen.

Introduction to Prayer

Leader: Let us now give thanks for the great mystery of the Incarnation by praying the *Angelus*.

Prayer

Leader: *Verse.* The Angel of the Lord declared unto Mary.

All: *Response.* And she conceived of the Holy Spirit.

All: Hail, Mary, full of grace, the Lord is with thee.
Blessed art thou among women and blessed is the fruit of thy womb, Jesus.
Holy Mary, Mother of God, pray for us sinners, now and at the hour of our death.
Amen.

Leader: *Verse.* Behold the handmaid of the Lord.

All: *Response.* Be it done unto me according to thy word.

All: Hail Mary. *(Pray the entire prayer.)*

Leader: *Verse.* And the Word was made flesh.

All: *Response.* and dwelt among us.

All: Hail Mary. *(Pray the entire prayer.)*

Leader: *Verse.* Pray for us, O holy Mother of God.

All: *Response.* That we may become worthy of the promises of Christ.

Leader: Let us pray;

All: Pour forth, we beseech thee, O Lord, thy grace into our hearts; that we, to whom the Incarnation of Christ, thy Son, was made known by the message of an angel, may by his Passion and Cross be brought to the glory of his Resurrection. Through the same Christ, our Lord. Amen.

Closing Song

Looking Back at Unit 2

In this unit you have learned that Jesus revealed the greatness and goodness of God perfectly. God wants us to become holy. We can do this by acting more like Jesus. We can show loving concern for others and worship the Father. In Reconciliation and the Eucharist, Jesus helps us become like him.

God made a covenant of love with us at Baptism. We respond to God by adoring and serving him. We offer our worship together with the worship that Jesus offered his Father. We show our love by trying to do what God asks. When we live by God's laws, we become holy and happy.

Word to Know
Angelus

Spreading the Word Around Town

Design a bumper sticker encouraging people to be with God or to follow his laws.

Living the Message

Check (✓) each sentence that describes you.

❑ 1.   I know the meaning of the Lord's Prayer and pray it with love.

❑ 2.   I can explain how my conscience can help me become like Jesus.

❑ 3.   I try to be aware of what is happening at Mass.

❑ 4.   I know many ways God has shown his greatness and goodness.

❑ 5.   I can explain ways to be like Jesus.

Planning to Grow

Fill in the blanks.

I can worship God by _____ and _____ him.

Gather and Go Forth

CHAPTER 9

Know and Proclaim

We look to Mary for guidance on how to live for Christ. Then we follow her example by what we say and do.

We Know Our Faith	We Proclaim Our Faith
The Virgin Mary is the best disciple. As mother of Jesus, she brought him into the world.	As Catholics, we repeat the words of the angel Gabriel when we pray, "Hail, Mary, full of grace, the Lord is with you."
Mary is the Queen of Heaven because she was taken into heaven when her life on earth was over.	As Catholics, we honor Mary and celebrate the mystery of the Incarnation by praying the *Angelus* morning, noon, and evening.
Mary is also called the Handmaid of the Lord because she did what God asked of her, even if she did not understand.	Many Catholic parishes honor Mary, the Blessed Mother, throughout the month of May by praying the Rosary daily.

Test Your Catholic Knowledge

Fill in the circle that best answers the question.

Whose words are repeated in the Hail Mary?

○ Jesus'

○ Saint Joseph's

○ Elizabeth's

○ the angel Gabriel's

Mary is a model for accepting God's plan. She shows us how to live our faith, even when it is not easy.

For he has looked upon his handmaid's lowliness; behold, from now on all ages call me blessed.

Luke 1:48

A Catholic to Know

Francis was born into a wealthy family in 1182. In his 20s, he went to war and was captured and held prisoner. Francis began thinking about the Gospel story in which Jesus tells the rich man to sell what he has and follow him. Francis returned home and did just that. He gave away all he had and rejoiced in God's creation. Known for his love of all creatures, Francis shows us how to be poor in spirit, depending only on God.

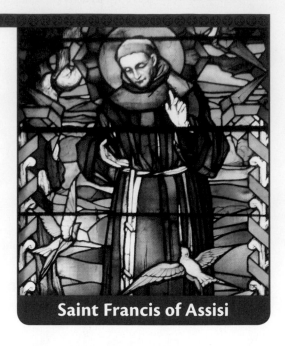

Saint Francis of Assisi

Witness and Share

These sentences describe what Catholics believe. Listen carefully as they are read. Ask yourself, "How strong are my Catholic beliefs?"

My Way to Faith

- I follow Mary's example because she is Jesus' first and greatest disciple.

- I believe Mary was taken into heaven when her life on earth was over.

- I look to Mary as a good example of how to say yes to God.

- I honor Mary by praying the Rosary.

- I trust that Mary prays to God for me.

Share Your Faith

What are your favorite ways to honor Mary? Make a list below. Share the list with family members. Invite them to suggest ways to honor Mary. Choose one of the ideas and prayerfully practice it this week.

_____

_____

_____

_____

_____

Family Feature

Give Thanks to God

The Ledet family has passed on African folklore and traditional African-American recipes for generations. One story they like to tell explains why people have to work for food.

Long ago the sky was close to the earth and was a source of food for the people. Anyone who was hungry could just reach up and break off a piece. Soon they began to waste their food. They would take a bite or two and throw the rest away. The sky warned that if people were not more careful with its gift of food, it would move far away. For a while the people changed, but then they again became greedy and careless. Finally the sky moved up so high that it could not be reached. At first the people waited for the sky to come down again, but as they grew hungry and the sky stayed out of reach, they began to make tools to plant and harvest their own food. To this day people must work for their food.

From generation to generation, these stories pass on important values, such as caring for the gifts of the earth and sharing them with one another. Were stories passed on in your family that helped shape your values? What stories are you telling your child?

Visit **www.christourlife.com** for more family resources.

Family Feature

Storytelling and mealtimes go together.

You can make a meal special by including a dish from your family's heritage or from another culture that interests you, and sharing stories as you enjoy the dish. Here's a delicious recipe for bread pudding, a popular dessert in Great Britain and in the southeastern United States that you can make with your child. You can add your favorite ingredients to make this your family's dessert tradition.

Bread pudding

2 cups milk
3 eggs, beaten
⅓ cup sugar
½ teaspoon salt
½ teaspoon vanilla extract
12–14 slices white bread, without crust
1 teaspoon cinnamon
dash nutmeg
½ cup raisins, optional
1 can of fruit-pie filling, optional

Heat the milk over low heat until it is hot but not boiling. In a bowl, combine eggs, sugar, and salt; stir well. Gradually stir about 1/4 of the hot milk into the egg mixture. Add remaining milk, stirring constantly. Stir in vanilla.

Place bread slices in a buttered, two-quart baking dish. Raisins or other dried fruit can be sprinkled over the bread. Pour the milk mixture over the bread. Combine cinnamon and nutmeg and sprinkle over the pudding mixture. Leave uncovered and bake at 300° for about 50 minutes. Serve warm with vanilla ice cream or other dessert topping, if desired. (serves 6)

The Gift of Family

Let the gingerbread people shown here represent different members of your family. (You can trace over these to make as many gingerbread people as you need. You can include grandparents and other close relatives as well.) Have everyone present write his or her name on his or her own gingerbread person. Then, on the lines provided, every member of the family can take a turn writing down traits of that person for which they are thankful.

When all the spaces are filled, your child can cut out the gingerbread people and give each person the one with his or her name and traits. You might want to post them all on the refrigerator as a reminder of the benefits of being a family.

Thanking God as a Family

Gratitude is an essential building block of all spirituality. When our hearts are thankful, we are more likely to care for the many gifts God offers in our lives. You can nurture the virtue of gratitude in your child and in your family. Here are two ways you can foster gratitude at home.

Draw Out Your Gratitude

Get an oversized sheet of paper or poster board and crayons, markers, or finger paints. Begin by writing a brief prayer of gratitude on the paper. Have every member of the family take a turn creating a work of art. Let your child begin by drawing one thing he or she is grateful for. Then, one by one, each takes a turn. Keep filling in the piece of art until the entire work is finished. Then have everyone explains the parts of the picture he or she contributed, telling what it means to him or her. Let everyone sign the masterpiece and display it in a prominent place in your home for the coming week.

Decorate Your Thanksgiving Day Tablecloth

Get a light-colored tablecloth and some permanent markers. Spread out the tablecloth on a table that has been protected by a piece of cardboard or similar material. After Thanksgiving dinner, or whenever you have the extended family over, have everyone present write a message of thanks and gratitude on the tablecloth. Encourage people to decorate the section of tablecloth in front of them in any way that expresses their thanks to God. You might even include the names of deceased family members who shared your table in years past.

You can use this tablecloth year after year on Thanksgiving and for other family gatherings. Every year people can add more decorations as well as the names of new family members to the tablecloth showing that it, like life and family and faith, is a work in progress.

We Love God

Let us love not in word and speech but in deed and truth.

1 John 3:18

A Letter Home

Dear Parents and Family,

Your child has studied the Ten Commandments over the years and, in Unit Two, learned that these instructions for living a good life are a sign of God's love. In Unit Three, the focus of the children's study will be the first three commandments—those that tell us how we should worship God.

The children will begin by recognizing the other gods in their lives, the people and things that claim their attention. They will learn to put God first by worshiping him with faith, hope, and love. Consider the ways you demonstrate in your home that God is first above all things.

As they continue in this unit with the Second Commandment, the children will learn that people who seek to honor God show reverence for his name and for the people, places, and objects related to his service and worship. The children will learn to become aware of their casual language as well as their attitudes and behavior in church.

Studying the Third Commandment, the children will explore ways to keep the Lord's Day holy, including worshiping at Mass and receiving Holy Communion, as well as putting aside those things that interfere with the rest and prayer for which the Lord's Day was intended. This can be a tall order in our busy society, but it can become a welcome custom and respite in your family.

The primary message your child will carry from Unit Three is that by keeping these three commandments, we show our love for God.

At the end of each chapter in this unit, the children will bring home a review of the chapter along with either the Building Family Faith page or the Family Feature section. These features give you a quick review of what your child learned and offer practical ways to reinforce the lesson at home so that the whole family may benefit.

Visit **www.christourlife.com** for more family resources.

We Show Our Love for God

God Gives Us Gifts

God our Father made us and gives us life. He gives us all the beautiful things in the world. Every good thing we have is a gift from God.

God wants us to love his good gifts because he made them. They show us God's glory and tell us of his love. God's gifts lead us to worship him.

I will praise the Lord with all my heart. . . .

Great are the works of the Lord.

Psalm 111:1–2

God Asks for Our Love

God is good and much greater than all his gifts. God wants us to love him more than everything else. He knows all things and tells us what is true. He wants us to believe in him. As our loving Father, God always cares for us. He wants us to hope in him.

In the First Commandment God says to worship only him.

> I, the Lord, am your God. . . . You shall not have other gods besides me.
>
> Exodus 20:2–3

God says, "Give me your love." He wants to be first in our lives.

Jesus is God's best gift to us. He shows us how to love God our Father above everything else. He shows us how to adore God. He shows us how to love God by loving and serving others.

My God and My All

Read the sentences and add the missing words.

1. God's gifts show us his _____ .

2. God calls us to _____ him.

3. God tells us what is true, so we can _____ in him.

4. God cares for us. He wants us to have _____ in him.

5. God wants us to _____ him more than his gifts.

6. We show our love when we _____ to God.

WORD BANK

adore	hope
love	believe
goodness	pray

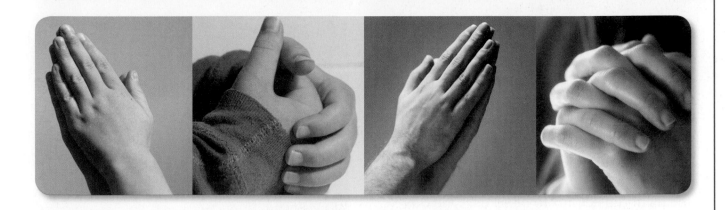

We Give God Our Love in Prayer

When we pray, we lift up our minds and hearts to God. We think of him and love him. God listens to us and speaks to us too. He loves us and wants us to pray.

Jesus teaches us how to pray. He often went off by himself to pray. Sometimes he prayed all night. Can you think of a time when Jesus prayed? Write it here.

_____

_____

_____

Jesus said,

> "Go to your inner room, close the door, and pray to your Father in secret."

Matthew 6:6

He also said,

> "Ask and it will be given to you."

Matthew 7:7

We ask God to give us all we need. A prayer in which we ask for something is called a **prayer of petition**, but there are three other kinds of prayer besides prayers of petition. In prayer we can praise God, thank God, and tell God we are sorry for our sins. A long time ago, God's people prayed all these ways. The prayers they wrote are called the psalms. We still pray them today.

A Moment with Jesus

Speak to Jesus in the quiet of your heart. Knowing that Jesus said that the Father will take care of all your needs, tell him what it is that you need most now. It could be a job for your dad or help with your math homework or good health for a friend who is sick. Jesus will take your need to the Father. Know that God will hear your prayer.

We Honor Mary, the Angels, and the Saints in Prayer

God wants us to love and to honor those who are in heaven with him. Mary, Jesus' mother and ours, lives there. Heaven is also home for the angels who bring us God's messages. God's special friends and ours, the saints, live there too. They pray for us and ask God to bless us. One day we will live with them in heaven.

We show our love for Mary, the angels, and the saints by asking them to pray for us and by imitating them. When we honor them, we honor God, who made them.

Mary, pray for us.

St. Michael, pray for us.

St. Julie, pray for us.

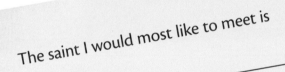

The saint I would most like to meet is

_____

_____

I would like to meet this saint because

_____

_____

_____

_____

_____

I would like to ask this saint

_____

_____

_____

We Pray the Psalms

Print on each blank the word that tells the kind of prayer each psalm verse is. The Word Bank will help you.

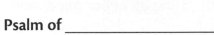

WORD BANK

petition   sorrow

praise   thanks

Psalm of _____

> Give thanks to the LORD, who
> is good,
> whose kindness lasts forever.
>> adapted from Psalm 106:1

Psalm of _____

> Shout joyfully to God, all you
> on earth;
> sing of his glorious name.
>> Psalm 66:1–2

Psalm of _____

> Have mercy on me, O God, . . .
> wipe out my sin.
>> adapted from Psalm 51:3

Psalm of _____

> Come quickly to help me,
> my Lord and my salvation!
>> Psalm 38:23

We Remember

What is prayer?
Prayer is the lifting up of our minds and hearts to God.

What is the First Commandment?
The First Commandment is

"I am the Lord your God: you shall not have strange gods before me."

Word to Know
prayer of petition

We Respond

Verse. **Come, Holy Spirit, fill the hearts of your faithful.**
Response. **And kindle in them the fire of your love.**
Verse. **Send forth your Spirit and they shall be created.**
Response. **And you shall renew the face of the earth.**

Building Family Faith

CHAPTER SUMMARY God is revealed as a loving father. Sometimes we let that which is not God take the place of God in our lives. God calls us into a right relationship with him, the one true God.

REFLECT
Everything the Lord has said, we will do.
Exodus 19:8

DISCUSS AS A FAMILY
• some of the other gods that might lead us away from the true God.
• what happens when people put that which is not God into the place that only God can fill.
• what God promises to those who keep his commandments.

PRAY
My God, I love and adore you above all things.

DO
• Review the four kinds of prayer—praise, contrition (sorrow), thanks, and petition (request). At dinner this week, have each member of the family mention one thing he or she praises God for, one thing he or she is sorry for, one thing he or she is grateful for, and one thing he or she is asking God for.

• Plan time for a cookie bake. Make cookies in the shape of the symbols for faith ✝, hope ⚓, and love ♥. Decorate them as you wish. Remind family members to ask God to help them grow in these virtues.

Visit **www.christourlife.com** for more family resources.

Gather and Go Forth

Know and Proclaim

We seek to know God and grow in friendship with him. This closeness makes us want to share God's love with others.

We Know Our Faith	We Proclaim Our Faith
God wants us to love him above all else. He always cares for us and wants us to hope in him.	During Lent, Catholics show that God is first in their lives by sacrificing something that seems important to them.
When we pray, we lift our minds and hearts to God. Everything we are and have comes from God.	Catholics pray in the morning and evening as a way to ask God's help as the first act of the day and thank him for his care as the last act of the day.
The saints are holy men and women who have died and now live with God in heaven.	We honor the saints by imitating their lives and their ways. Catholics often choose a patron saint at Confirmation to guide their words and actions.

With God first in our hearts, we cannot help but tell others the Good News.

But sanctify Christ as Lord in your hearts. Always be ready to give an explanation to anyone who asks you for a reason for your hope.

1 Peter 3:15

Test Your Catholic Knowledge

Fill in the circle that best completes the sentence.

Prayers, written long ago by God's people, that praise God and tell him we are sorry for our sins are called the:

○ Acts of the Apostles.

○ psalms.

○ letters.

○ Gospels.

A Catholic to Know

Teresa was a friendly girl from Spain in the 1500s who loved to sing and dance. As a young woman, she liked pretty clothes and took special care of her hair and hands. Even so, Teresa could not ignore that God was calling her to religious life. Teresa eventually followed God's call to became a nun, and she discovered that all the things that made her happy in her earlier life were nothing compared to her happiness in the service of God. Teresa, however, struggled with prayer. Then she put God first in her life. She said, "Prayer is an act of love; words are not needed." We can be like Saint Teresa when we pray with joy and love.

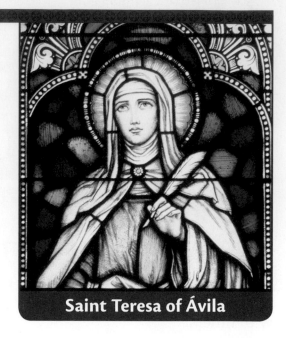

Saint Teresa of Ávila

Witness and Share

These sentences describe what Catholics believe. Listen carefully as they are read. Ask yourself, "How strong are my Catholic beliefs?"

My Way to Faith

- I love God above all things.

- I adore God with my prayers.

- I study the lives of the saints to strengthen my faith and gain courage.

- I pray at night to reflect on my actions during the day.

Share Your Faith

Think of a way to put God first in your life this week. List your ideas below. Share them with a friend. Invite a friend to join you in doing one of the things on your list.

_____

_____

_____

_____

We Love All That Is Holy

We Praise the Name of the Lord

We give our love to God when we keep the Second Commandment.

> You shall not take the name of the LORD, your God, in vain.
>
> Exodus 20:7

In vain means "for no good reason."

Our names are important because they stand for us. We do not like it when others make fun of our names. We are pleased and happy when our names are said with love. God's name is holy because God is holy. Because of their great respect for God, Jewish people would never say God's name.

Jesus taught us to call God our Father and to pray: "Hallowed be thy name."

We honor God's name as "hallowed," or holy, when we use it with love and respect. We do not say God's name carelessly in everyday speech. We do not use God's name in anger or to curse. Cursing is using God's name to wish harm to someone or something. If we love God, we say his name only in prayer or for another good reason. For instance, in court people are sometimes asked to swear. In this case swearing means calling on God to witness that what they say is true.

> O LORD, our Lord,
>   how awesome is your name through all
>   the earth!
>
> Psalm 8:2

God Has Many Names

When we sing and pray, we use many of the names of God. Each name that we call God tells how good or powerful he is.

Unscramble the letters and write the name of God that belongs on each blank.

1. _____

   SUJES

   means "God saves."

2. Another name for Jesus is

   _____ .

   HCRSTI

3. The Third Person of the Blessed Trinity is the

   _____

   YHOL

   _____ .

   TRISPI

4. We call God

   _____

   DLOR

   because he rules heaven and earth.

5. Jesus told us to call God our

   _____ .

   HAFTRE

When you pray, what holy name for God do you use the most?

_____

Use that name now to tell God that you love him.

The Name of Jesus Is Holy

The name of Jesus is powerful. When Jesus walked the earth, blind men who called his name with faith were given sight. Later Peter and John healed a crippled man in the name of Jesus. Other disciples did many marvels in his holy name.

The Bible says that God gave to his Son the name

> that is above every name,
> that at the name of Jesus
> every knee should bend,
> of those in heaven and on earth and
> under the earth.
>
> Philippians 2:9–10

Because the name of Jesus is so holy and powerful, repeating it is itself one of the oldest and best prayers. When praying the name of Jesus, people come to feel his love and presence.

A Moment with Jesus

Imagine that you are in a quiet place and that Jesus is with you. You are so happy to be with him that you just say his name over and over softly and reverently. Close your eyes and let the word "Jesus" be your prayer. Then just sit quietly in the presence of Jesus. When you are ready, open your eyes and pray "Amen."

We Respect All That Is Holy

One day when Jesus went to the **Temple** to worship, he saw people buying and selling for their own profit. Jesus was angry when he saw that people were not honoring God in that holy place. He knocked over tables with piles of money on them and ordered people who were selling things to leave the Temple.

Then Jesus said, "My Father's house shall be a house of prayer. You are making it a den of thieves."

adapted from Matthew 21:12–13

Jesus wanted the people to respect the Temple as a holy place. Today, he wants us to respect all holy, or sacred, people, places, and things. In the Second Commandment, God our Father taught us the same thing. Holy people, places, and things help us think of God. When we honor what is holy, we praise and honor God.

All people are called to holiness. Some are called to give themselves entirely to God and to his work.

Complete the help wanted ad below. Fill in some qualities you think would be found in a person seeking holiness.

HELP WANTED

Needed: Holy People

Job: To do God's work and help make our world a better place

Qualities:

Be kind, help others, respect people,
Be nice, be helpful, care for others, be loving
always obey

Reward: Happiness on earth and in heaven

Our Homes Are Holy

Certain places are called holy because they are special places where people pray and worship. Our homes are holy too because we often pray together there as a family.

Certain things are called holy because they remind us of God or because they are used when we pray.

Think about your own home. On the line, write the name of a fourth room in your house. Then draw a picture of some holy things that can be found in each of the rooms.

Bedroom

_____

Kitchen

Living Room

Living the Second Commandment

Circle the names of the children who are showing reverence for what is holy.

1. Winston laughed and said Jesus' name when his friend struck out.

2. Labelle played with her rosary by swinging it around and making designs with it.

3. Before taking a test, Claire prayed for help.

4. When a friend said God's name in anger, Brigitte said in her heart, "Praised be Jesus Christ."

5. Emma bowed her head whenever she heard the name of Jesus.

6. During Mass, Christopher kept kicking the kneeler, disturbing people nearby.

We Remember

What is the Second Commandment?
The Second Commandment is "You shall not take the name of the Lord your God in vain."

Word to Know
Temple

We Respond

I will honor God's name and respect all that is holy.

Western Wall of the Temple in Jerusalem, built by King Herod the Great.

Building Family Faith

CHAPTER SUMMARY Christians are called to give special respect to people, places, and things related to God. We should especially revere God's name and not use it carelessly or in anger.

REFLECT
"You shall not take the name of the LORD, your God, in vain."

Exodus 20:7

DISCUSS AS A FAMILY
- some ways you misuse God's name.
- how to handle anger and frustration constructively.
- how to give proper respect to holy things at home, school, and church.

PRAY
You are holy, Lord. Blessed be your holy name.

DO
Talk about the importance of names, the reasons you reverence God's name, and what you can do when you hear God's name being misused or abused.

Name the holy things you have in your house. Talk about how you show respect for them.

Sing "Holy God We Praise Thy Name" or another song that shows reverence for God.

Visit **www.christourlife.com** for more family resources.

Gather and Go Forth

Know and Proclaim

When we respect God and set apart what is holy for worship, we tell him and the world he is first in our lives.

We Know Our Faith	We Proclaim Our Faith
We praise the name of the Lord.	Catholics refer to God with reverence and respect by using names such as God the Father, God the Son, and God the Holy Spirit.
Jesus' name is holy and powerful.	As Catholics, we call on Jesus' name for help in times of need and to praise him with joy.
Jesus wants us to respect all sacred places and things.	We show reverence for God in our homes by displaying holy objects, like religious statues or the Bible.

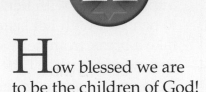

How blessed we are to be the children of God!

Hear, O Israel! The LORD is our God, the LORD alone! Therefore, you shall love the LORD, your God, with your whole heart, and with your whole being and with your whole strength.

Deuteronomy 6:4–5

Test Your Catholic Knowledge

Fill in the circle that best completes the sentence.

The Second Commandment tells us to:

○ speak the Lord's name with love and respect.

○ honor our fathers and mothers.

○ have no other god besides the Lord.

○ keep the Lord's Day holy.

A Catholic to Know

Having good friends who love and welcome you is one of the most precious gifts in life. Martha was a good friend to Jesus. She wanted everything to be perfect for the Lord. She cooked, cleaned, and served Jesus when he visited her family. Jesus appreciated Martha's devoted care and developed a special bond with her. However, he told her not to be upset with her sister Mary, who chose to take a break from her work to sit with him. Jesus reminded Martha of the importance of resting from one's work to spend time in his presence.

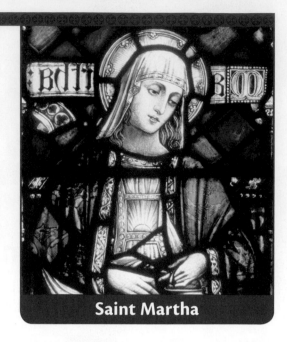

Saint Martha

Witness and Share

These sentences describe what Catholics believe. Listen carefully as they are read. Ask yourself, "How strong are my Catholic beliefs?"

My Way to Faith

- I praise God's name in prayer.

- I call on Jesus when I am joyful and when I am in need.

- I show respect for holy people, places, and things because they help me know God.

- I treat the holy objects in my home with reverence and respect.

- I pray together with my family at home.

Share Your Faith

Think of one way to show Jesus how much you love him. Write your idea below. Invite a family member to join you in putting your idea into practice this week. Offer your actions to Jesus as a prayer for those who have separated themselves from him.

_____

_____

_____

_____

CHAPTER 12

We Keep the Lord's Day Holy

God Tells Us to Keep His Day Holy

When God created the world, he worked for six days and rested on the seventh. God blessed the seventh day and made it holy.

> So God blessed the seventh day and made it holy, because on it he rested from all the work he had done in creation.
>
> Genesis 2:3

In his Third Commandment God told his people to do as he had done.

> Remember to keep holy the sabbath day.
>
> Exodus 20:8

God explained, "You may work for six days, but the seventh day is the Sabbath of the Lord." God's people loved him and were careful to keep Saturday, the **Sabbath** day, holy. They went to the temple or the synagogue to worship together. They rejoiced with others. They rested from work. They did all their work before the day of rest.

The early Christians kept Sunday as the Lord's Day because Jesus rose from the dead on Easter Sunday. Christians celebrated Sunday to show they believed in Jesus. They came together for the Breaking of the Bread, the Eucharist. At this celebration the risen Christ offered himself to the Father for them, united them, and nourished them with himself.

We Celebrate Sundays and Holy Days

In his Third Commandment God tells us that he wants us to keep his day holy. The Church tells us to keep Sunday holy by celebrating Mass and resting from our work. As Catholics, we praise and thank God together at the Eucharist on Saturday evening or on Sunday. We celebrate the new life Jesus won by his dying and rising. We make Sunday a day of rest and celebration by enjoying ourselves and being with others. Celebrating each Sunday reminds us of the big celebration we will enjoy in heaven one day.

Here are three good reasons for celebrating Sunday with the Eucharist, making time to rest, and having fun with others.

- God tells us to keep the Lord's Day holy.
- Rest, prayer, and fun are good for our physical and mental health.
- Celebrating the Eucharist and spending fun time with others builds up the community.

As Catholic Christians, we also come together for Mass to celebrate special feasts in honor of Jesus, Mary, and the saints. These feasts are called holy days. There are certain laws of the Church that are called **Precepts of the Church**. One of these laws requires Catholics to go to Mass on specific holy days.

Name some holy days that we celebrate in our country.

_____

_____

_____

Keeping the Lord's Day Holy

Answer the questions, using the words in the Word Bank.

WORD BANK

resting   Jesus' rising
Sunday   the Eucharist
praying   the Sabbath
rejoicing

1. What was the Lord's Day first called?

_____

2. How did God's people keep the Sabbath holy?

a._____

b._____

c._____

3. What day do Christians keep as the Lord's Day?

_____

4. What happened on that day?

_____

5. What do Christians share?

_____

A Moment with Jesus

Quiet your body and your mind. Think of some special gifts that you have been given. Have you ever thought of Sunday as a gift? On Sunday, God gives you the opportunity to spend extra time with him, to rest, and to do fun things with your family. Share with Jesus how you spend your Sundays. Ask him to help you use your day of prayer and rest well.

The Eucharist Is Our Greatest Prayer

As we celebrate the Eucharist, we pray prayers of praise, thanks, sorrow, and petition. Beside each numbered part of the Mass, write the letter identifying the kind of prayer it is.

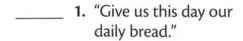

KINDS OF PRAYER

A. Praise   B. Thanks
C. Sorrow   D. Petition

_____ **1.** "Give us this day our daily bread."

_____ **2.** Lamb of God

_____ **3.** Holy, Holy, Holy

_____ **4.** Prayer of the Faithful

_____ **5.** *Gloria*

_____ **6.** "Let us give thanks to the Lord our God."

_____ **7.** ". . . And graciously grant [the Church] peace and unity in accordance with your will."

_____ **8.** "Lord, have mercy."

_____ **9.** "Through him, and with him, and in him, O God, almighty Father, in the unity of the Holy Spirit, all glory and honor is yours, for ever and ever."

_____ **10.** "The Word of the Lord." "Thanks be to God."

May the Lord accept the sacrifice at your hands for the praise and glory of his name, for our good, and the good of all his holy Church.

Make the Sun Shine on the Lord's Day

On each sun ray, print one way in which you can celebrate Sunday with your family. Print *Celebrate the Eucharist* in the center of the sun.

Saint Margaret Valued the Eucharist

Long ago in England and Wales, it was a crime to be a Catholic. Many people risked being sentenced to a cruel death if they celebrated the Eucharist. Hundreds of priests and laypeople were killed for their faith. Margaret Clitherow was one of these laypeople.

Margaret became a Catholic shortly after she married. She hid priests in her house, where they would celebrate Mass in secret. She hired a Catholic to tutor her children in the faith. This too was against the law.

One day officers came to search the house while the children were being tutored. Margaret was imprisoned, but she refused to give up her Catholic faith to save her life. In 1586 she was put to death. Saint Margaret Clitherow was canonized by Pope Paul VI in 1970.

We Remember

What is the Third Commandment?
The Third Commandment is "Remember to keep holy the Lord's Day."

Words to Know
Precepts of the Church   Sabbath

We Respond

I will keep the Lord's Day holy by celebrating the Eucharist on Sundays or Saturday evenings and on holy days.

Building Family Faith

CHAPTER SUMMARY Christians set aside Sunday as a special day to worship God, to receive the Eucharist, and to rest and relax. We do this to celebrate Jesus' Resurrection and to build up our community of faith.

REFLECT
"Remember to keep holy the sabbath day. Six days you may labor and do all your work, but the seventh day is the Sabbath of the LORD, your God."
Exodus 20:8–10

DISCUSS AS A FAMILY
• why it is important to take time to rest and relax with family and friends.
• how your family observes Sunday.
• the ways you celebrate other holy days of the Church.

PRAY
Thank you, Lord, for the great gift of your Sabbath.

DO
Plan something special for the family to do together on Sundays.

Prepare for Sunday Mass by reading the Gospel together the night before. Talk about the reading as a family.

Spend some time on Sunday with fellow parishioners. Mingle with them after Mass. Invite another family for Sunday brunch.

Visit **www.christourlife.com** for more family resources.

Gather and Go Forth

Know and Proclaim

Knowing God's laws helps us live good and holy lives. We grow stronger in faith and can spread his love to the world.

We Know Our Faith	We Proclaim Our Faith
When God created the world, he worked for six days and rested on the seventh.	As Catholics, we keep Sunday holy by celebrating the Eucharist at Mass.
Jews observe the Sabbath with a special meal, prayer, and rest. Sunday is the day Catholics fulfill the Third Commandment. The holy sacrifice of the Mass replaces the practices of the Sabbath.	Catholics keep this day holy by celebrating the Eucharist and refraining from work in order to praise and thank God for his gifts. Sunday is the "eighth day," the Lord's Day of new creation that celebrates Christ's Resurrection.
Throughout the year the Church celebrates special feasts in honor of Jesus, Mary, and the saints.	Catholics celebrate All Saints Day on November 1 to honor all the saints in heaven.

God told us to celebrate together in his name and rest one day each week. We follow his command to show others we put him first.

So whether you eat or drink, or whatever you do, do everything for the glory of God.

1 Corinthians 10:31

Test Your Catholic Knowledge

Fill in the circle that best completes the sentence.

Catholics are required to:

○ go to Mass on Sundays and holy days.

○ wear a religious medal.

○ do something fun with your family on Sunday.

○ attend Mass the first Friday of every month.

A Catholic to Know

Luke spoke Greek and wrote one of the four
Gospels as well as the Acts of the Apostles. Though
Luke was not an eyewitness to what he wrote
about, he learned about Jesus from Saint Paul and
interviewed people who knew Jesus. Luke's Gospel
tells of the angel Gabriel visiting Mary and of
Mary's visit to Elizabeth. Luke also wrote about
Jesus' birth and his being lost and then found in
the Temple when he was 12 years old. In the Acts of
the Apostles, Luke tells us about what the apostles
and friends of Jesus did after his Ascension into
heaven. Like Saint Luke, we are called to tell others
about Christ.

Saint Luke

Witness and Share

**These sentences describe what Catholics believe. Listen carefully as they are read.
Ask yourself, "How strong are my Catholic beliefs?"**

My Way to Faith

- I keep Sunday holy by attending Mass and receiving the Eucharist.

- On the Sabbath, a day of rest, I am grateful for the many ways God cares for me.

- I know and follow the Precepts of the Church.

- I pray to Jesus, Mary, and the saints.

Share Your Faith

**What activities can you do with your family to keep Sunday holy? Write two ideas on
the lines. Share the list with family members and invite them to add their own ideas.
Try at least one activity this Sunday. Give thanks to God as a family.**

_____

_____

_____

_____

We Grow in Holiness

We Receive the Word of the Kingdom

Jesus told the parable of the sower.

"Hear this! A sower went out to sow seed. As he sowed, some seed fell on the path and the birds came and ate it up. Other seed fell on rocky ground where it had little soil. It sprang up at once because the soil was not deep. And when the sun rose, it scorched the little plants. Not having roots, they withered and died. Some seed fell among thorns, and the thorns choked the plants so they produced no grain. And some seed fell on rich soil and produced fruit—thirty, sixty, and a hundredfold. Whoever has ears to hear ought to hear!"

adapted from Mark 4:3–9

Then Jesus explained the parable.

"The sower is anyone who spreads God's word. The seed is God's word. The people on the path hear the word, but Satan comes and takes it from them. The people who receive the word on rocky ground are those who listen with joy at first. But it does not stay with them. When it is hard to keep God's word, they give up. The people who receive the word among thorns listen to the word, but it is choked by the worries of this world and the desire for riches. But the people who receive the word on rich soil are those who hear the word, accept it, and bear fruit.

adapted from Mark 4:14–20

How Well Do You Understand?

Match the sentences with the pictures of Jesus' parable. Write the number of your choice in the small box.

1. This person spreads God's word.

2. Satan steals the seed from some people as soon as they hear it.

3. Some people listen to God's word at first with joy. But when it becomes hard to keep God's word, they give up.

4. Some people worry about money and what people think of them. The word of God is choked.

5. Some people hear the word and accept it. It produces a harvest of good works.

The sower went out to sow.

Some seed fell on rocky ground. It started to grow, but the plants soon withered.

Some seed fell on the path. The birds took it away.

Some seed fell on good soil. It grew and produced fruit.

Some seed fell among thorns. It grew, but thorns choked the plants.

Is God's Word Growing?

Read these stories and tell what these children will do if God's word is growing in them.

1. When Eduardo plays with friends, he uses words that are not respectful of God or others. He says the boys will tease him if he doesn't do what they do.

   Eduardo should

   _____

   _____

   _____

2. An elderly man on Sam's street lives alone. Sam often stops in to visit or to run errands for him rather than playing with his friends.

   Sam should

   _____

   _____

   _____

3. All during Mass, Su Lin is thinking about the fun she will have at the pool with her friend that afternoon.

   Su Lin should

   _____

   _____

4. Madeline likes to watch television. When her mother calls, she doesn't even hear her. She hardly notices all the work her mother has to do.

   Madeline should

   _____

   _____

   _____

Word Search

Find and circle the words from the Word Bank that refer to the first three commandments.

WORD BANK

believe	Easter	God	holy
honor	hope	Jesus	love
Mary	Mass	name	petition
praise	pray	rest	saints
sorrow	thanks	worship	

```
L C N O P R A I S E Q U A D
P R A Y O E L Z S A I N T S
B I M O A S T W U L H C F O
E P E T I T I O N H O N O R
L L J G O D M R D I P S I R
I O E H M A S S A L E T P O
E V S I V B C H Y U S I C W
V E U H O L Y I T H A N K S
E A S T E R Q P N A M A R Y
```

Jigsaw Puzzle

Print a motto on one side of a card and decorate it. Draw lines on the other side to divide the card into 10 pieces. Cut apart the card on the lines and put the pieces in an envelope. Exchange your envelope with that of a classmate and work each other's puzzle.

Some Mottos You Could Use

Love God with all your heart.   Lift up your hearts.

Trust in the Lord.   Pray to the Lord.

Love the Eucharist.

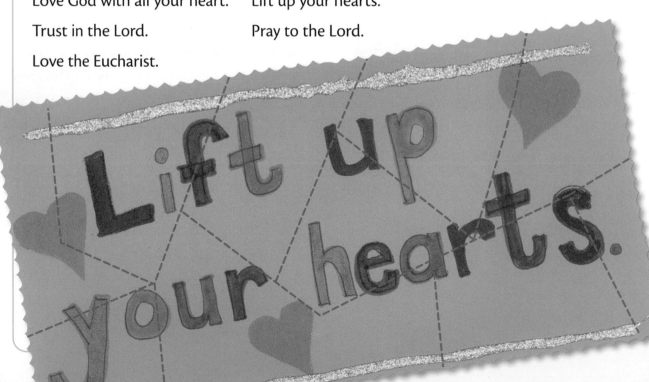

Follow the Footsteps

Use the words in the footsteps to complete the sentences.

1. God gave us the Ten Commandments to help us reach _____ .

2. The first three commandments tell us to love _____ .

3. In the First Commandment God said, "I am the _____ your God."

4. "You shall not have strange _____ besides me."

5. Prayer is lifting our minds and _____ to God.

6. When we honor Mary, the angels, or the _____ , we honor God, who made them.

7. In the Second Commandment God tells us not to use his name in _____ .

8. We respect holy _____ , places, and things.

9. In the Third Commandment God tells us to keep holy the _____ Day.

10. Catholics celebrate the Eucharist on Saturday evenings or Sundays and on _____ days.

A Prayer Puzzle

Complete the puzzle, using the words in the Word Bank to name the kinds of prayer.

WORD BANK

petition	praise
sorrow	thanks

P _ _ _ _ _

_ _ R _ _ _

_ _ A _ _ _

Y

_ _ E _ _ _ _ _

R

From Tiny Seeds the Kingdom Grows

Procession and Song

Leader: In the name of the Father, and of the Son, and of the Holy Spirit.

All: Amen.

Leader: Praise be to God who gives such abundant growth.

All: Now and forever.

Leader: Loving God, we want to serve your kingdom with joy in all we think, say, and do. Help us be fruitful soil so that the kingdom Jesus preached might continue to grow. We ask this in Jesus' name.

All: Amen.

Reading from Mark 4:1–9

Reader: A reading from the holy Gospel according to Mark.

All: Glory to you, O Lord.

Reader: On another occasion he [Jesus] began to teach by the sea. A very large crowd gathered around him so that he got into a boat on the sea and sat down. And the whole crowd was beside the sea on land. And he taught them at length in parables, and in the course of his instruction he said to them, "Hear this! A sower went out to sow. And as he sowed, some seed fell on the path, and the birds came and ate it up. Other seed fell on rocky ground where it had little soil. It sprang up at once because the soil was not deep. And when the sun rose, it was scorched and it withered for lack of roots. Some seed fell among thorns, and the thorns grew up and choked it and it produced no grain. And some seed fell on rich soil and produced fruit. It came up and grew and yielded thirty, sixty, and a hundredfold." He added, "Whoever has ears to hear ought to hear."

The Gospel of the Lord

All: Praise to you, Lord Jesus Christ.

All: I will share the stories of my faith, sharing lessons from of old.

Side A: We have heard them, we know them; our ancestors have recited them to us.

All: I will share the stories of my faith, sharing lessons from of old.

Side B: We do not keep the stories to ourselves; we tell them over and over.

All: I will share the stories of my faith, sharing lessons from of old.

Side A: We tell others the wondrous deeds of Jesus, the miracles he performed.

All: I will share the stories of my faith, sharing lessons from of old.

Side B: So that children still to be born know these stories.

All: I will share the stories of my faith, sharing lessons from of old.

[adapted from Psalm 78:2–6]

Intercessions

Leader: Let us pray that we continue to serve God's kingdom.

That your Word will grow in our hearts, we pray to the Lord.

Response: Lord, we love and serve in your kingdom.

Leader: That bishops, priests, deacons, missionaries, and all of us may spread your Word, we pray to the Lord . . . ℞

That we may continue to make sacrifices for others, we pray to the Lord . . . ℞

That we may love and serve with joy in your kingdom, we pray to the Lord . . . ℞

That we may grow and produce a harvest of good works, we pray to the Lord . . . ℞

Leader: As members of the kingdom, we pray to the Father in the words our Savior taught us:

All: Our Father, . . . Amen.

Closing Song

Looking Back at Unit 3

You have studied the first three commandments in this unit. They tell us to respond to God's love by putting God first in our lives. This means praying to God to express praise, thanksgiving, and sorrow for sin—as well as to ask for things for ourselves and others. Loving God means using his name with reverence and showing respect for sacred persons, places, and things. It also means making the Lord's day holy through rest, recreation, and the celebration of the Eucharist.

Living the Message

Check (✓) each sentence to which you can say yes.

❏ 1. I pray each day.

❏ 2. I try not to take God's name in vain.

❏ 3. I make my Sundays special in different ways.

❏ 4. I pray to Mary and the saints.

❏ 5. I join in the prayers and songs at Sunday Mass.

Planning Ahead

When in the morning is a good time for you to pray?

_____

What prayers will you say?

_____

When in the evening is a good time for you to pray?

_____

What prayers will you say?

_____

Which weekend Mass at your parish is best for you to attend?

_____

How can you better take part in this celebration?

_____

_____

_____

Gather and Go Forth

Know and Proclaim

One reason we learn who we are as Catholics is so we can feel confident in sharing the faith with those who do not yet know Christ.

We Know Our Faith	We Proclaim Our Faith
We receive the Word of God in many ways.	As Catholics, we hear God's message in many ways, including by attending Mass, studying Sacred Scripture, and listening to the teachings of the Church.
In the parable of the sower, Jesus teaches us that we should hear God's Word with joy, even when it is difficult to do so.	We find support for our faith in our parish community where we give one another strength through service and fellowship.
Although we experience hardships in life, God's Word is there to support and guide us.	Catholics spread God's Word through acts of kindness and service to those in need.

We follow the commandments to show love and respect for God. Our hearts become open for the Holy Spirit who sends us out to share the Good News with others.

Children, let us love not in word or speech but in deed and truth.

1 John 3:18

Test Your Catholic Knowledge

Fill in the circle that best answers the question.

Which of the following are we **NOT** called to do as Christians?

○ share stories of our faith with others.

○ keep the commandments

○ only talk about God with other Christians

○ serve those in need

A Catholic to Know

Isaac Jogues was a Jesuit missionary in North America in the 1600s. He struggled through dangerous conditions to bring the Gospel to the Huron, a Native American tribe. He built schools for the Huron and taught them medical and farming skills. One day while Isaac was on a canoe journey, an Iroquois war party captured Isaac. They tortured him and sold him into slavery, but he escaped. When he had recovered, Isaac went back to continue his work. He was martyred shortly after his return. The Indian who killed him, however, was later baptized and took the name Isaac in his memory. Isaac Jogues's sacrifice teaches us that the sufferings of the missionaries are the seeds of the Church.

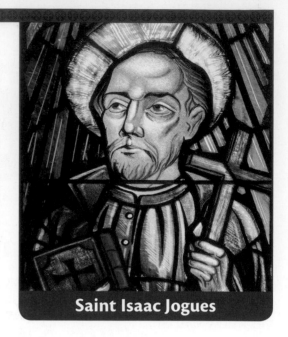

Saint Isaac Jogues

Witness and Share

These sentences describe what Catholics believe. Listen carefully as they are read. Ask yourself, "How strong are my Catholic beliefs?"

My Way to Faith

- I listen for God's Word in Sacred Scripture and in the teachings of the Church.

- I find support for my faith in my parish community.

- I witness to God's kingdom through service and acts of kindness.

- I keep God's Word even when it is hard.

Share Your Faith

Think of ways to be more involved in Mass on Sunday. Write ideas below and share the list with a family member. Invite him or her to join you in putting one idea into practice.

Family Feature

God's Care Shines Through the Darkness

Each year the Sher family celebrates Hanukkah. This is an eight-day feast of lights that takes place in December when Jewish people remember a marvelous deed God worked for them in a time of great peril. It happened more than a hundred years before Jesus was born.

A pagan king was persecuting the Jews and had offered sacrifices to Zeus in the Jewish temple. Led by the Maccabees (Mattathias and his five sons), the Jewish people rebelled, held fast to their faith, and defeated the enemy. The Maccabees wanted to relight the lamps in the Temple and hold a rededication ceremony, but only enough oil to light the lamps for one day could be found. Miraculously, the lamps burned for eight days. In remembrance of this miracle, on each day during Hanukkah another candle is lit on a multibranched candleholder called a menorah.

Family Feature

At Hanukkah the Sher children play a game with a spinning top called a dreidel. The dreidel has four sides, each marked with a Hebrew letter. Taken together, the letters refer to the miracle celebrated at Hanukkah and stand for the phrase, "a great miracle happened there." Players take turns spinning the top. When it stops, the letter at the top of the dreidel tells the spinner what to do.

You can make a dreidel out of a four-inch square of heavy paper or cardboard. On each of the four sides write one of the following letters: N, G, H, S. The code for these is below. Insert a pencil or other stick in the center of the sheet with the point down.

Each player starts with the same amount of tokens (which can be chips, raisins, nuts, pennies, or chocolate coins) and places one in a central pot. Then each player takes a turn spinning the dreidel and doing what it says at the top of the dreidel when it falls to its side. If during play the pot goes down to one token, everyone adds another one. The player who ends up with all the tokens wins. Then redistribute the tokens and play again.

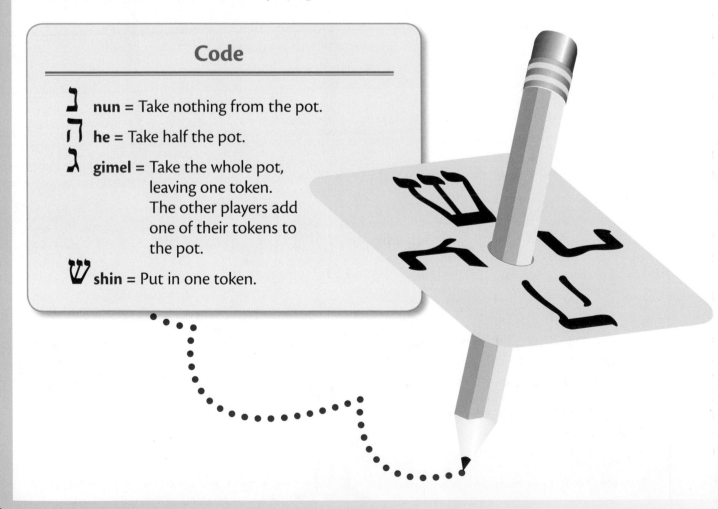

Code

נ **nun** = Take nothing from the pot.

ה **he** = Take half the pot.

ג **gimel** = Take the whole pot, leaving one token. The other players add one of their tokens to the pot.

ש **shin** = Put in one token.

Let It Glow, Let It Glow, Let It Glow

The symbol of light in the darkness is a central part of the Christian faith. Jesus said, "I am the light of the world." During Advent, when the days grow shorter and the nights longer, the Church waits in confident hope for the coming of Jesus, our Lord and our light.

Visit **www.christourlife.com** for more family resources.

Here's a family activity that you can do to experience the power of light shining in the darkness. Gather some candles, two or three times the number of people in your family. The easiest to use are tea lights or vigil lights, but other candles, including birthday candles, will do. Make sure the candles are securely placed for safety. Have matches or a lighter on hand.

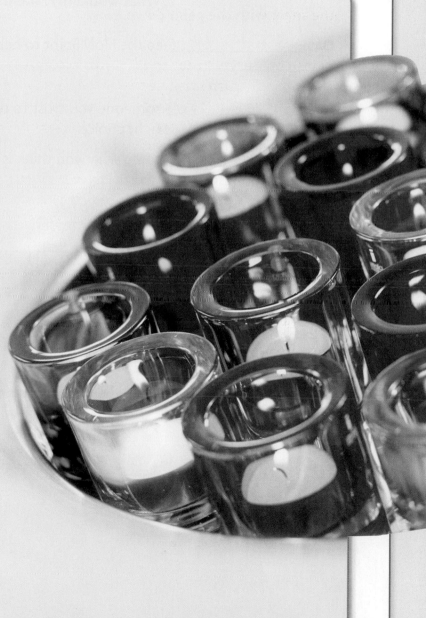

Get everyone in the family settled in a comfortable place with the candles situated close by. Ask everyone to think about reasons he or she is thankful for being part of this family. Tell them you're going to give them a minute to think about it and then turn down the lights. After a short time sitting in the dark, have each person tell a reason why he or she is thankful. When the person is finished, he or she lights a candle. (Be ready to help younger family members light their candles safely.) Keep taking turns until all the candles are lit. As each person describes why he or she is thankful, the light grows and grows.

Finish by having a favorite family treat together.

Family Feature

Decisions

Unscramble the words in each step to help you in making good decisions.

1. _____ for a moment.
   psot

2. _____ Why do I want to do what I feel is wrong?
   ktnih   What will happen if I choose to do it? How will I feel?
              What would my parents and best friends think?

3. _____ to the Holy Spirit to help you make a good choice.
   aryp

4. _____ someone you trust to tell you what he or she thinks is the
   sak   right choice.

5. _____ to do what you think is the right thing.
   ohoesc

(Answers: Stop; Think; Pray; Ask; Choose)

114d

We Love God's People

Beloved, if God so loved us, we must also love one another.

1 John 4:11

A Letter Home

Dear Parents and Family,

Unit Four brings your child to a discussion of the remaining commandments. In Unit Three, the children studied the first three commandments, which give us direction in how to show love for God. Now the children will learn about how to show love for others.

In addition to loving and obeying our parents, the Fourth Commandment calls for us to be considerate of and to respect people in authority. In reviewing the Fifth Commandment, the children will be guided to show appreciation for the gift of life by showing kindness and concern for others. When studying the Sixth and Ninth Commandments, the children will learn to respect themselves and others and to be faithful in their personal relationships.

The Seventh and Tenth Commandments ensure the right to own property, to receive just compensation for work, and to share in the world's natural resources. The children will learn to respect others' property, to care for the gifts of the earth, and to share their own gifts freely. The children will learn that the Eighth Commandment charges us to speak the truth in all things and to keep our promises.

The activities and the closing celebration encourage the children to appreciate the Ten Commandments and to show their love for God by keeping them.

At the end of each chapter in this unit, the children will bring home a review of the chapter along with either the Building Family Faith page or the Family Feature section. These features give you a quick review of what your child learned and offer practical ways to reinforce the lesson at home so that the whole family may benefit.

Visit **www.christourlife.com** for more family resources.

We Honor and Obey

We Bring Happiness to Our Families

We belong to God's large family. God wants us to help make his family happy by loving everyone in it. The last seven commandments help us do this. The Fourth Commandment helps us bring happiness to our own family.

Families are different in many ways, but they should all have one thing in common: members of a family should love and care about one another. Children should honor and respect their parents.

Jesus belonged to a family. Mary was his mother, and Joseph was his foster father. Jesus loved the parents his heavenly Father had given him. He showed his love for them through his **obedience**. He kept the Fourth Commandment.

> Honor your father and your mother.
>
> Exodus 20:12

Jesus respected and obeyed his parents, although he was greater than they were because he was God's Son.

God shows us how precious the gift of life is by giving us this commandment. God wants us to honor our mothers and fathers. Through our parents' marriage and their love for each other, they created our family. They helped give us life. God promises special blessings if we honor them.

God asks our parents to love and care for us. They are to give us what we need to grow as God's children. Our parents make many sacrifices for us. When we honor and respect them, we please God. When we obey them, we obey God and bring happiness to our families and ourselves.

Wheel of Happiness

The words on the Wheel of Happiness tell how we honor our parents. We love, respect, help, and obey them. We also pray for our parents.

Match the words in the wheel with the sentences below. On the line after each sentence, print the word that tells best how we honor our parents when we do what the sentence says.

1. We do what our parents tell us.

   _____

2. We talk politely to our parents.

   _____

3. We do the dishes.

   _____

4. We do kind things for our parents.

   _____

5. We listen politely to our parents.

   _____

6. We ask God to bless our parents.

   _____

7. We carry out the trash.

   _____

8. We say nice things about our parents.

   _____

9. We clean our rooms and pick up our things.

   _____

10. We come when our parents call us.

   _____

A Moment with Jesus

Imagine that you can see Jesus at home with Mary and Joseph. He is your age. What is he doing? Is he helping around the house? Is he talking with Mary and Joseph, or are they playing a game together? Tell Jesus how things are at your home. He is always interested in what is going on in your life. Ask Jesus to bless your home and all who live there.

We Respect Our Leaders

There are other people besides our parents who guide and protect us. We also keep the Fourth Commandment when we respect and obey those in authority, such as our teachers or crossing guards. Jesus taught us to honor our leaders. The Holy Spirit helps us honor and obey them.

One day some men asked Jesus whether they should pay taxes to Caesar, the leader of their country.

Jesus said to them, "Bring me a coin to look at." When they brought one to him, he asked, "Whose image and inscription is this?"

They replied, "Caesar's."

So Jesus said to them, "Repay to Caesar what belongs to Caesar and to God what belongs to God."

adapted from Mark 12:13–17

Jesus wants us to respect and obey the leaders in our country and our Church. God guides us through these leaders.

Leaders Have Duties

Our leaders must show respect to us too. They must always love and respect those whom they lead and never ask others to do something that is wrong. They must do their jobs the best way they can, and they must be honest and trustworthy.

A good leader will try to be like Jesus and help others follow him more closely. Leaders should pray for their people, and we should pray for our leaders.

Write in each blue-ribbon award a word that tells what a good leader is like. Use the words you chose to write a prayer for someone who is your leader.

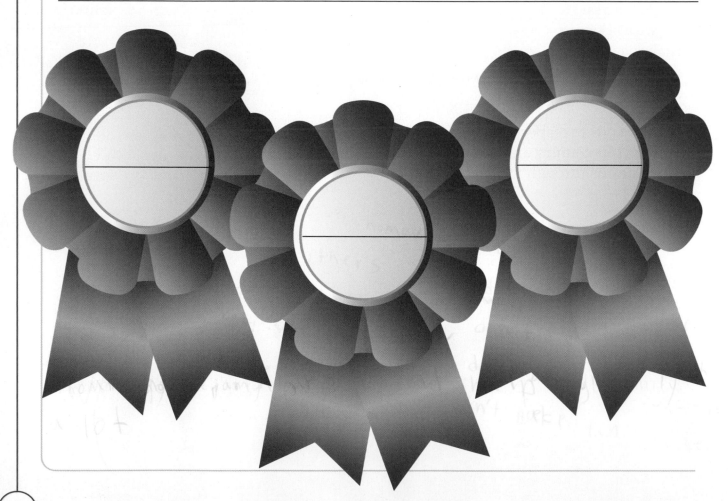

We Respect and Obey
Those Who Guide Us

Teacher: Today we are going to talk about leaders. Has anyone here ever been chosen to be a leader in a game?

Jack: *(Smiling proudly, raises his hand)* Me! I'm always team captain!

Teacher: I can see that you like being a leader, Jack. Can you tell the class why?

Jack: I enjoy telling others how to play a good game. It's fun when everybody plays hard to win. I like everybody to listen and do as I say.

Teacher: *(Laughing)* I also like everyone to listen and do as I say! Does that make me a leader too?

Megan: Yes, but you're not like *him!*

Teacher: Jack and I guide you in different ways. There are many different leaders who try to guide us to do what is right. Can you think of some others?

Ethan: People such as the mayor.

Olivia: And the pope!

Teacher: That's right, we have leaders in our Church and government—and there are even more. All leaders need the help of those they lead in order to do a good job. For instance, how can you help Jack lead well during a game?

Owen: Watch for his signals and try to work well with each other as a team.

Ethan: Always listen to what Jack says.

Olivia: What if someone who is our captain asked us to cheat to win a game?

Jack: I would never do that!

Teacher: I know you wouldn't, Jack, but we must always remember never to obey *anyone* who tells us to do something we know is wrong.

Fourth Commandment Word Scramble

Complete the sentences by writing the correct word next to the scrambled letters.

1. The | ortufh | _____ commandment tells us how to honor our fathers and mothers.

2. | nohro | _____ means to love, respect, and obey.

3. The Fourth Commandment helps us bring | piespahsn | _____ to our families.

4. Besides our parents, | daeresl | _____ guide and protect us.

5. We should never do | rgnow | _____ even if a leader says we should.

We Remember

What is the Fourth Commandment?
The Fourth Commandment is "Honor your father and your mother."

Word to Know
obedience

We Respond

I will love, respect, and obey my parents and others who guide and protect me.

Building Family Faith

CHAPTER SUMMARY Christians respect and obey those in authority. Children owe respect and obedience to their parents. Everyone honors those who lead our country and our Church.

REFLECT

"Honor your father and your mother, as the LORD, your God, has commanded you, that you may have a long life and prosperity in the land which the LORD, your God, is giving you."
Deuteronomy 5:16

DISCUSS AS A FAMILY

- how everyone in the family respects and obeys those in authority.
- the ways children honor their parents.
- the reasons why respect for authority is important for your whole family.

Visit **www.christourlife.com** for more family resources.

PRAY

Father, bless our family. Show us how to love and honor each other.

DO

Discuss your family's history. Draw a family tree. View pictures of your ancestors and tell stories about them. Find out how your ancestors came to America.

Ask each person to share an experience that made him or her happy to be a member of the family.

Draw names. In the coming week, do something special for the person whose name you drew.

Gather and Go Forth

Know and Proclaim

Studying Scripture and celebrating the sacraments fill us with strength and the desire to share God's love with others.

We Know Our Faith	We Proclaim Our Faith
God wants us to honor our mothers and fathers. They formed our family and helped give us life.	As Catholics, we can bring happiness to our families by treating our mothers and fathers with honor and respect.
Jesus taught us to honor our parents and leaders. The Holy Spirit helps us honor and obey them.	We keep the Fourth Commandment when we respect and obey our parents and leaders because they represent God's authority.
Leaders must love and respect those whom they lead. They must never ask others to do wrong.	Catholics live the values of God's kingdom when they lead in an honest, trustworthy, and respectful way.

God has given us many gifts. We worship and praise him by using those gifts to love and serve others.

As each one has received a gift, use it to serve one another as good stewards of God's varied grace.

1 Peter 4:10

Test Your Catholic Knowledge

Fill in the circle that best completes the sentence.

According to Catholic social teaching:

○ leaders have a responsibility to be honest and just.

○ a leader's only job is to tell others what to do.

○ leaders should do anything necessary to be successful.

○ leaders do not need to concern themselves with the needs of those who follow them.

A Catholic to Know

When Emperor Constantine became a Christian and ended the persecutions in the Roman Empire, his mother Helena converted as well. Helena soon became known for her great piety and just leadership. She was called by many people "empress to the poor" because she cared for those who were poor and performed acts of charity. Helena oversaw the building of many churches, including one at Golgotha, the place where Jesus was crucified. When Helena also found what is believed to be the Cross that Jesus died on, she saw that the Cross was venerated there. Helena is a witness to Christ's love and an example for all leaders because of her generosity to those in need and her dedication to justice.

Saint Helena

Witness and Share

These sentences describe what Catholics believe. Listen carefully as they are read. Ask yourself, "How strong are my Catholic beliefs?"

My Way to Faith

- I honor and obey my parents.

- I ask the Holy Spirit to help me respect and obey leaders.

- I witness to God's kingdom by being honest and just.

- I pray for my leaders and all of God's people.

Share Your Faith

How can you respect leaders in your home, school, and community? Write one idea below. Compare it with a classmate's and invite him or her to join you in putting one of your ideas into action this week. Work together to show respect for those who lead you.

Treat your parents good and help your family a lot

We Respect the Gift of Life

Life Is God's Precious Gift

> God said, "Let us make man in our image, after our likeness."
>
> Genesis 1:26

Life is not a gift we keep for ourselves. It always belongs to God. He created all life out of love. The life of every person belongs to God.

All life is precious to God: tiny babies still inside their mothers, men and women who are too sick to move, people in other countries, people you do not like, and even dogs and whales. God wants us to take care of our own lives and those of others.

God tells us in the Fifth Commandment to respect life and to protect it.

> You shall not kill.
>
> Exodus 20:13

How can you tell that the people in these pictures love life?

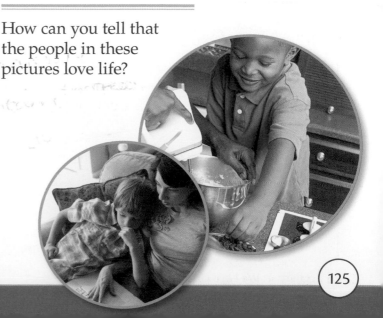

We Take Care of Ourselves

Do you know how wonderful you are? Think of some amazing facts about your body. It changes food into skin and bones. When it is cut or bruised, it heals itself. It has parts like eyes and ears that are cleverly designed to put you in touch with the world and other people. Think of some of the amazing things you can do. You can speak and sing. You can create new and beautiful things. You can experience the joy that comes from loving and being loved.

God wants us to be healthy, happy people and to love ourselves. We are to take care of our bodies. We are to use our minds and our talents, and we are to grow. Then we will be able to enrich the world, help others, and give glory to God, our Maker.

Prescription for Healthy Living

Write a prescription for a long, healthy life, as though you are a doctor. Under Do's, list ways to care for your life. Under Don'ts, list things to avoid.
(Hint: Recall things that your parents often tell you.)

For _____

Address _____

R

Date _____

Do's

Do your homework

help others

do exersice

respect God

love God

Don'ts

Don't eat too much candy

don't color on the wall

don't watch tv too much

don't be mean to others

don't make fun of others

SUBSTITUTION PERMITTED

REFILL _____ TIMES

DISPENSE AS WRITTEN

DEA No. _____

God Wants Us to Take Care of Others

People who really love Jesus do nothing to harm others or to hurt others' feelings. Instead they protect others and help them enjoy life. They are kind to others.

Peter Claver was a Spanish priest who spent his life helping Africans in the West Indies. Many had been brought there to be slaves. Father Claver saw how cruel slavery was. He met the slave ships as they arrived from Africa. Sometimes the slaves were starving. Father Claver gave them fresh fruit. He gave medicine to the sick and helped the dying.

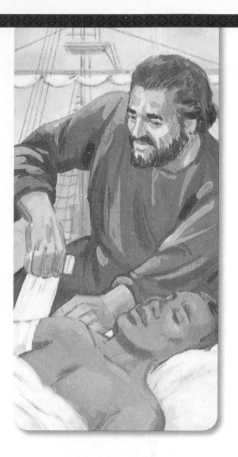

After Father Claver helped these people, he told them about Jesus. He taught them to offer their sufferings to God and told them that one day they could join God in heaven. God wants all people to be saved. Many slaves asked to be baptized. Father Claver baptized more than 40 thousand slaves. Now he is in heaven, and we call him Saint Peter Claver.

The terms in the jar are like poison. They harm and destroy life. Choose two of these terms. Circle them and write how you would act instead. Use examples.

teasing
holding a grudge
taking revenge
playing mean jokes
arguing
being prejudiced
fighting
refusing to speak to someone

1. _____

_____

_____

_____

2. _____

_____

_____

_____

Christians Are Kind and Merciful

A lawyer asked Jesus what to do in order to win eternal life. Jesus told him to love God and his neighbor. Then the lawyer asked Jesus, "Who is my neighbor?" Jesus answered by telling this story:

A man going down the road was attacked by robbers. They took the man's money and clothes and left him half dead. Soon a religious man came by. He saw the man but went right on. Another traveler saw the dying man, but he passed by too.

Then a man from Samaria came along and felt sorry for the man. He cleaned and bandaged the man's wounds. The Samaritan put the man on a donkey and rode to an inn, where he cared for the wounded man. The next day the Samaritan gave two silver coins to the innkeeper and said, "Take care of this man. If you need more money, I will repay you on my way back."

Jesus then asked, "Which of these three was a good neighbor to the wounded man?"

The lawyer replied, "The man who treated him with kindness and mercy."

Jesus said, "Go and do the same."

adapted from Luke 10:25–37

A Moment with Jesus

Did you find an opportunity to be a Good Samaritan today? Did you pick up something someone else dropped? Did you share with someone who needed a pencil? Were you helpful at home? Jesus wants you to know that you don't have to do big things to be a Good Samaritan. Little things count too. Ask Jesus to help you do caring things for others. Thank him for always being there for you.

How Are These People Like the Good Samaritan?

1. Mr. and Mrs. Ortiz, an elderly couple, lived next door to Peter. One night it snowed very hard. Peter and his friend Julius shoveled the Ortizes' deck. When Mr. Ortiz offered to reward them, Peter and Julius refused to take any money.

2. Sarah and Bo Yun met Mrs. Reynolds in the store. Mrs. Reynolds was trying to watch her three small children and shop too. The two girls took care of the children so that Mrs. Reynolds could do her shopping.

3. Mara's brother had prepared supper for the family. When Mara sat down to eat, she noticed some food she did not like. Mara ate it anyway, without complaining, and thanked her brother for the meal.

A Puzzle About Life

WORD BANK

God	respect
mercy	life
kindness	

Work the puzzle on the globe, using the Word Bank.

Down

1. All life belongs to _____ .

2. The Fifth Commandment tells us to care for _____ .

3. When we forgive others, we show _____ .

Across

4. When we say or do loving things, we show _____ .

5. We are to show _____ for all forms of life.

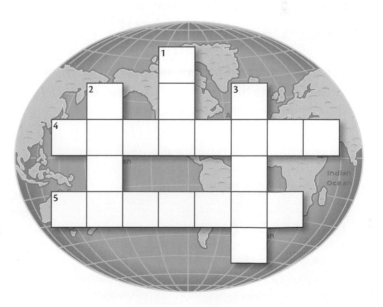

Award for Bravery

Awarded to

_____

for

_____

Life Givers Are Heroes

Ten-year-old Betty Ruth Hood awoke in the middle of the night to see her bed on fire. She woke up her mother. She took her sister out of her crib and carried her to safety. Then she returned to the house to rescue her brother.

In 1996 Betty was awarded one of the Young American Medals for Bravery by the president. That same year, Shivon Kershaw received the Young American Medal for Service. She organized teenagers to collect and ship relief packages to orphanages across the United States.

Not all life givers receive rewards in this life. Do you know someone who has done something brave or special to help others live a better life?

Write the person's name on the award and the reason he or she deserves it.

We Remember

What is the Fifth Commandment?
The Fifth Commandment is "You shall not kill."

We Respond

I thank God for the gift of life. I will respect life and show kindness toward others.

Building Family Faith

CHAPTER SUMMARY All life is sacred and belongs to God. We show our appreciation for the gift of life by taking good care of ourselves and by protecting and cherishing others, especially those who are vulnerable and weak.

REFLECT
When the Samaritan traveler came upon the injured man in the road, he "was moved with compassion at the sight."
Luke 10:33

DISCUSS AS A FAMILY
- how we care for each other when someone is sick or in need in other ways.
- the people in our family or in our neighborhood whom we know need help and how we can help them.
- ways we can take good care of ourselves.

Visit **www.christourlife.com** for more family resources.

PRAY
Lord Jesus, thank you for giving us life. Keep us safe and strong. Show us how to care for others.

DO
Determine ways to avoid things that endanger us, such as smoking, taking drugs, poor eating habits, and risky behavior.

Prepare healthy meals and snacks for the family.

Identify someone who is in need, such as an older person who has trouble getting around or a parishioner or neighbor who is ill. Give aid to that person.

Gather and Go Forth

Know and Proclaim

The stories of our faith inspire us to show the world Christ's love by following his kind and merciful example.

We Know Our Faith	We Proclaim Our Faith
Life is God's precious gift. The life of every person belongs to God.	As Catholics, we keep the Fifth Commandment when we serve those in need and protect those who are helpless.
God wants us to be healthy, happy people and to love ourselves.	We honor God's gift of life by using our minds and talents to help heal the world.
God wants us to care for others. People who love Jesus respect and protect others and are kind to them.	Catholics spread Jesus' love by showing kindness and mercy to those who are weak and sorrowful.

Christ reminds us that we are all God's children. We follow his example by caring for one another and helping one another reach his kingdom.

Bear one another's burdens, and so you will fulfill the law of Christ.

Galatians 6:2

Test Your Catholic Knowledge

Fill in the circle that best answers the question.

What lesson did Jesus teach when he told the story of the Good Samaritan?

○ We only have a responsibility to care for those who are like us.

○ Our job is always our first responsibility.

○ God commands us to serve only the needs of our family members.

○ We must treat all people with kindness and mercy.

A Catholic to Know

Bonaventure was born in Italy in the 11200s. As a young boy, he was cured of a serious illness through the prayers of Francis of Assisi. When he was old enough, he went to the University of Paris to study theology. The friars at the university and Saint Francis inspired Bonaventure to join the Franciscan Order. Bonaventure was eventually chosen as minister general of the Franciscans. He felt God calling him to bring a deeper understanding of the way of Saint Francis to the Order. Bonaventure wrote a biography of Saint Francis and many other books explaining the ideals of the Franciscans. He is an example on our way of faith because of his learning, kindness, and compassion.

Saint Bonaventure

Witness and Share

These sentences describe what Catholics believe. Listen carefully as they are read. Ask yourself, "How strong are my Catholic beliefs?"

My Way to Faith

- I make a habit of helping those in need.

- I enrich the world by using God's gifts to serve others.

- I praise and thank God for the talents he gave me.

- I show Jesus' love by being kind and respectful to those who need protection.

Share Your Faith

How do you show your love of life? List your ideas below. Share the list with your family. Invite them to join you in planning an activity to enjoy together the life God has given you.

_____

_____

_____

_____

We Are Faithful to Ourselves and Others

Our Bodies Are Good

Have you ever watched the Olympics? The beauty and grace of the gymnasts, divers, ice skaters, and other athletes amaze and inspire us. They make us realize just how wonderful our human bodies are.

God gave us the gift of our bodies when he made us. Scripture tells us:

> God created man in his image;
> . . . male and female he created them.
>
> Genesis 1:27

God wants us to be happy with who we are. Each of us can be proud to be a boy or a girl and be happy with the wonderful body God has given us. We can thank God by treating our bodies with respect. This way we can live and grow as human beings.

Another great gift we have is the ability to form friendships. We let others know who we are, and we come to know and love others. In our friendships God asks us to be true to ourselves and others. We are true to ourselves and to others when we treat our bodies with respect.

We Are True to Ourselves

Long ago Saint Paul wrote a letter to some people who had been Christians for only a short time. He wanted them to know that they were holy. He gives three good reasons for respecting their bodies. This letter in the Bible is meant for us too. Saint Paul tells us how to be true to ourselves.

Dear Friends in Christ,

God raised the Lord and will also raise us by his power. Do you not know that your bodies are members of Christ? . . . Keep yourselves holy and pure. . . . Your body is a temple of the Holy Spirit. You do not belong to yourselves but to God. He bought you at a great price. So use your body to give glory to God. My love to all of you in Christ Jesus.

Paul the Apostle

adapted from 1 Corinthians 6:14,15,18–20

How Can We Keep Ourselves Holy?

Draw a line to connect the beginning of each sentence with the right ending.

1. Look at •   • to the Holy Spirit for guidance.

2. Make •   • movies, TV shows, books, and pictures with good values.

3. Pray •   • sacrifices to show love for God and others.

4. Receive •   • your body and those of others.

5. Respect •   • the Eucharist and the Sacrament of Penance often.

Church

We Are Faithful to Others

Friends are people who care about each other. They like to be together and to do things together. They also help each other in times of need. Good friends can always count on each other. They are faithful. They help each other to love God and to do what is right.

God wants us to have many good friends. He is pleased when we are true to them.

Scripture says,

A faithful friend is beyond price.

Sirach 6:15

The Sixth and Ninth Commandments help us be faithful.

You shall not commit adultery.
You shall not covet your neighbor's wife.

Exodus 20:14 and 17

A Moment with Jesus

Speak to Jesus in your heart, naming all your friends for him. Does a friend need help because of something going on in school or in his or her family? Is there something special you need? If so, tell Jesus about it. He always listens; he always understands. Let Jesus know how glad you are to be his friend.

Marriage Is a Special Friendship

Sometimes a man and a woman have a special kind of friendship. They want to share their lives and start a new family. They get married in order to do this.

At their wedding a husband and wife make special promises to each other before God. They promise to love and care for each other always. Through the Sacrament of Matrimony, the Holy Spirit helps the husband and wife keep their promises.

Marriage Vows

Read the sentences and fill in the missing words from the Word Bank.

WORD BANK

love	promises
care	other
God	

At their wedding a man and woman

make special _____

to each _____

before _____ .

They promise to _____

and _____ for

each other always.

A Heartfelt Discovery

To discover what is at the heart of every marriage, follow the strings of the heart-shaped balloons. Only four strings will find their way to the spaces below.

___ ___ ___ ___ · ___ ___ ___

We Are Temples of the Holy Spirit

Mia: Hi, Mom. We're home!

Alex: Hi! We had a great class today. Try to guess what I learned. I'll give you some hints. It's about something that is like a temple or a church. It belongs to God because he made it. He came to live in it at Baptism. Do you know what it is?

Mom: Could it be your body or the body of anyone who is baptized?

Alex: Right, Mom. Think about it: I'm a temple of the Holy Spirit.

Mia: Am I a temple too?

Mom: Yes, Mia. It's so wonderful that I hope you'll always remember it.

Alex: That's just what Saint Paul told us to do. Do you know what else he said?

Mia: No. What else?

Alex: He said we respect our bodies when we act in ways that give glory to God. We should care for our bodies because they are a gift from God. *(Suddenly smiling)* Mom, do you think I would be caring for my body if I ate some of your great pizza?

Mia: Yeah, me too, Mom!

Mom: *(Laughing)* I think it would be good if you both changed your clothes first, washed your hands, and then ate some of my pizza.

Alex: Awesome!

Mia: Okay, Mom!

Respecting Our Bodies

Finish this sentence that is based on Saint Paul's letter on page 104.

We do not want to use our bodies the wrong way because one day they will

_____ . Our bodies are

parts, or members, of _____

and _____ of the Holy Spirit.

We Remember

What is the Sixth Commandment?
The Sixth Commandment is "You shall not commit adultery."

What is the Ninth Commandment?
The Ninth Commandment is "You shall not covet your neighbor's wife."

We Respond

I will respect myself and others and be faithful to my friends.

Building Family Faith

CHAPTER SUMMARY We have a special dignity because we are made in the image and likeness of God. We honor God and ourselves when we take good care of ourselves, when we are faithful, and when married people are true to their marriage promises.

REFLECT

"Do you not know that your body is a temple of the holy Spirit within you . . . ? Therefore, glorify God in your body."
1 Corinthians 6:19–20

DISCUSS AS A FAMILY

• the ways we give honor to God by the way we use and care for our bodies.

• how we have been faithful to friends through hard times and troubles.

• what it means to be a good friend.

PRAY

Jesus, help me be true to myself, to others, and to you.

DO

Take a careful look at the television programs and movies your family watches. Choose to watch those that show proper respect and reverence for people.

Write letters to television station managers encouraging them to offer more appropriate programming.

Visit **www.christourlife.com** for more family resources.

Gather and Go Forth

Know and Proclaim

We learn our faith well so we will have the power to share it with others who may not yet know God's love for them.

We Know Our Faith	We Proclaim Our Faith
God gives us the gift of our bodies. He wants us to be happy with who we are and to take care of ourselves.	As Catholics, we honor God by living healthy lives and treating our bodies with respect.
God wants us to have many good friends. He is happy when we are true to ourselves and others.	Catholics reflect God's justice and love when they are honest with their friends.
A man and a woman marry to share their lives and start a family. Theirs is a special friendship.	Catholics honor God through the Sixth and Ninth Commandments when they keep the promises made in the Sacrament of Matrimony.

Test Your Catholic Knowledge

Fill in the circle that best answers the question.

In which sacrament does a man and a woman make special promises before God to be faithful to each other?

○ Sacrament of Baptism

○ Sacrament of Holy Orders

○ Sacrament of Penance and Reconciliation

○ Sacrament of Matrimony

God blesses each of us with a wonderful body made in his image. By respecting ourselves and others, we can live and grow as human beings.

For God did not give us a spirit of cowardice but rather of power and love and self-control.

2 Timothy 1:7

A Catholic to Know

Monica was raised Christian in the 300s, but she was given in marriage to a pagan named Patricius. Despite many hardships, Monica lived her calling as a loving wife. Her example of piety and charity eventually inspired her husband and his mother to become Christians. Monica also served as a powerful example to her son, Augustine, who spent his youth ignoring God's call and living immorally. Monica dreamed he would one day follow the one true faith, so she stayed close to him, praying and fasting. Eventually, Augustine became a Christian and went on to become a bishop and saint.

Saint Monica

Witness and Share

These sentences describe what Catholics believe. Listen carefully as they are read. Ask yourself, "How strong are my Catholic beliefs?"

My Way to Faith

- I treat my body as a temple of the Holy Spirit.

- I give glory to God when I respect my body.

- I please God when I am true to my friends.

- I live a healthy life because my body is a gift from God.

- I trust that the Holy Spirit helps me keep my promises.

Share Your Faith

How can you be a good and faithful friend? Write some ideas below. Share this list with a friend and invite him or her to join you in acting on one or more of your ideas this week.

_____

_____

_____

_____

We Respect What God Has Given Us

God Gives Us the Things We Need

God loves all the people he made. God put into the world everything we need to lead good lives. All of us have a right to what we need, but God wants us to use his gifts in the proper way. We should take care of our belongings and those of others. We should share with others.

How can we take care of what we have?

When can we share with others?

We show love for others when we respect what they own. It is wrong to take what belongs to them. In the Seventh Commandment God tells us this.

> You shall not steal.
>
> Exodus 20:15

How do others feel when we respect their things?

If we are living good, healthy lives, we should be satisfied with what we have. We should not covet. In other words, we do not envy others for things or talents they have that we do not. We also should not envy them because they have more things than we do. God tells us this in the Tenth Commandment.

> You shall not covet your neighbor's goods.
>
> adapted from Exodus 20:17

We Respect the Property of Others

Everyone has a right to own things. God wants us to respect others' rights. He wants us to respect other people's belongings and to be honest and fair in all we do.

We show respect for other people's belongings by using them the right way. We should be careful not to damage, ruin, or lose what belongs to others. If we damage anything, we must repair it or pay for it.

It is wrong to steal from people or to cheat them. A person who takes anything that belongs to someone else must always return it to the owner or pay for it.

We ask others before using their things. We return what we borrow. When we find things that are not ours, we try to return them to their owner.

When we take tests, we do not cheat. When we play games, we are fair and follow the rules.

Signs of Respect

Read the sentences and fill in the letters to complete the missing words.

1. We respect others and share because we c __ __ __ .

2. We respect the b __ __ __ __ __ __ __ __ __ of others.

3. When we take a test, we are h __ __ __ __ __ ; we do not cheat.

4. We make up to others for d __ __ __ __ __ to their property.

5. We are satisfied with all we have and t __ __ __ __ God for his gifts.

Choosing to Do Right or Wrong

The decision to do right or wrong, to sin or not, is a **moral choice**. God gave us the commandments as guides for living holy lives. God also gave us **free will,** which allows us to choose to do right or wrong. The Holy Spirit will help us make good decisions.

Put a check (✓) on the blank if the sentence is about someone who is following either the Seventh or Tenth Commandment. If the sentence is about someone not keeping either commandment, write the letter of the answer that tells what wrong is being done.

A. stealing
B. cheating
C. envy
D. damaging property

____✓____ 1. Tawanda told the librarian that she had accidentally torn a page in a book.

____A____ 2. Joe took a CD from the store, hid it under his coat, and left without paying for it.

____✓____ 3. After accidentally breaking Mr. Joyce's window, some boys offered to pay for it.

____A____ 4. Nathan took money from his dad's dresser to buy an ice-cream cone.

____C____ 5. Catherine was angry because she could not have Gerald's new CD.

____B____ 6. To get a higher grade, Claire copied an answer from Brigitte's test paper.

____✓____ 7. Rosalita shared her new jewelry-making kit with her friends.

_____ 8. Emma left her friend's new bike out in the rain.

____✓____ 9. Aida returned the pencil she had borrowed.

____D____ 10. With his skateboard, Max rolled over the flowers in his neighbor's garden.

Dorothy Becomes a Hero for Justice

Dorothy Day was born in New York City in 1897. Her family moved around a lot. They were living in California when a terrible earthquake occurred. The quake left many families homeless and without food. Dorothy remembers her mother jumping in to help them. This memory stayed with young Dorothy.

As she grew older, Dorothy came to realize that taking care of the poor was the most important thing anyone could do. Later, when she became a Catholic, she decided to be a worker for justice. She wanted to follow the example Jesus gave.

Dorothy and a friend created a newspaper called the *Catholic Worker.* This newspaper told what life was like for the poor and how to make their lives better.

Dorothy believed that it wasn't enough just to give money to people in need. You should take them in and treat them as you would treat Jesus. So she created hospitality houses where the poor could live and get help.

Dorothy Day died in 1980. During her life, she didn't just talk about justice. She worked for justice. She became one of the poor herself. She lived with them and became their friend.

A Moment with Jesus

Share with Jesus what you think about Dorothy Day. Ask him to help you find ways to make things easier for the people in your life. Jesus knows you try to be good. Maybe he wants you to try a little harder. Talk this over with Jesus. Then share with him anything else that's on your mind.

Unjust Acts Cause Harm

Respecting people's rights is just. Acts against the Seventh and Tenth Commandments are unjust. They cause harm and make us sad and fearful. They break down peace in the world and in our hearts.

Read each unjust act in the first column. Find each one's unhappy result in the second column. Write the letter of the answer on the line.

_____ 1. Houses on a block are broken into.

_____ 2. People shoplift.

_____ 3. Gangs cover public walls with words and pictures.

_____ 4. A company cheats its customers.

_____ 5. Items are stolen at school.

_____ 6. Someone does not play fair.

A. People do not trust salespeople.

B. The game is ruined.

C. Prices are raised to cover the cost.

D. Rooms and lockers must be locked.

E. People live in fear.

F. Neighborhoods are no longer beautiful.

Peace Walk

Find your way to peace by keeping the commandments and avoiding unjust acts.

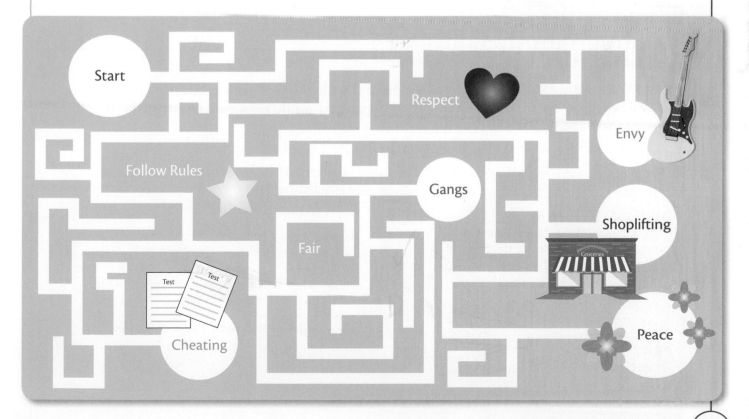

My Own Book

Imagine you are writing a book about the Seventh and Tenth Commandments. What would be a good title? Write it on the book cover.

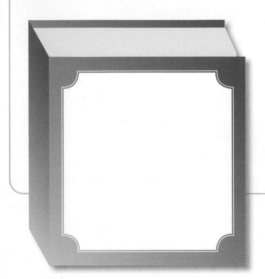

We Remember

What is the Seventh Commandment?
The Seventh Commandment is "You shall not steal."

What is the Tenth Commandment?
The Tenth Commandment is "You shall not covet your neighbor's goods."

Words to Know
free will   moral choice

We Respond

I will be honest and fair. I will be satisfied with what I have.

Building Family Faith

CHAPTER SUMMARY All of us have the right to share in the goodness of the earth's resources, to own property, and to receive just compensation for our work. We should be satisfied with what we have and respect the property and rights of others.

REFLECT
"You shall not steal."
Exodus 20:15

DISCUSS AS A FAMILY
• the possessions we have that are most important to us. Why are they important?
• how we take care of the things we have.
• the ways we show respect for the possessions of others—in our family, at school, among our friends.

PRAY
"The Lord will surely grant abundance; our land will yield its increase."
Psalm 85:13

DO
Work through a charity supported by your parish, if possible, and have the children get personally involved in making the donation.

Participate as a family in a community beautification or conservation project.

At dinner or bedtime, pray prayers of thanks for God's generosity to your family.

Visit **www.christourlife.com** for more family resources.

Gather and Go Forth

Know and Proclaim

We have a responsibility to know our faith so we can share the gifts God has given us with others.

We Know Our Faith	We Proclaim Our Faith
God created the world with everything we need to lead good lives. He wants us to use his gifts properly.	As Catholics, we show love for our neighbor when we keep the Seventh Commandment and respect what others own.
God wants us to respect other people's belongings and to be honest and fair in all we do.	Catholics show respect for other people's belongings by using them the right way.
God gives us free will to choose to do right or wrong, to sin or not to sin.	We study the Seventh and Tenth Commandments and pray for guidance from the Holy Spirit to make good choices.

God blesses us with many gifts. We show gratitude by respecting what we and others have been given.

Then he said to the crowd, "Take care to guard against all greed, for though one may be rich, one's life does not consist of possessions."
Luke 12:15

Test Your Catholic Knowledge

Fill in the circle that best completes the sentence.

Deciding not to cheat on a test is an example of:

○ coveting someone's things.

○ respecting life.

○ damaging property.

○ making a moral choice.

A Catholic to Know

Cecilia lived in Rome in the late 100s. At an early age, she dedicated her life to God. Cecilia's parents, however, insisted that she marry. An account of her wedding says that while musicians played, Cecilia sang to the Lord in her heart. Cecilia's faith soon persuaded her husband to be baptized. He, in turn, converted his brother. Sadly, all three were eventually arrested and martyred for their faith. Today, Saint Cecilia is often pictured with a small organ, a harp, or a viola because she is the patroness of music and musicians. We learn from Saint Cecilia's example that we can lead others to Christ when we proclaim our faith even under difficult circumstances.

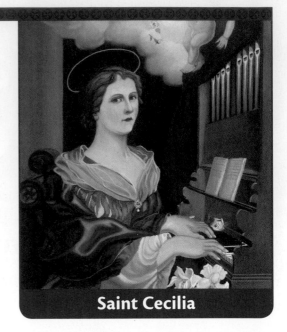

Saint Cecilia

Witness and Share

These sentences describe what Catholics believe. Listen carefully as they are read. Ask yourself, "How strong are my Catholic beliefs?"

My Way to Faith

- I am honest and fair in all I do.
- I make good decisions with the help of the Holy Spirit.
- I know it is wrong to take what does not belong to me.
- I study the Ten Commandments to make the right moral choices.

Share Your Faith

Write a prayer thanking God for the many gifts he has given you. Share your prayer with family members. Invite them to pray it with you each morning this week.

_____

_____

_____

_____

We Respect the Gifts of the Earth

We Care for Our Earth Home

God made all things on earth. In the Bible we read about it.

> God looked at everything he had made, and he found it very good.
>
> Genesis 1:31

God put all the wonderful gifts of the earth in our care. He wants us to respect them and use them the right way. At the end of time they will be changed and share in God's glory too.

We use God's gifts the right way when we are not wasteful and when we take good care of them. It is right to share them with other people. If we use God's gifts properly, earth will be a pleasant place to live, and we will reach heaven.

The Poor Man Gets His Reward

Jesus told a story about a rich man and Lazarus. The rich man had fancy clothes and fine feasts with his friends. Lazarus, a poor and sick man, begged at the door for scraps of food from the rich man's table. He was given nothing.

Both the rich man and Lazarus died. Lazarus was taken to a place of happiness for all eternity. The rich man was taken to a place of suffering.

The rich man begged, "Send Lazarus down with a drop of water to cool my tongue and relieve my suffering."

The answer came, "You received what was good during your life. Lazarus received what was bad. Now he is comforted and you are suffering."

adapted from Luke 16:19–31

God gives the gifts of creation to everyone. He wants those who have more to share with those who have less. By not sharing even the smallest portion of what he owned with Lazarus, the rich man was keeping for himself the gifts God had given him. He did not show real gratitude.

A Moment with Jesus

Close your eyes and relax. Tell Jesus about some of your favorite things. He might ask if you are willing to share what you have with someone who has little. What is your answer? Jesus knows that it can be hard to give up the things you like. He promises to help. Jesus loves you.

Operation Rice Bowl Helps People Live Better Lives

Every day on the news we see stories about children who need help. God has given us our world to share, but what can we do to help other people?

In 1975, Catholics in the Diocese of Allentown, Pennsylvania, decided to do something about helping others during the season of Lent. They began a program that became known as Operation Rice Bowl. It gives families the opportunity to pray with one another. The families are also asked to make small sacrifices and donate the money saved to help meet the needs of others.

The money that is collected by Operation Rice Bowl helps people live better lives.

Farmers are given the opportunity to produce better crops. Mothers and children are given health and dental care. It also helps people create a better water supply, a serious need in some parts of the world.

Operation Rice Bowl has been very successful in helping others. More than 15,000 parishes, schools, and faith communities participate every year. About eight million dollars a year is collected to help people locally and worldwide.

Participating in Operation Rice Bowl is a great way to be part of the big picture in answering God's call to share with people in need.

Alphabet Soup

Fill in the word from the steaming bowl of soup that best completes each sentence.

1. We treat the gifts God has given us with _____ .

2. We _____ God's gifts with others.

3. We do not _____ things.

4. We take good _____ of them.

5. God found all he had made _____ .

care   respect   waste   good   share

We Share God's Gifts with Others

We call the earth our planet, but the earth and everything on it really belong to God. He has given the earth to his creatures to use in order to live and grow. There are some people in our world, however, who have no homes. Others have no clothing, no food, no medicine, no education.

Some people are in need because they have been treated unfairly. Others are very lonely. They are not loved or cared for by anyone.

Many people in the world have not heard the Good News. They need someone to teach them about Jesus.

We belong to God's big family of people with the earth as our home. God wants all his people to be happy. All of us, including future generations, have a right to the world's gifts. So we must use the riches of the earth carefully and wisely. Those of us who have more should share with people in need. When we do this, we show that we are all brothers and sisters in God's family.

Words of Wisdom

Print in the boxes the message from Saint Paul that will help you share God's gifts with others. Use the code to help you.

Code

A	C	D	E	F	G	H	I	L	O	R	S	U	V
1	2	3	4	5	6	7	8	9	10	11	12	13	14

6 10 3   9 10 14 4 12

1 2 7 4 4 11 5 13 9

6 8 14 4 11 .

2 Corinthians 9:7

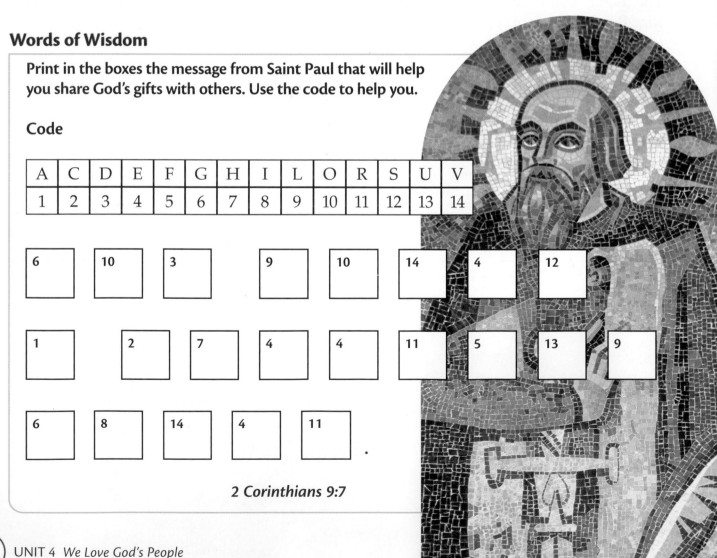

You Are Never Too Young

People may stare at Michael Munds. Sometimes kids tease him. That's because Michael has a disease that causes the bones in his face to not fit together like other people's do. He looks different. Since being born in 1989, he has had many operations on his face, and he has more to go. That doesn't stop Michael from helping others.

Michael raises and donates money for people who need it. He started when he was very young. At age five, he donated all his stuffed animals to children who had lost theirs in a flood. Then when he was six years old, there was a bombing in Oklahoma City. He organized a bowling game, and he asked people to donate money for every pin knocked down. He raised $37,649. He has raised money for the Children's Miracle Network and for the victims of 9/11. In all, he has raised and donated close to $200,000 for different people and organizations. And he doesn't plan to stop.

When people ask Michael why he does all this, he answers, "If we all make a difference—even a little bit—one person at a time, then maybe when I grow up the world will be a better place to live."

It's Your Turn Now

**Is there a person or a group of people that you could help?
Write down whom you can help and describe what you would do.**

_____

_____

_____

_____

_____

_____

Reminder Notes

Fill in what you will respect in each place.
Choose from the words listed on the right.

water	walls	clothes	dishes
toys	animals	books	trees
birds	lawn	desks	paper

At school

_____

_____

_____

_____

At home

_____

_____

_____

_____

Outside

_____

_____

_____

_____

_____

We Remember

How do we use the gifts of the earth in the right way?

We use the gifts of the earth in the right way by sharing them, not wasting them, and taking care of them.

We Respond

Lord, our world is full of your goodness. Help me use the gifts of the earth in the right way.

Building Family Faith

CHAPTER SUMMARY God created a world rich in beauty, resources, and wealth. He expects us to use these resources wisely and to care for them responsibly.

REFLECT
"The land will yield its fruit and you will have food in abundance, so that you may live there without worry."

Leviticus 25:19

DISCUSS AS A FAMILY
- how our family benefits from the natural abundance of the earth.
- how the labor of others serves us.
- the ways we waste things—at home and in our community.
- the ways we can conserve and care for the good things of the earth.

PRAY
"Give us this day our daily bread."

DO
Organize a family beautification day. Clean up the house or the yard.

Find old or damaged household items. Whenever possible, fix them up and use them again instead of throwing them out.

Learn about recycling. Take old items to the recycling center and ask for a quick tour.

Visit **www.christourlife.com** for more family resources.

Gather and Go Forth

Know and Proclaim

By knowing the truths of our faith, we come to understand how to use and share the great gifts God has given us.

We Know Our Faith	We Proclaim Our Faith
God put the wonderful gifts of the earth in our care.	As Catholics, we honor God by using the earth's resources wisely and sharing them with others.
God gives the gifts of creation to everyone. He wants us to share with those who have less.	We answer God's call to charity by organizing our faith communities to share with those in need.
We are all brothers and sisters in God's family.	Catholics are witnesses to Jesus' Great Commandment by showing gratitude to others for their generosity and service to us.

The gifts God gives are many. Through his Word, we learn to share with others so that we will be blessed in this life and the next.

Do not neglect to do good and to share what you have; God is pleased by sacrifices of that kind.

Hebrews 13:16

Test Your Catholic Knowledge

Fill in the circle that best answers the question.

What lesson can we learn from the story of the rich man and Lazarus?

○ We show God real gratitude by sharing what we have with those in need.

○ We are not obligated to share with those who do not work.

○ God wants us to use the gifts we have been given for our own best interest only.

○ There was nothing the rich man could have done to change.

A Catholic to Know

Miguel was born in Ecuador in 1854. He had an unknown disability early in life that made it impossible for him to stand and walk like other children. At age five he is said to have experienced a vision of Our Lady and was healed. A bright student educated by the Christian Brothers, Miguel published his first book at age 17. He eventually became an understanding and patient teacher who always laughed with his students. Despite his academic honors and writings, Miguel always considered his students to be most important. He followed Jesus' example of a kind and patient teacher of all students, whether rich or poor.

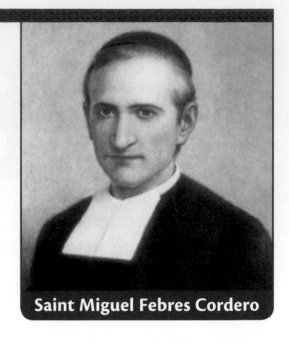
Saint Miguel Febres Cordero

Witness and Share

These sentences describe what Catholics believe. Listen carefully as they are read. Ask yourself, "How strong are my Catholic beliefs?"

My Way to Faith

- I use God's earthly gifts wisely.

- I am generous with the things I have.

- I work with my parish community to serve those in need.

- I show God gratitude in prayer for all he has given me.

- I follow Jesus' Great Commandment to treat others with respect and dignity.

Share Your Faith

What could you share with others? Make a list below. Compare your list with a classmate's and discuss them together. Invite your family to join you in sharing with someone in need.

_____

_____

_____

CHAPTER
19

We Speak the Truth with Love

God Wants Us to Speak the Truth

God is always true. He loves the truth and God is truth. We trust God because everything he says is true. God is always faithful to his promises.

God wants us to tell the truth and to keep our promises. He tells us this in the Eighth Commandment.

> You shall not bear false witness against your neighbor.
>
> Exodus 20:16

To bear false witness means to tell a lie. God tells us to be always truthful. It is especially important to tell the truth when we are talking about others.

When we tell the truth and keep our promises, we show love for God and for others. Our trust in one another grows. We trust those who tell the truth.

Jesus, Sermon on the Mount, ❯ Church of the Annunciation, Nazareth, Israel.

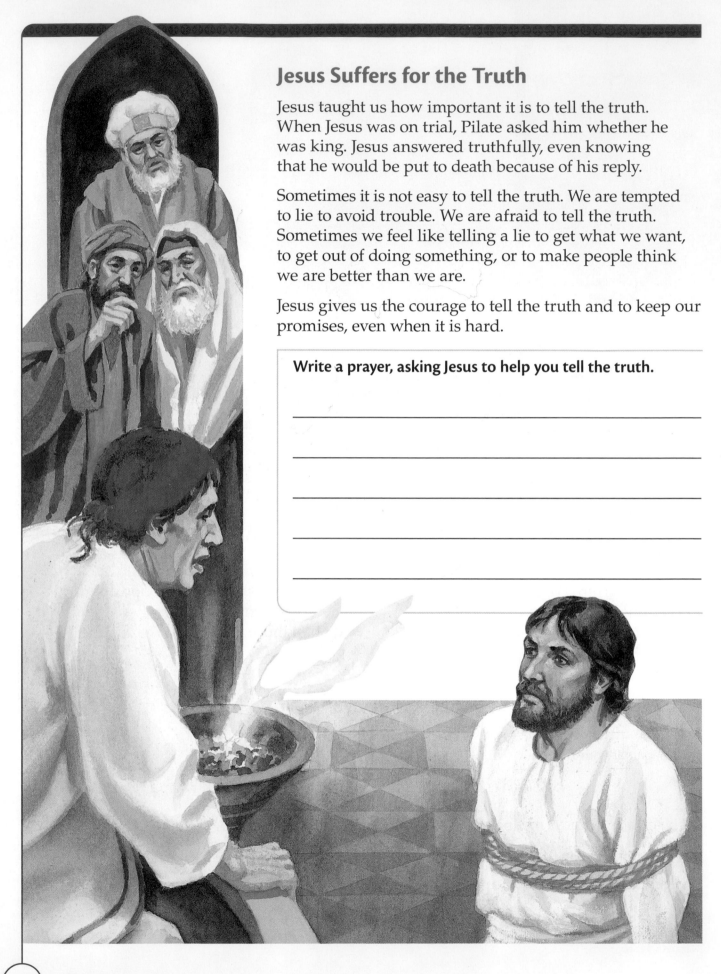

Jesus Suffers for the Truth

Jesus taught us how important it is to tell the truth. When Jesus was on trial, Pilate asked him whether he was king. Jesus answered truthfully, even knowing that he would be put to death because of his reply.

Sometimes it is not easy to tell the truth. We are tempted to lie to avoid trouble. We are afraid to tell the truth. Sometimes we feel like telling a lie to get what we want, to get out of doing something, or to make people think we are better than we are.

Jesus gives us the courage to tell the truth and to keep our promises, even when it is hard.

Write a prayer, asking Jesus to help you tell the truth.

_____

_____

_____

_____

_____

Sometimes We Suffer for the Truth

Thomas More was a lawyer and a helper to the king of England. The people loved him because he was fair to all and good to the poor. Thomas prayed at Mass every day and asked God to help him do what was right. He wanted to never offend God.

Henry VIII was king when Thomas lived. The king liked Thomas. He knew that Thomas would do whatever he could to help him.

Then King Henry made himself the head of the Church in England. When Thomas heard this, he would no longer work for the king. King Henry was very angry at Thomas and had him put into prison. Thomas still would not say that the king was the head of the Church, because it was not true. When the judges could not make Thomas say what was not true, they said he must die. Thomas's last words were, "I die the king's good servant, but God's first."

A Man of Truth

Work the puzzle about Saint Thomas More. Find the answers in the story above.

M Every day Thomas prayed for

God's help at _____ .

O Thomas loved God and would

not _____ him.

R Thomas prayed that God would help him

do what was _____ .

E Thomas More lived in _____ .

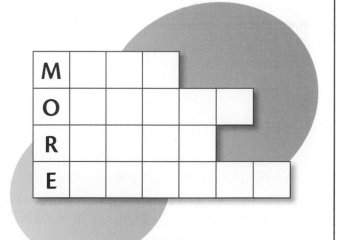

God Wants Us to Speak with Love

God gave us the wonderful gift of speech. With it we can help others learn, speak to them with love, and bring them good news and happiness.

Saint Paul wrote a letter that tells how to speak with love. This is what he said:

> Love is patient, love is kind. It is not jealous; it is not boastful. It is not rude, selfish, or quick-tempered. Love is never happy with evil but is happy with the truth.

adapted from 1 Corinthians 13:1,4–6

Our words are *true* when we are honest. Our words are *patient* when we speak calmly and hold back anger. Our words are *unselfish* when we praise others or share their joy. Our words are *kind* when we say polite and thoughtful things to others.

God wants us to say only what is true and good. He wants us to protect others' good names. Sometimes we show love just by being quiet. When someone does something wrong, we show love by not talking about it, except to protect that person or someone else. God wants us to say only what will bring happiness and peace to others.

Look at the two scenes below. Fill in the bubbles with what you think the children are talking about. Write some kind words in the bubbles.

A Moment with Jesus

Listen to Jesus as he speaks to you in your heart about what it means to tell the truth. Did he remind you to write only what is true as well? Whether we are speaking or writing, Jesus wants us to be truthful, kind, and encouraging. Sometimes that is hard to do, especially if we are angry with someone or have hurt feelings. Ask Jesus to send his Holy Spirit to help you. He never refuses a call for help. He loves you so much!

We Have Fun with Words

We like to hear tall tales. We listen to people say the strangest things, such as "I didn't sleep a wink."

Sometimes people say what is not true just to tease. Make-believe stories are not wrong, because everyone knows that they are not really true.

Color the clouds around the sentences that tease or that are make-believe.

Ernesto said that it was raining cats and dogs.

Luke told his little brother that there is a pot of gold at the end of the rainbow.

The bell rang to announce the end of the school day.

Josh liked carrots. His father said, "One day you'll turn into a rabbit."

Mother told Alexis that elves must have made her doll's new clothes.

Helena said that she has a pet dinosaur on her farm.

The horse spread its wings and flew over the steep mountain.

Nicole's mother is a police officer.

True or False?

Check (✓) the box under T if the sentence is true. Check the box under F if the sentence is false.

T F

☐ ☐ 1. The truth makes trust grow.

☐ ☐ 2. We do wrong when we pretend or play make-believe.

☐ ☐ 3. Jesus told the truth at his trial.

☐ ☐ 4. It is all right to talk about what others did wrong.

☐ ☐ 5. We keep the secrets of others.

We Remember

What is the Eighth Commandment?
The Eighth Commandment is "You shall not bear false witness against your neighbor."

We Respond

I will speak the truth with love, saying only things that are kind and true.

Building Family Faith

CHAPTER SUMMARY It is important to speak the truth and to keep our promises. We do this in imitation of God, who loves truth and who commands us to always say what is true, good, and loving.

REFLECT
"Speak the truth to one another; let there be honesty and peace in the judgments at your gates."

Zechariah 8:16

DISCUSS AS A FAMILY
• the negative consequences of lying.
• how you felt when someone told a lie about you.
• how keeping a promise is a way of speaking the truth.

PRAY
Jesus, you are the way, the truth, and the life. Give me the strength to always be truthful.

DO
Think of people who had the courage to tell the truth, such as Abraham Lincoln or Dominic Savio. Who are some current examples?

As a family, adopt and live by the motto of the knights of King Arthur: "Live pure, speak true, right wrong, follow the King!"

Visit **www.christourlife.com** for more family resources.

Gather and Go Forth

Know and Proclaim

Truth and love are principles of our Catholic faith. We learn them and then live them in our words and deeds.

We Know Our Faith	We Proclaim Our Faith
God wants us to speak the truth and to keep our promises.	When Catholics are honest and truthful, they bear witness to the just nature of Jesus' teachings.
Jesus suffered for the truth. He refused to deny the Word of God and accepted the consequences.	We study the lives of the martyrs for examples of courage to spread the Good News. They help us when we feel pressured to keep silent or deny our belief in God.
God gave people the gift of communication to help others learn and to act with love.	As Catholics, we engage and support ministries that spread Jesus' message of love around the world.

Our words and actions show others who we are. The Holy Spirit guides us in speaking truth and love.

Therefore, putting away falsehood, speak the truth, each one to his neighbor, for we are members one of another.

Ephesians 4:25

Test Your Catholic Knowledge

Fill in the circle that best completes the sentence.

We use our gift of communication the way God wants when we:

○ say everything we think.

○ tell people what they want to hear.

○ speak calmly and express anger appropriately.

○ point out the mistakes of others.

A Catholic to Know

Gertrude lived in Delft, the Netherlands, in the 1300s and worked as a servant girl. She focused her life on pursuing worldly satisfaction. Like many others, however, Gertrude's life took unexpected and difficult turns until she arrived on her true path of faith. When she joined the Béguine Sisters, she started a new life dedicated to works of mercy. As she opened herself to God in prayer, she felt him take a deep presence in her heart. Through God's comfort and love, Gertrude lost all desire for wealth and her former life. Before she died, Gertrude whispered, "I am longing to go home."

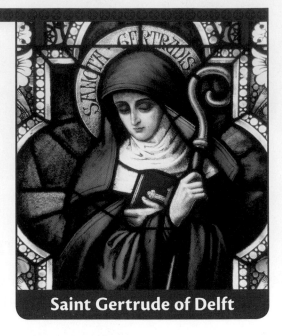

Saint Gertrude of Delft

Witness and Share

These sentences describe what Catholics believe. Listen carefully as they are read. Ask yourself, "How strong are my Catholic beliefs?"

My Way to Faith

- I am always truthful in everything I say.

- I spread Jesus' message of love whenever I can.

- I support the Church's ministries with donations and service.

- I draw courage from the lives of martyrs to proclaim God's words.

Share Your Faith

What sincere, loving things can you say to the people in your life? Make a list below. Invite a friend to add to your list. Together promise to be truthful, patient, unselfish, and kind in what you say this week.

_____

_____

_____

_____

We Live God's Laws

God's Laws Bring Happiness

The Ten Commandments show us how to love. The first three tell us how to love God, and the rest spell out how to love others.

A Song About God's Laws
(To the melody of "If You're Happy")

O be prayerful and give honor to God's name.
O be prayerful and give honor to God's name.
You'll be happy and will know it,
And your life will surely show it.
O be prayerful and give honor to God's name.

Go to Mass and celebrate the Sabbath day.
Go to Mass and celebrate the Sabbath day.
You'll be happy and will know it,
And your life will surely show it.
Go to Mass and celebrate the Sabbath day.

Be obedient, kind, and truthful every day.
Be obedient, kind, and truthful every day.
You'll be happy and will know it,
And your life will surely show it.
Be obedient, kind, and truthful every day.

O be faithful and respectful every day.
O be faithful and respectful every day.
You'll be happy and will know it.
And your life will surely show it.
O be faithful and respectful every day.

O be honest and be careful with all things.
O be honest and be careful with all things.
You'll be happy and will know it,
And your life will surely show it.
O be honest and be careful with all things.

Climb the Mountain

How to Play

- Roll the die and move your marker the number of spaces it shows.

- Read what is on the space and name the commandment it matches.

- A person acting as Moses checks the answers against the commandments listed on page 247. If you are correct, keep your marker on the space. If you are incorrect, move back one space. Read what is on that space and name the commandment it matches.

- If you are incorrect again, move back one more space; your turn is now over.

- The player who reaches the top of the mountain first wins.

What You Need

Marker for each player

Die

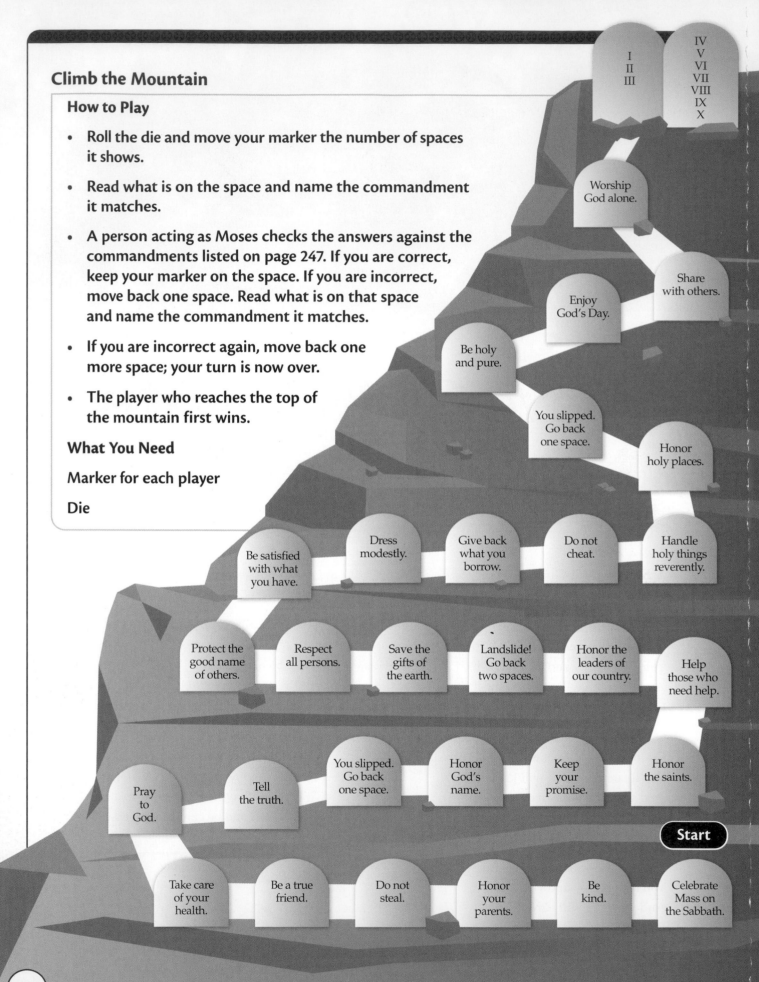

I II III

IV V VI VII VIII IX X

Worship God alone.

Share with others.

Enjoy God's Day.

Be holy and pure.

You slipped. Go back one space.

Honor holy places.

Be satisfied with what you have.

Dress modestly.

Give back what you borrow.

Do not cheat.

Handle holy things reverently.

Protect the good name of others.

Respect all persons.

Save the gifts of the earth.

Landslide! Go back two spaces.

Honor the leaders of our country.

Help those who need help.

Pray to God.

Tell the truth.

You slipped. Go back one space.

Honor God's name.

Keep your promise.

Honor the saints.

Start

Take care of your health.

Be a true friend.

Do not steal.

Honor your parents.

Be kind.

Celebrate Mass on the Sabbath.

An E-Mail Message

Write the message on the lines, using the code.

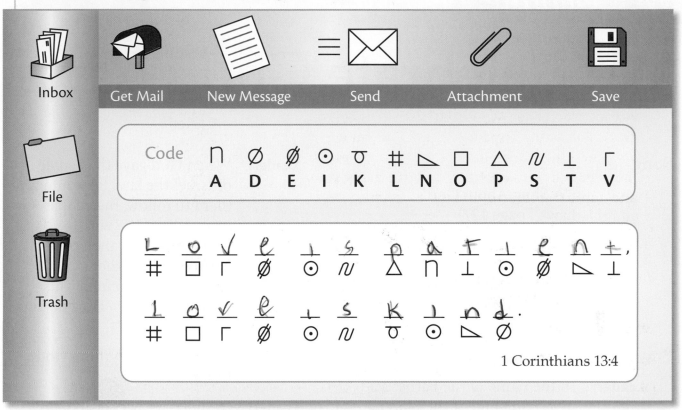

Code	∩	∅	∅	⊙	ꝋ	#	▷	□	△	⋈	⊥	Γ
	A	D	E	I	K	L	N	O	P	S	T	V

Love is patient,
love is kind.

1 Corinthians 13:4

A Path for Life

Find the words on the sidewalk and write them on the lines.

1. The First Commandment is to ___love god___ .

2. The Second Commandment is to honor God's ___name___ .

3. The Third Commandment is to keep the Lord's Day ___holy___ .

4. The Fourth Commandment is to ___obey___ our parents.

5. The Fifth Commandment is to be ___honest___ to others.

6. The Sixth and Ninth Commandments are to be ___kind___ .

7. The Seventh and Tenth Commandments are to be ___thankfull___ .

8. The Eighth Commandment is to speak the ___truth___ .

honest
pray
holy
kind
truth
name
faithful
obey

We Celebrate God's Laws

Song

("A Song About God's Laws," page 127)

The children process with, and then put in place, the Bible, the Ten Commandments tablets, and candles.

Prayer

Leader: In the name of the Father and of the Son and of the Holy Spirit. Amen.

Let us join together as we pray:

All: Lord God, we raise our hearts to you with joy. We want to live as you have told us. Put your love into our hearts today. Keep us faithful to your laws. We ask this through Jesus our Lord. Amen.

Leader: When God gave the people of Israel the laws he wanted them to follow, the people responded, "We will do everything that the LORD has told us." (Exodus 24:3) God asks you to follow his commandments. How do you respond?

All: We will do everything God has told us.

Leader: In the letter we are about to hear, Saint Paul tells us that when we keep the commandments, we are like runners in a race trying to win a prize. But the prize we win will last forever, because it is heaven.

Reading adapted from 1 Corinthians 9:24–25

Leader: A reading from the first letter of Saint Paul to the Corinthians

All the runners in a race are trying to win, but only one gets the prize. They do many difficult things to train for the race. They run fast to win a prize that will not last long. But we run for a prize that will last forever. Run so as to win.

The Word of the Lord

All: Thanks be to God.

Homily

(in dialogue with the children)

Silent Prayer

Awards

Leader: Accept this medal as a sign that you will live God's laws with joy.

Each child (upon receiving the medal):

Child: I want to keep God's laws.

Prayer with Commandments

All: Your Word, O Lord, is the joy of my heart. I sing your praises and walk with gladness.

For each commandment, a child prays and holds up a picture. Response to each prayer:

All: Lord, teach us to love your laws.

Final Prayer

Leader: Let us now pray together with joyful voices.

All: Lord, we rejoice because we have your laws. They are better than great riches. We will follow them closely. Help us obey them, O Lord. Amen.

Closing Song

Looking Back at Unit 4

Jesus reminded us that love for God is shown in love for our neighbor. The last seven commandments tell us how to love others in our daily lives. Keeping them brings us happiness and also helps bring God's kingdom of peace, justice, and joy to others.

In the Ten Commandments, God tells us to care for the gifts of the earth, to use them the right way, and to share them. God tells us to value life in all forms as a precious gift. God tells us to be faithful to ourselves and to others and to respect others' rights. We ask God's help in following these laws with love.

Living the Message

Check (✓) each sentence that describes you.

❏ 1. I can explain what the last seven commandments tell me to do and not to do.

❏ 2. I show that I value God's earthly gifts and my own life by the way I treat them.

❏ 3. I treat others with respect and kindness.

❏ 4. I try to be honest and truthful.

❏ 5. I can recite the Ten Commandments by heart.

Planning Ahead

Fill in the Don't Forget list with ways you can show Jesus' love in words or deeds.

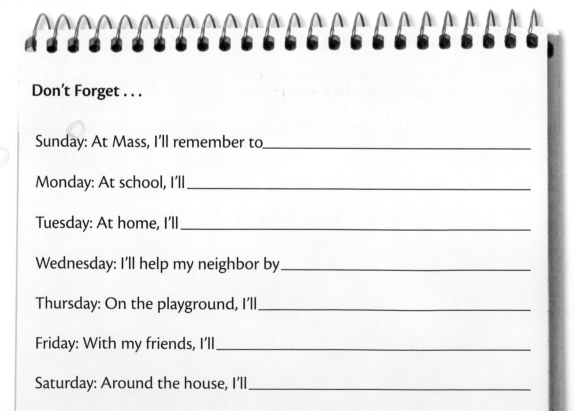

Don't Forget . . .

Sunday: At Mass, I'll remember to_____

Monday: At school, I'll_____

Tuesday: At home, I'll_____

Wednesday: I'll help my neighbor by_____

Thursday: On the playground, I'll_____

Friday: With my friends, I'll_____

Saturday: Around the house, I'll_____

Gather and Go Forth

Know and Proclaim

God's law is the basis of our faith. Knowing it and proclaiming it is our Christian duty.

We Know Our Faith	We Proclaim Our Faith
The Ten Commandments are God's laws. They show us how to love and bring happiness.	As Catholics, we listen to the priest's Homily at Mass for inspiration on how to live God's laws every day.
The first three Commandments teach us how to love God.	We put God first in all we do. We speak his name with reverence and celebrate his gifts on the Sabbath.
The last seven Commandments teach us how to love others.	Catholics practice God's law in everything they do. They are honest and respectful and look for opportunities to serve others.

Test Your Catholic Knowledge

Fill in the circle that best completes the sentence.

Jesus' New Commandment teaches us to:

○ pray.

○ love God.

○ receive the sacraments.

○ love one another as he loves us.

As Catholics, we learn God's law through Scripture and the Church's teachings. By the power of the Holy Spirit, we are able to live God's law when we love God and our neighbor.

The law of the LORD is perfect refreshing the soul.

Psalm 19:8

A Catholic to Know

The name *Irenaeus* means "peace." This saint held true to his name. As a priest and later bishop of Lyon, France, Irenaeus's chief concern was unity among churches. He fought against a group of Christians known as Gnostics who taught that eternal life was reserved for a chosen few who had special knowledge of God. Instead he pointed out that Scripture tells us that God wants all people to be saved and to know the truth. Throughout his life, Irenaeus was an important writer and a strong witness to the teachings of the Church as they came from Peter and the other apostles.

Saint Irenaeus

Witness and Share

These sentences describe what Catholics believe. Listen carefully as they are read. Ask yourself, "How strong are my Catholic beliefs?"

My Way to Faith

- I am guided by God's laws in everything I do.

- I honor the Lord above all else.

- I am wise and generous with the gifts God has given me.

- I always treat others with dignity and respect.

- I give witness to Jesus by how I live my life.

Share Your Faith

Choose one of the Ten Commandments. Write a pledge below telling how you can follow it this week. Invite a friend to join you in putting your pledge into action. Post your pledge somewhere as a daily reminder.

_____

_____

_____

_____

The Ten Commandments Are Gifts from God

Your first thought about the commandments might be that they are obligations. Though we are obliged to understand, accept, and obey them to the best of our ability, we do so because following them is the way to our truest happiness. That's the real gift of the commandments. Here is a look at the commandments along with some of the wisdom they hold for our lives.

1. I am the Lord your God: you shall not have strange gods before me.

There's good news and even better news. The good news is that there is a God, and the better news is that it's not me. It's a human temptation to want to make ourselves gods. Instead, we have a Creator who loves us, cares for us, and calls us to be one with him.

2. You shall not take the name of the Lord your God in vain.

When we are careless in our use of God's name, we demean the truth about him.

3. Remember to keep holy the Lord's Day.

With our culture's frantic workaholic tendencies, we need the Sabbath as a spiritual antidote. We need to stop, rest, and get in tune with the reality that we are at our core deeply spiritual beings.

4. Honor your father and your mother.

A culture grows shallow when it fails to honor its elders. When life becomes all about "me, me, me," we fail to become the human beings we were created to be—people for others.

5. You shall not kill.

There are many ways to do mortal damage to others. We can kill people's spirits, their reputations, their hopes, and their dreams. God calls us to choose life.

6. You shall not commit adultery. and
9. You shall not covet your neighbor's wife.

These are commandments about respect for other people, their inherent dignity, and their relationships.

7. You shall not steal. and
10. You shall not covet your neighbor's goods.

These are commandments about respect for other people and for what belongs to them.

8. You shall not bear false witness against your neighbor.

Ours is a God of truth. Telling lies about others is unjust and unfair. Lies harm not only the person we lie about, but they also undermine society as a whole.

Family Feature

Respect for Material Gifts

"You'd be surprised what people throw away," says John Havlicek, a man who sells rescued treasures at a local flea market. "People in our society have just so much stuff that they fail to appreciate what they're tossing in the alley. They throw things out just to make room for their next round of purchases."

Saint Benedict

God's laws tell us to love God, other people, and ourselves. In their great wisdom, these laws tell us to take care of and to share the gifts of the earth so that there is enough for everyone. We are to treat the gifts that God gives us with care. Saint Benedict (480–547) was the founder of many monasteries. He taught his monks to treat the everyday objects in the monastery, such as forks and spoons, clothing, and furniture, as though they were the vessels (chalice, paten, and ciborium) used on the altar. He wanted the monks to be able to recognize the inherent worth and sacredness of such common household items. This is a lesson we ought to model and teach to our children.

Visit **www.christourlife.com** for more family resources.

Gifts on Loan

Catholic wisdom tells us that the material items in our possession are gifts on loan from God. We are told to care for them. We must not hoard them but share them with others. We must realize they are given to us to serve the common good. Saint Basil (329–379) said, "The extra cloak that hangs in the closet belongs to the one who has none."

Steps your family can take to show greater care for the gifts God has given:

Participate in your area's recycling efforts. Some common objects in your home that you might not realize can be recycled or refurbished are old cell phones, used printer cartridges, prescription eyeglasses, batteries, and even running shoes.

Treat the possessions in your home with respect. Gently remind one another to turn off the lights when you leave a room or to pick up clothes that are crumpled on the bedroom floor.

Teach your child the importance of sharing with others. When your family bakes cookies, put some on a plate for your neighbor.

Have your child help you gather and deliver donations of used and well-cared-for items to charities that help families in need. Your children can take a few minutes to look in their closets and pick a few toys that they don't play with anymore. They can pass them along for another child to enjoy (even if it's only one toy).

Thank God regularly for all that you've been given in life. Ask for help in using these gifts for the greater honor and glory of God.

Family Feature

Love of Others

For each saying write the number of the commandment it matches.

1. _____ Don't let your parents down. They brought you up.

2. _____ He who lives by the sword dies by the sword.

3. _____ Don't let Sunday pass without going to Mass.

Saint Thomas More

4. _____ "I die the king's good servant, but God's first." (St. Thomas More)

5. _____ If friends are true, they don't envy what belongs to you.

6. _____ _____ Honesty is the best policy.

7. _____ Never in anger, only in love, do we say the name of God.

8. _____ _____ The greatest gift parents can give a child is to love each other.

9. _____ O what a tangled web we weave, When first we practice to deceive! (Sir Walter Scott)

10. _____ _____ The measure of life is not length, but honesty. (John Lyly)

1. I am the Lord your God: you shall not have strange gods before me.

2. You shall not take the name of the Lord your God in vain.

3. Remember to keep holy the Lord's Day.

4. Honor your father and your mother.

5. You shall not kill.

6. You shall not commit adultery.

7. You shall not steal.

8. You shall not bear false witness against your neighbor.

9. You shall not covet your neighbor's wife.

10. You shall not covet your neighbor's goods.

(Answers: **1.** 4, **2.** 5, **3.** 3, **4.** 1, **5.** 10, **6.** 7 and 8, **7.** 2, **8.** 6 and 9, **9.** 8, **10.** 7 and 8)

Jesus Leads Us to Happiness

Jesus said to him, "I am the way and the truth and the life."

John 14:6

A Letter Home

Dear Parents and Family,

In this final unit, the children will study the Beatitudes, Jesus' lessons for happiness. They will learn that by following in the footsteps of Jesus, Mary, and the saints, they can achieve happiness.

The first beatitude advises us to be detached from material things and to feel satisfied with what we have. The children will be encouraged to share with others and to trust in God for all their needs.

Suffering is part of daily life. In the second and third beatitudes, Jesus calls blessed those who mourn and the meek. By imitating Jesus, who is gentle and humble of heart, they can learn to meet life's challenges with patience and to comfort others who are suffering.

In the fourth and fifth beatitudes, Christ calls us to purity and holiness so that we can share in his happiness. The children will learn just what it means to seek God alone: doing what God wants, aligning their intentions with him, and following the example of the Blessed Virgin Mary and the saints.

The following two beatitudes share the ways in which the children can express mercy, through love and compassion. Jesus' word and example encourage them to become peacemakers in their schools, their homes, and the world around them.

The last beatitude tells us that God can bring good from evil and happiness from suffering. The children are encouraged to trust in God's grace for the strength to bear suffering with love, keeping in mind the example of the martyrs and Jesus' promise of happiness.

The children end this unit with a celebration, motivating them to live the Beatitudes and thus achieve the happiness promised to the faithful.

At the end of each chapter in this unit, the children will bring home a review of the chapter along with either the Building Family Faith page or the Family Feature section. These features give you a quick review of what your child learned and offer practical ways to reinforce the lesson at home so that the whole family may benefit.

Visit **www.christourlife.com** for more family resources.

Happy Are the Poor in Spirit

Jesus Showed Us the Way to Happiness

While he was on earth, Jesus showed us what it means to be happy. He showed us that true happiness comes from being willing to love God as our Father.

Jesus worked for low wages as a carpenter. He faced suffering in his life. He showed us that happiness is not found in owning many things or in having only pleasant things happen to us. The true source of Jesus' happiness was his Father's love.

Jesus wants us all to share his happiness. While teaching on a mountainside, he gave us the eight **Beatitudes** to help us live in hope and love. They lead us to God's kingdom, where we will share God's life forever. Jesus' teaching of the Beatitudes is part of his **Sermon on the Mount.**

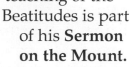

175

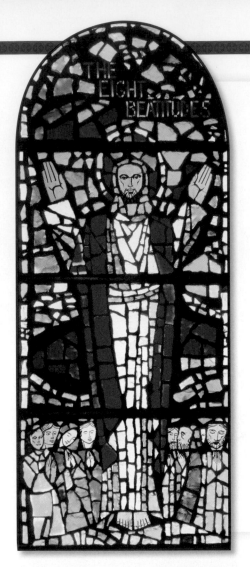

The Beatitudes

Happy are the poor in spirit,
    for theirs is the kingdom of heaven.
Happy are they who mourn,
    for they will be comforted.
Happy are the meek,
    for they will inherit the land.
Happy are they who hunger and thirst
      for righteousness,
    for they will be satisfied.
Happy are the merciful,
    for they will be shown mercy.
Happy are the clean of heart,
    for they will see God.
Happy are the peacemakers,
    for they will be called children of God.
Happy are they who are persecuted
      for the sake of righteousness,
    for theirs is the kingdom of heaven.
          adapted from Matthew 5:3–10

Saint Francis Was "God's Little Poor Man"

"Happy are the poor in spirit,
for theirs is the kingdom of heaven."
adapted from Matthew 5:3

Francis was a very rich young man who lived in the Italian town of Assisi. His father, who had a good business, wanted Francis to follow in his footsteps. But God had other plans; he called Francis to follow the example of his Son, Jesus.

One time, Francis met a poor man who was dressed in rags. He felt so sorry for the man that he exchanged clothes with him. The poor man walked away wearing Francis' fine coat, belt, and sandals. When Francis put on the poor man's ragged clothes, he felt the happiness promised to those who are poor in spirit.

The Holy Spirit led Francis to understand that he could show his love for Jesus by giving up his riches. So Francis left behind all that he owned to live as a poor man.

Francis did not miss his worldly riches, because he loved God above all things. He saw God's love and care in everything around him. Saint Francis wanted to share God's love with others. Most of all, he wanted to share it with the people in the world who were hungry, poor, and sad. He wanted to bring them happiness by sharing his food, clothing, and joy with them. God wants us to do the same.

Fill in the word that tells what we will want to do if we are poor in spirit.

If we are poor in spirit, we will

_____ with others.

Jesus Promises Happiness

People are foolish to think that riches can bring them happiness. If we remember that Jesus told us to love God above everything, we can be poor in spirit. To be "poor in spirit" means to realize that we always need God's help. It is to be satisfied having what we need, to be grateful for God's gifts, and to share with others. When we do these things, we will have the happiness that Jesus promised.

Write the word on each line that tells how the people in these stories are poor in spirit. Use the Word Bank to help you.

> **WORD BANK**
>
> generous   grateful
> content   God

1. Samantha received a new bike for Christmas. She took it over to show Angela. Angela was happy for Samantha, but Angela was just as happy with her own gift, a puzzle. Angela was poor in spirit because she was

   _____ .

2. Andrew planned to buy a new baseball with the money he had earned. At Sunday Mass, Andrew gave part of his money to help hungry people in the missions. Andrew was poor in spirit because he was

   _____ .

3. Mr. and Mrs. Marino own a large department store and a beautiful house. Each day before going to their store, they ask God to help them be honest and fair to their customers. They are poor in spirit because they show they need

   _____ .

4. Hannah lives alone with her mother, who works hard to support them. Hannah always has clean clothes, enough food, and people who love her, but not many extras. At night Hannah thanks God for caring for her mother and herself. She is poor in spirit because she shows she is

   _____ .

A Moment with Jesus

Spend this special time with Jesus. Ask him to help you find ways to be poor in spirit. Jesus wants you to know that it is all right to have things. After all, God gave you the gifts of creation. He wants you to enjoy what you have while still being generous to those who have less. Talk this over with Jesus and then just rest in his love.

Saint Francis realized that God had given him all the wonders of the universe. He was rich! With a grateful heart, he prayed a beautiful prayer.

Canticle of the Sun (adapted)

Be praised, my Lord,
For all your creatures,
For Brother Sun,
Who is beautiful and radiant in all
    his splendor.
Be praised for Sisters Moon and Stars.

Be praised for Brothers Wind and Air,
For the clouds, and for all kinds
    of weather.

Be praised for Sister Water,
Who is so useful and precious and
    pure.

Be praised for Brother Fire,
Who is so beautiful, bright, and strong.

Be praised for Sister Earth, our
    mother,
Who gives us fruit and plants
    and flowers.

Be praised for those
Who forgive others for love of you,
And who endure sickness and trial.

Praise and bless the Lord,
All you children.
Serve him and give him thanks.

Word Jumble

Unscramble the letters to discover Jesus' promise to those who live the Beatitudes.

The _____
gtihe

Beatitudes lead us to God's

_____ where
idognkm

we will live _____
rrefvoe

in _____ .
ppinhaess

We Remember

What do we call the way to happiness that Jesus gave us?

We call Jesus' way to happiness the Beatitudes.

What did Jesus say about the poor in spirit?

Jesus said, "Happy are the poor in spirit, for theirs is the kingdom of heaven."

Words to Know

Beatitudes
Sermon on the Mount

We Respond

Happy are they who . . . seek the Lord with all their heart.

adapted from Psalm 119:2

Building Family Faith

CHAPTER SUMMARY Much of Jesus' teaching about happiness is summarized in the Beatitudes. The first beatitude, "happy are the poor in spirit," speaks to the importance of being detached from material things.

REFLECT

"Do not worry about your life, what you will eat [or drink], or about your body, what you will wear. Is not life more than food and the body more than clothing?"

Matthew 6:25

DISCUSS AS A FAMILY

• the ways God provides for our family's needs, as he promises he will. Read Matthew 6:25–34.

• the ways we take care of one another's needs in our family.

• how we can avoid worrying about how our needs will be met.

PRAY

Father, you care for us. Show us how to care for others.

DO

Ask each family member to complete the sentence, "Happiness is . . . ." Discuss the answers.

Have family members name as many blessings from God as they can in two minutes. Write them down and discuss the list when finished.

Regularly pray prayers of thanksgiving to God for the resources your family has.

Visit **www.christourlife.com** for more family resources.

Gather and Go Forth

Know and Proclaim

We learn our Catholic faith. Then we proclaim it by the way we live each day.

We Know Our Faith	We Proclaim Our Faith
Jesus shows us that true happiness comes from loving God as our Father.	As Catholics, we find happiness in putting God before all else. One way we can celebrate his love is through our acts of kindness and generosity.
In the first Beatitude, Jesus blesses the poor in spirit, promising that the Kingdom of Heaven shall be theirs.	We show our gratitude to God for his gifts by sharing with others.
Saint Francis of Assisi was the son of a rich merchant. He found joy by walking away from wealth and following Jesus' example.	Catholics show their love of Jesus when they are generous with their possessions and give selflessly to those who are in need.

God gives so much to us. We find true happiness when we share his love with those in need.

"For I was hungry and you gave me food, I was thirsty and you gave me drink, a stranger and you welcomed me."

Matthew 25:35

Test Your Catholic Knowledge

Fill in the circle that best completes the sentence.

God calls us to be poor in spirit because he:

○ wants us to sell all we have and live in poverty.

○ is telling us to be serious.

○ wishes for us to share our gifts with others and depend only on him.

○ wants us to desire more than we have.

A Catholic to Know

From a young age, Rose only wanted to live for Jesus. Flowers played a big part in her life in the 17th century. Instead of attending school, Rose stayed home to work in her parent's garden growing flowers. She embroidered floral designs on silk too. When Rose's parents wanted her to marry to help them financially, she sold her needlework and flowers instead so she could give herself completely to God. Rose became a religious sister and moved into a small hut in her garden that she had built as a place of prayer. She used a room in her parent's home to care for the sick. Her work was the beginning of social service in her country of Peru.

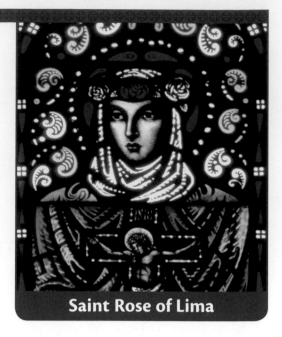

Saint Rose of Lima

Witness and Share

These sentences describe what Catholics believe. Listen carefully as they are read. Ask yourself, "How strong are my Catholic beliefs?"

My Way to Faith

- I put God first in my life.

- I give thanks to God for his gifts every day in my prayers.

- I learn how to show my love of Jesus from the saints, such as Saint Francis of Assisi.

- I am generous to those who are in need.

Share Your Faith

What are you grateful for? List some ideas below. Share your list with your family and invite them to join you in praying a prayer of gratitude to God for his gifts every day this week.

_____

_____

_____

_____

God's Sorrowing and Meek People Receive a Special Promise

Sorrowing People Will Be Comforted

By his life, Jesus taught us to trust that God our Father will comfort us in times of sorrow. In one of the Beatitudes, he promised a special peace to sorrowing or suffering people.

> "Happy are they who mourn,
> for they will be comforted."

adapted from Matthew 5:4

Jesus had sorrows and sufferings just as we do, but he put his trust in his Father. When he suffered in the garden on the night before he died, he prayed:

> "My Father, if it is possible, take this suffering away from me! Yet, let it be not as I will, but as you will."

adapted from Matthew 26:39

Jesus faced Death with courage. The Father accepted his sacrifice for our **salvation.** Jesus' suffering saved us from our sin. In heaven his sorrows are turned into joy.

Mary has the title Mother of Sorrows because she suffered so much when she stood at the foot of the Cross. But her sorrow was changed into joy when Jesus rose from the dead.

Jesus let us know that his followers would have to suffer too. He said,

> "Take up your cross and follow me."

adapted from Mark 8:34

In the Beatitudes, however, Jesus promises that in the midst of our suffering we will be comforted.

Jesus Helps Suffering People

Jesus felt sorry for people who were suffering. Once he looked out over the city of Jerusalem and saw that many people suffered because they did not believe in him. Jesus did all he could to help them. He prayed for them, taught them, and forgave them. He even gave his life to save them from sin and death.

God's people feel sorry when they see others suffer. They feel sad when they see that others are unhappy because they do not know or love Jesus. They pray and offer sacrifices to bring these people to him.

A Moment with Jesus

Think about all that Jesus suffered because of his love for you. Do you want to thank him? You can do it now. Then ask Jesus to help you through the hard times in your life. Jesus reminds you that he will always be at your side to help and to comfort you. Rest now in the love of Jesus and your heavenly Father.

Veronica Mourned for Jesus

In the Stations of the Cross we hear about a woman named Veronica who felt sorry for Jesus when she saw him carrying the heavy Cross. She comforted him by wiping his face with her veil. Later she found the face of Jesus imprinted on the veil.

Jesus calls us to help those who suffer. Even though it may be difficult for us, he wants us to help those who need our kindness, prayers, and sacrifices. By showing love and concern for others, we show our love for Jesus. This is one way we show that we belong to God's people.

When we help those who suffer, Jesus gives us a greater share in his life and love. In heaven, we will find that he has changed all our sorrows into joy!

Words for Those Who Mourn

It is not easy to be one of God's sorrowing people. Jesus tells us what to do when we have sorrow.

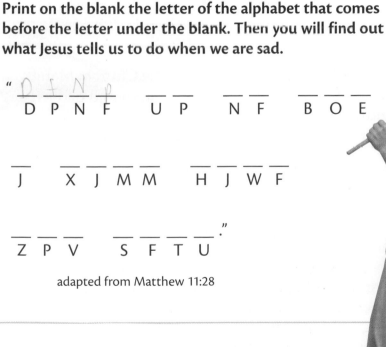

Print on the blank the letter of the alphabet that comes before the letter under the blank. Then you will find out what Jesus tells us to do when we are sad.

" _C_ _O_ _M_ _E_   __ __   __ __   __ __ __
   D P N F   U P   N F   B O E

__   __ __ __ __   __ __ __ __
J   X J M M   H J W F

__ __ __   __ __ __ __ ."
Z P V   S F T U

adapted from Matthew 11:28

Meek People Are Humble and Gentle

In one of the Beatitudes, Jesus spoke about people who are meek.

"Happy are the meek,
for they will inherit the land."

adapted from Matthew 5:5

Jesus also said,

"Learn from me, for I am meek
and humble of heart."

Matthew 11:29

Francis de Sales Was a Gentleman Saint

Francis was born into a noble Catholic family in France in 1567. Francis' father thought his son should be a soldier, so he was trained to use a sword. Francis had other ideas about his life; he wanted to be a priest. Yet he didn't want to give up his fancy clothes for the humble clothes of a priest. Finally he decided that, no matter what, it was time to answer God's call.

Some people thought that Francis was too proud to be a priest. Others thought he had too hot a temper. But Francis was serious. He really wanted to follow God's calling. He decided to ask Jesus for help whenever he felt himself getting angry or upset. He began to make up for hurting someone by doing something kind for that person. Over the years, Francis became so kind and gentle that people could hardly believe he once had a bad temper.

Francis lived during hard times for the Church. Many people were opposed to the Catholic faith and had left the Church. Francis left his own country and went to Switzerland to teach and preach. There he walked the countryside speaking to anyone who would listen. People threw rocks at him as he passed. So he wrote pamphlets and slid them under the doors of the homes.

Francis knew that in these troubled times, he needed to be meek and gentle. He began teaching the children. Soon their parents were also drawn to his gentle manner. When he became a bishop, Francis continued to work in his gentle way, and many more people were drawn to his writings and teachings. His manner won over their hearts. Because of him, more than 70,000 people returned to the Catholic faith. Francis was not always meek and humble, but with God's help, he changed his ways. That is why today we know him as Saint Francis de Sales.

Learning to Be Gentle

When we are gentle and humble like Jesus, Mary, and the saints, we show that we understand what Jesus said about meek people.

Fill in the blanks in these sentences with words from the Gentle Savings Bank to find out how you can become more gentle and humble.

GENTLE SAVINGS BANK

pray   patient   quiet   praise   serve

forgive

1. If you are upset, be _____quiet_____ until you can speak kindly.

2. Be _____patient_____ when people do not understand you.

3. Be willing to _____forgive_____ those who are unkind.

4. Be ready to _____serve_____ those who need help.

5. When others play well and win, _____praise_____ them.

6. To control hurtful feelings, _____pray_____ for grace.

Draw a ☺ if the sentence describes a way to be gentle or humble.
If it does not, draw a ☹.

◯ 1. Say "I'm sorry. Please forgive me."

◯ 2. Say "You really did a good job."

◯ 3. Push yourself ahead of someone in line.

◯ 4. Share something you like.

◯ 5. Pout when someone else wins a game.

◯ 6. Offer to do a chore for someone.

◯ 7. Pray for someone who has been unkind to you.

◯ 8. Let someone have the first turn doing something you like.

We Remember

What did Jesus say about the sorrowing?
"Happy are they who mourn, for they will be comforted."

What did Jesus say about the meek?
"Happy are the meek, for they will inherit the land."

Word to Know
salvation

We Respond

Jesus, meek and humble of heart, make my heart like yours.

Building Family Faith

CHAPTER SUMMARY Suffering is part of our daily life. We accept it and look to God for the strength to bear it and learn from it.

REFLECT
"Blessed are they who mourn,
    for they will be comforted.
Blessed are the meek,
    for they will inherit the land."
                    Matthew 5:4–5

DISCUSS AS A FAMILY
• a recent difficulty, frustration, or failure in the family and the positive results of these experiences.
• how God uses us and other people we know to bring comfort to sorrowing people.

PRAY
Our hearts are open to you, Jesus. Fill them with your love.

DO
Help alleviate pressures and difficulties people in your family have right now.

Comfort someone who is suffering physically, in your extended family, your neighborhood, or elsewhere.

Pray regularly for the suffering people you have talked about.

Visit **www.christourlife.com** for more family resources.

Gather and Go Forth

Know and Proclaim

As we learn more about our Catholic faith, we tell others so they too can be comforted by God's loving care.

We Know Our Faith	We Proclaim Our Faith
In the Beatitudes, Jesus teaches us that trusting God the Father will comfort us in times of suffering.	We receive God's comfort when we are in need. As Catholics, we are called to give comfort and love to others who suffer.
God's people help others when they are suffering.	We bring comfort to those who suffer through acts of kindness in Jesus' name. In addition, we ask Mary, Mother of Sorrows, to intercede for them.
Jesus gives us the grace to be compassionate to those who suffer.	As Catholics, we give witness to Jesus' love and comfort by supporting Church missionaries and serving those in need.

Test Your Catholic Knowledge

Fill in the circle that best answers the question.

In the Stations of the Cross, which Beatitude does Veronica model in her compassion for Jesus?

○ Blessed are the poor in spirit, for theirs is the kingdom of heaven.

○ Blessed are those who mourn, for they will be comforted.

○ Blessed are the meek, for they will inherit the land.

○ Blessed are the peacemakers, for they will be called children of God.

We put our trust in God and show the world how much he loves and cares for us.

Do not fear: I am with you;
do not be anxious: I am
your God.
I will strengthen you, I will
help you,
I will uphold you with my
victorious right hand.

Isaiah 41:10

A Catholic to Know

Thomas was born into a wealthy family in 1225. At age five, he was sent to a Benedictine monastery in hopes that some day he would be the abbot. But Thomas had other dreams. Against his family's wishes, he joined the Dominicans, whose life of prayer and study fascinated him. Thomas became a brilliant but humble scholar. He knew his gifts came from God. Thomas's writing about the Christian mysteries showed great reason and understanding. He wrote prayers and hymns that are still used today. A scholar for Christ, Saint Thomas Aquinas is the patron of Catholic schools.

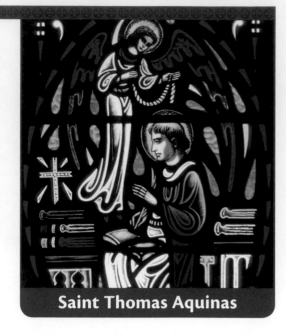

Saint Thomas Aquinas

Witness and Share

These sentences describe what Catholics believe. Listen carefully as they are read. Ask yourself, "How strong are my Catholic beliefs?"

My Way to Faith

- I remember Jesus' teaching in the Beatitudes when I feel sorrow.

- I show love and care for others who suffer.

- I pray the Litany of the Blessed Virgin Mary.

- I experience Jesus' love when I show love to others.

- I show compassion for others by supporting parish ministries.

Share Your Faith

Write a prayer asking the Holy Spirit to help you bring comfort to someone who is hurting. Share your prayer with your family. Invite them to pray it with you every day this week.

_____

_____

_____

_____

Holy Trinity, Dominican Church, Krakow, Poland.

CHAPTER 23

God's People Long to Be Clean of Heart and Holy

The Clean of Heart Will See God

The pure of heart are God's happy people. Jesus spoke of them.

> "Happy are the clean of heart, for they will see God."
>
> adapted from Matthew 5:8

Jesus' heart was filled with love for his Father. He saw God our Father in everything, and everyone saw the Father's love in Jesus. Jesus gave glory to the Father by his life and his Death on the Cross.

Mary's heart was free from sin too. From the moment God made her, she belonged entirely to him. Her heart was full of love, so Mary pleased God in everything she did. She thought of others and made them happy. Now Mary is with God in heaven, where she sees him in all his beauty and glory. Mary will help us be clean of heart. We can say to her, "Mother most pure, pray for us."

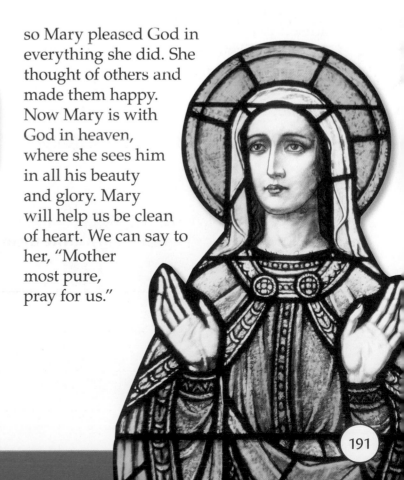

191

Saint Aloysius Was Clean of Heart

In the 16th century, a boy named Aloysius lived in Italy. His family was rich, and he had everything he wanted. One summer, when he was seven, his father took him to a camp where soldiers trained. Aloysius heard some bad words from these men. After he returned home, he repeated these words in school. When his teacher scolded him for speaking this way, Aloysius learned how wrong it was to offend God, even in a small way. From that time on, he was careful not to say or do anything that would offend God or hurt others. He tried to please God and to keep his heart pure.

Aloysius grew in love for God by praying to him often during the day. He especially loved to pray the psalms, and he prayed special prayers to Mary each day. Once he went to a shrine of Mary in the city of Florence. When he knelt before her beautiful statue, he was filled with a great desire to be pure and holy. He wanted to serve God always and to please our Blessed Mother. Aloysius promised God that he would never sin and asked Mary to help him. He often went to church to pray and was happy when he could receive Jesus in Holy Communion.

Aloysius loved Jesus so much that he decided to give himself to Jesus in a special way by becoming a priest. He left his rich home and gave up his money to become a member of the Society of Jesus, also known as the Jesuits.

While Aloysius was studying in Rome to be a priest, a terrible disease broke out. Aloysius helped care for the sick until he became sick himself. After suffering for three months, he died at the age of 23. Now Aloysius is with God in heaven, where he sees him in all his glory. He has received the wonderful reward Jesus promised the pure of heart.

Color the medal of Mary. Make a design around the frame of the medal. Print the words *Mary, pray for us* on the lines.

We too can become pure of heart like Jesus, Mary, and the saints. When our hearts are pure, we are able to see God in the beautiful world around us, in ourselves, and in other people. One day we will see God in heaven. Until then, we can ask Mary and Saint Aloysius to pray for us.

Finish the beatitude by naming the reward of the pure of heart.

"Happy are the clean of heart, for they will

_____ _____."

A Moment with Jesus

Share with Jesus the story you just read about Saint Aloysius. Now imagine Jesus asked you if you would like to be holy as this saint was. What would you answer? Jesus reminds you that wanting to be holy is the first step. The other steps will be harder, but Jesus promises to walk with you. Thank him and then share with him anything else you would like.

We Hunger and Thirst for Righteousness

Jesus told us about people who desire to be holy.

> "Happy are they who hunger and thirst for righteousness, for they will be satisfied."
>
> adapted from Matthew 5:6

We show our desire to be holy when we try to love God with all our hearts, please God in all things, and work to spread peace and justice in the world.

Once Jesus sat down at a well to rest. His disciples knew that he was hungry and said, "Master, have something to eat." But Jesus told them:

> "My food is to do the will of the one who sent me. I am hungry to finish his work."
>
> adapted from John 4:34

Jesus loved his Father, so he tried to please God in everything. He pleased his heavenly Father by obeying his parents. He showed love for the Father when he prayed to him alone on the mountain or with others in the Temple.

Jesus did the work his Father wanted him to do. He healed the sick, told people how much God our Father loved them, and forgave those who were sorry for their sins. He finished his Father's work when he suffered and died on the Cross to gain heaven for us. Jesus worked hard to bring God's kingdom of love to earth.

Mary Desired to Be Holy

Mary was holy. Because she loved God so much, her greatest desire was to do his will. When the angel told her that God wanted her to be the mother of Jesus, she said,

> "May it be done to me according to your word."
>
> Luke 1:38

Mary was happy because she always did what God wished. Now she is happy with God in heaven. We pray to her, "Holy Mary, Mother of God, pray for us."

Mary's joy in the risen Lord was greater than anyone else's because she loved and believed more deeply than anyone else. The glorious risen Jesus, the Son of God, was and always will be her son. She now shares his glory.

Thérèse Desired to Be Holy

In 1873, a girl named Thérèse Martin was born in France. Even as a child, Thérèse wanted to be holy. She knew that, to become a saint, one had to love God and to suffer like Jesus.

Thérèse also understood that she was free to sacrifice much or little for Jesus, but she loved Jesus so much that she told him: "I choose everything you want me to do. I am not afraid to suffer for you."

All her life Thérèse made sacrifices for Jesus. She always tried to be like him. Once Thérèse said, "My heart does not wish for riches or glory. What I ask for is love. Only one thing, my Jesus, to love you."

When Thérèse was 24 years old, she died from tuberculosis. Now Saint Thérèse is with God in heaven.

Ponder This

Using the words in the Word Bank, complete the sentences below. Then circle those words in the puzzle.

God's _____ tells us how to be holy.

A desire to be holy is like a _____ for food.

A desire is a strong _____ .

We want to do God's _____ .

We can be _____ for holiness.

To become holy, we must give God our _____ .

WORD BANK

wish	Word	will
hunger	love	thirsty

L	R	S	H	U	N	G	E	R	A
O	D	W	M	G	W	O	R	D	L
V	S	I	T	H	I	R	S	T	Y
E	K	L	U	D	S	Q	E	Q	Z
G	B	L	U	P	H	J	N	U	E
D	I	H	Z	Q	U	N	I	L	O

We Remember

What did Jesus say about the pure of heart?

"Happy are the clean of heart, for they will see God."

What did Jesus say about those who hunger and thirst for righteousness?

"Happy are they who hunger and thirst for righteousness, for they will be satisfied."

We Respond

Those who seek the LORD want for no good thing.

adapted from Psalm 34:11

Building Family Faith

CHAPTER SUMMARY We are called to be pure and holy so that we may share in the joy God intends for us. This means putting God first. We follow Jesus, and we imitate him, Mary, and the saints.

REFLECT

"Blessed are the clean of heart, for they will see God."
Matthew 5:8

DISCUSS AS A FAMILY

- the story of Saint Aloysius from pages 148–149, after reading it together as a family. What kind of person was Aloysius? How can we be like him?
- the quality of Jesus you would most like to imitate.

PRAY

Holy Mary, Mother of God, pray for us sinners.

DO

What person living today would you call holy? Discuss why.

Review the television programs the family watches. Do they reflect the values that promote purity of heart? Should we do something else for entertainment?

Visit **www.christourlife.com** for more family resources.

Gather and Go Forth

Know and Proclaim

As we examine the truths of our faith, we are able to tell others of the blessings God wants to share with us all.

We Know Our Faith	We Proclaim Our Faith
Jesus teaches us that "Happy are the clean of heart, for they will see God."	As Catholics, we can form a clean heart by examining our daily actions in prayer. We can seek to understand whether our motivation is to truly follow God's will.
In the Beatitudes, we learn that God's people hunger and thirst for righteousness.	We seek righteousness by trying to spread the peace and justice of the Lord in the world. We support Church ministries in our parish communities and in faraway lands.
Mary loved God so much that her greatest desire was to do his will.	Catholics seek Mary's strength in prayer because they believe that she is the person closest to Jesus. They honor her commitment to God's will when celebrating the Annunciation.

Test Your Catholic Knowledge

Fill in the circle that best answers the question.

Which Beatitude best describes someone who sees God in themselves, others, and the beautiful world?

○ Blessed are the poor in spirit.

○ Blessed are the peacemakers.

○ Blessed are the meek.

○ Blessed are the pure of heart.

Knowing God's love makes us desire to be close to him. Our hearts are full!

Although you have not seen him you love him; even though you do not see him now yet believe in him, you rejoice with an indescribable and glorious joy.

1 Peter 1:8

A Catholic to Know

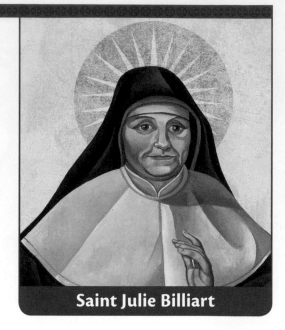

Saint Julie Billiart

Julie showed an early interest in religion and teaching about Jesus. When she needed to help support her family as a teenager, she taught the faith to those she worked with. Even when a serious illness left her paralyzed, Julie continued to teach the faith to her village's children from her bed. When the French Revolution forced Julie to leave her home, she and a friend began a Christian school for girls who were poor even as Julie continued to suffer great pain. Julie dedicated the rest of her life to opening convents and schools throughout France that served all people of faith.

Witness and Share

These sentences describe what Catholics believe. Listen carefully as they are read. Ask yourself, "How strong are my Catholic beliefs?"

My Way to Faith

- I form a clean heart by examining my conscience to understand if I am following God's will.

- I provide examples of God's justice by being fair to people and caring for others.

- I know Mary always did what God wanted.

- I pray to Mary and ask her to intercede so that I can be holy.

Share Your Faith

Make a list of places, people, and things in which you recognize God's presence. Share your list with a friend. Invite him or her to join you in saying a prayer to the Holy Spirit, asking him to open your heart to God's presence around you each day.

_____

_____

_____

_____

CHAPTER 24

God's People Bring Mercy and Peace to Others

Jesus tells us to show mercy.

> "Happy are the merciful,
> for they will be shown mercy."

adapted from Matthew 5:7

Jesus was merciful like his Father. When he was dying on the Cross, he said,

> "Father, forgive them, they know not what they do."

Luke 23:34

Jesus had mercy on people who were sick and suffering. List two people who were helped by Jesus.

_____

_____

Jesus told us how to show mercy. He said:

> "Love your enemies. Do good to those who hate you and pray for those who mistreat you. Give to those who are in need. Do not wish for anything in return. Be merciful as your heavenly Father is merciful. Forgive, and you will be forgiven. Give, and gifts will be given to you."

adapted from Luke 6:27–38

Mother Cabrini Was Merciful

Frances Cabrini wanted to help everyone. She left her home in Italy to be a missionary sister in the United States. Some people from her country had moved to America hoping to find a better life, but many of them could not find jobs. They lived in very poor places and went without the food and clothes they needed. Many became weak and ill.

Mother Cabrini and her sisters begged for food and clothing for these people. They started hospitals, homes for children, and schools.

Before Mother Cabrini died, she became an American citizen in 1909. Now she is Saint Frances Cabrini, the first United States citizen to be named a saint.

We Are Called to Be Merciful

The **Corporal Works of Mercy** are ways we can meet the material needs of people. We do what we can to help feed, clothe, and find homes for those who have none. We also visit and comfort people who are sick.

The **Spiritual Works of Mercy** include teaching, consoling, comforting, forgiving, and being patient when others do wrong to us. The Church has been doing these acts of mercy following the example of Jesus.

Work the puzzle. The clues below will help you.

Down

1. Merciful people _____ those who hurt them.

3. They _____ their enemies.

4. They do_____ to those who hate them.

Across

2. Merciful people _____ for those who mistreat them.

4. They _____ to everyone in need.

God's Children Are Peacemakers

"Happy are the peacemakers,
for they will be called children of God."

Matthew 5:9

In this beatitude, Jesus speaks of the peace that comes from loving God and others, and from doing what is right.

God sent Jesus into the world to give us his peace. Jesus often greeted his apostles by saying "Peace be with you."

Isaac Jogues Was a Missionary of Peace

All God's saints were peacemakers. Isaac Jogues, a 17th-century French priest of the Society of Jesus, left France to bring God's peace to the North American tribes. Father Jogues lived as the American Indians lived. He ate the kinds of food they ate and slept on a bed of bark chips. He helped those who were sick, and he shared his food with those who were hungry.

Father Jogues and other missionaries often smoked the ceremonial peace pipe with their American Indian friends as a sign that they could trust one another. One Iroquois tribe would not smoke the peace pipe with the French. They captured Father Jogues, but while their prisoner, Father Jogues prayed for them, taught them about God's love, and offered his sufferings to God for them.

One day Father Jogues escaped and returned to France. He was so thin and sick that his friends did not know him. As soon as he was well, he went back to work with the American Indians again. He tried to help enemy tribes make peace with one another. Father Jogues even went to help the Iroquois who had taken him prisoner. He had forgiven them.

One night someone in the camp invited Father Jogues to his home for supper. As Father Jogues entered the tent, another Iroquois Indian struck him with a tomahawk and killed him. Isaac Jogues, God's peacemaker, died a martyr for Jesus.

Doing Things to Make Peace

Read each story and underline the choice that shows what each child could do to bring God's peace to others.

1. At supper Dylan told the family that his sister, Emily, had been in trouble for playing after the school bell had rung. Emily felt embarrassed and angry. Their father told Dylan that he didn't have to tell on Emily. Dylan said he was sorry, but Emily's anger could make the evening meal unpleasant. What should Emily do?

   • Tell something mean about Dylan.

   • Forgive Dylan.

   • Keep being angry.

2. Maribel's little sister Jasmine took off the best dress from Maribel's doll to put on her teddy bear. She tore the dress. When Maribel came home, Jasmine was in tears about the accident. What should Maribel do?

   • Say she will mend it if she can.

   • Scold Jasmine.

   • Take something away from Jasmine.

3. Abigail saw that her baby brother's toys were all over the floor. She knew her mother would not like such a mess. What should Abigail do?

   • Leave the toys on the floor.

   • Tell her mother.

   • Help pick up the toys.

4. Patrick went out to play at recess. He wanted to play a game of Keep Away. The other boys wanted to play basketball. What should Patrick do?

   • Quarrel with the boys.

   • Play basketball.

   • Refuse to play.

A Moment with Jesus

Think of the example of peacemaking Jesus gave us. He was silent when people made fun of him, forgiving when they hurt him. Can you be a peacemaker in your home? in school? on the playground? What would you have to do? Talk about this with Jesus. Then ask him to send the Holy Spirit to help you.

Bringing-Mercy-and-Peace Game

Throw a die and move a marker as many spaces as the die tells you. Write on the scorecard the number of spaces moved. If you land on a space that names a good act, add the number given there to your score. Each player gets six turns; the one with the highest score wins.

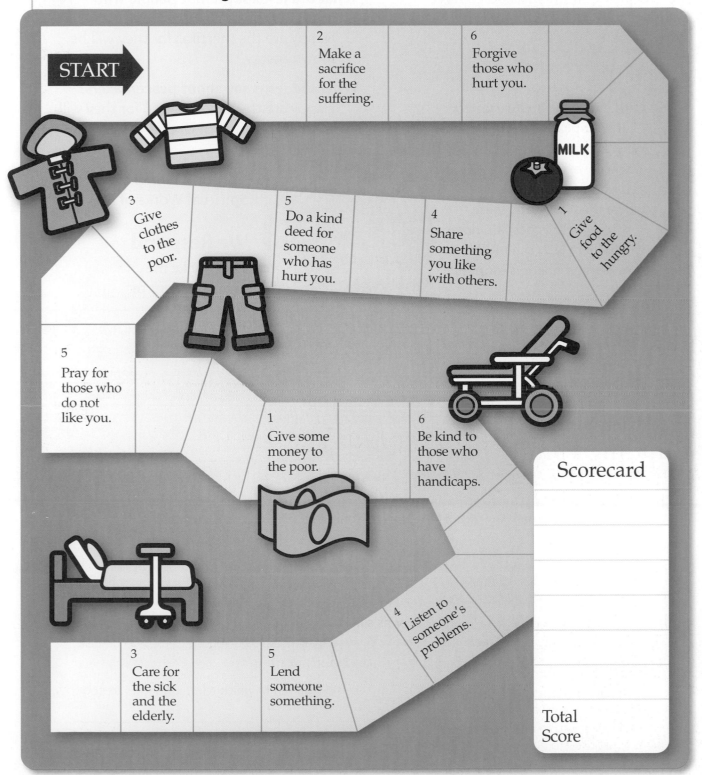

START

2 Make a sacrifice for the suffering.

6 Forgive those who hurt you.

3 Give clothes to the poor.

5 Do a kind deed for someone who has hurt you.

4 Share something you like with others.

1 Give food to the hungry.

5 Pray for those who do not like you.

1 Give some money to the poor.

6 Be kind to those who have handicaps.

3 Care for the sick and the elderly.

5 Lend someone something.

4 Listen to someone's problems.

Scorecard

Total Score

Prayer for Peace

Here is part of a prayer said to have been written by Saint Francis of Assisi. Pray it often.

Lord, make me an instrument
   of your peace.
Where there is hatred, let me
   sow love; where there is injury,
   pardon;
where there is doubt, faith;
   where there is despair, hope;
where there is darkness, light;
   and where there is sadness,
   joy.

We Remember

What did Jesus say about people who are merciful?

"Happy are the merciful, for they will be shown mercy."

What did Jesus say about peacemakers?

"Happy are the peacemakers, for they will be called children of God."

Words to Know
Corporal Works of Mercy
Spiritual Works of Mercy

We Respond

Lord, make me an instrument of your peace.

Building Family Faith

CHAPTER SUMMARY **Our relationship with God causes us to bring love, peace, and mercy to others. We do this through the gifts of the Holy Spirit and by striving to be like Jesus.**

REFLECT

"Blessed are the peacemakers,
   for they will be called children of God."
                Matthew 5:9

DISCUSS AS A FAMILY

• how Jesus showed mercy to others. Refer to his parables, such as the Good Samaritan, and to the miracles he performed.

• how we have seen disputes and disagreements settled peacefully. What made the difference?

• disagreements we presently have at home or in school that need to be resolved.

PRAY

Lord, make me an instrument of your peace.

DO

Make the prayer of Saint Francis your family's prayer. Take advantage of opportunities to bring peace to others, to bring hope to those in despair, and to bring joy to those who are sad.

Decide as a family which television shows are too violent to watch.

Visit **www.christourlife.com** for more family resources.

Gather and Go Forth

Know and Proclaim

We seek to learn the truths of our Catholic faith so that we can tell others of the Good News, leading all to God's kingdom.

We Know Our Faith	We Proclaim Our Faith
Jesus teaches us in the Beatitudes that those who are merciful shall receive mercy.	As Catholics, we give our time and possessions to meet others' needs. We help by feeding, clothing, and finding homes for those who need them.
Jesus asked his Father to forgive all, even those who crucified him. Jesus tells us to show mercy.	We follow Jesus' example of forgiveness by practicing Spiritual Works of Mercy. We witness to God's kingdom by offering care, love, and counsel to all his people.
God sent Jesus into the world to give us his peace. Jesus calls us to be peacemakers.	Many Catholics work for peace as missionaries in places suffering from war and violence. Catholics support them through donations and service.

We are called to follow Jesus' example and continue his work on earth. The Holy Spirit is our strength and our guide to help us in this mission.

"Be merciful, just as [also] your Father is merciful."
Luke 6:36

Test Your Catholic Knowledge

Fill in the circle that best completes the sentence.

When we teach about Christ, comfort, console, forgive, and are patient with others, we perform the:

- ○ Corporal Works of Mercy.
- ○ Spiritual Works of Mercy.
- ○ the Precepts of the Church.
- ○ the Ten Commandments.

A Catholic to Know

Polycarp was a bishop in what would become Turkey in the second century. He was one of the most respected leaders in the early days of the Church. Polycarp was a disciple of John the Apostle and worked fearlessly to spread the Good News. Polycarp spoke clearly in defense of Christ among nonbelievers, even when threatened with persecution and death. When Polycarp was arrested for being a Christian, he was sentenced to death by fire. When he was unharmed by the flames, Polycarp was finally killed by a sword. Like the Good Shepherd, Polycarp laid down his life for his flock.

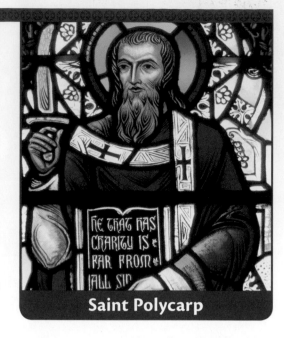

Saint Polycarp

Witness and Share

These sentences describe what Catholics believe. Listen carefully as they are read. Ask yourself, "How strong are my Catholic beliefs?"

My Way to Faith

- I show mercy to those who have wronged me by forgiving them.

- I follow Jesus' example by showing care and love to all his people.

- I help my parish feed and clothe those in need.

- I spread God's peace in the world through my prayers, actions, and words.

Share Your Faith

List some ways that you can practice the Corporal or Spiritual Works of Mercy. Invite family members to join you in following Jesus' example by putting your ideas into action.

_____

_____

_____

_____

God's People Are Happy

Jesus Shows Us the Way

Jesus loved us so much that he suffered and died for us. He told his followers to love others as he did and not to be afraid:

> "People will hate you because of my name. They will make you suffer. They may put some of you to death."
>
> adapted from Luke 21:16–17

In one of the Beatitudes, Jesus spoke about those who would suffer for him.

"Happy are they who are persecuted for the sake of righteousness,
for theirs is the kingdom of heaven."

adapted from Matthew 5:10

Our Blessed Mother loved and suffered as Jesus did. We call her the Queen of Martyrs. The saints loved God as Jesus did. Those who suffered and died for Jesus are **martyrs.**

Fill in the puzzle. Use the clues in the sentences to help you.

M _____ is the Queen of Martyrs.

A We _____ Jesus to help us face suffering bravely.

R The Kingdom of Heaven will be our _____ .

T We must _____ others kindly.

Y We should say _____ to what God wants us to do.

R We must be willing to suffer for what is _____ .

Saint Joan of Arc Was God's Soldier

Joan of Arc was a brave girl who lived in a village in France during the 1400s. At the time she lived, her country was at war with England. The king of France was weak and afraid that his armies could not save France. Joan began hearing the voices of saints, urging her to save her country. She said that Saint Michael the Archangel had told her, "Daughter of God, go and save France."

Although Joan was afraid, she did what God wanted. Carrying a banner, she led the French army into battle. On the banner were written the names of Jesus and Mary. Joan won battles that helped save France.

Many people did not believe that God had spoken to Joan in a special way. They called her a witch and other wicked names. But Joan kept on doing what she thought was right.

Soon she was captured by the enemy and put in prison. Although she was treated unfairly, she forgave and prayed for her enemies. When she was put to death by fire, her last word was "Jesus." Joan suffered bravely for God and for her country. Today we call her Saint Joan of Arc.

Print the names that appeared on Saint Joan's banner, and then decorate it.

A Happy-Heart Puzzle

Work this puzzle. Use the clues and the Word Bank.

WORD BANK

merciful	peace	comfort	meek	suffer
clean	right	happy	poor	Mary
holy	Arc	children		

Across

4. Jesus said, "_____ be with you."

6. We should be _____ like our heavenly Father.

8. The Beatitudes help us be _____ .

11. We please God when we do what is _____ .

12. Peacemakers will be called _____ of God.

Down

1. Sometimes Christians must _____ for the name of Jesus.

2. We become _____ by doing God's will.

3. _____ people are gentle.

5. The _____ of heart will see God.

6. _____ is the holiest woman.

7. God's sorrowing people will receive _____ .

9. The Kingdom of Heaven belongs to the _____ in spirit.

10. The saint who fought for France was Saint Joan of _____ .

Beatitudes Review in Code

Print in the boxes the letters that match the numbers.

A	B	C	D	E	F	H	I	L
1	2	3	4	5	6	7	8	9

M	N	O	P	R	S	T	U	Y
10	11	12	13	14	15	16	17	18

1. Jesus gave us the Beatitudes to help us share

   his __ __ __ __ __ __ __ __ __ .
      7 1 13 13 8 11 5 15 15

2. People are __ __ __ __ __ __ __ to think that riches will make them happy.
      6 12 12 9 8 15 7

3. Sorrowing people will be __ __ __ __ __ __ __ __ __ .
      3 12 10 6 12 14 16 5 4

4. Meek people are gentle and __ __ __ __ __ __ of heart.
      7 17 10 2 9 5

5. People who hunger and thirst to be holy __ __ __ __ __ __ to please God.
      4 5 15 8 14 5

6. Jesus said, "Be __ __ __ __ __ __ __ __ as your heavenly Father is merciful."
      10 5 14 3 8 6 17 9

7. Peacemakers will be called __ __ __ __ __ __ __ __ of God.
      3 7 8 9 4 14 5 11

8. Jesus said, "They will make you __ __ __ __ __ __ for my name."
      15 17 6 6 5 14

We Are Glad in the Lord

Leader: In the eight Beatitudes, Jesus calls us to the greatest happiness—joy in the Lord. He and his blessed Mother have shown us the way. The saints who followed their example found happiness both in this life and in heaven. Jesus wants us to be happy now and always.

Procession and Song

(The child carrying the Bible leads the children who are carrying flowers.)

Leader: Saint Paul was happy like Jesus. He taught the early Christians what they must do to have joy in the Lord.

First Reading from Philippians 4:4–7

Reader 1: A reading from a letter of Saint Paul

Rejoice in the Lord always. I shall say it again: rejoice! Your kindness should be known to all. The Lord is near. Have no anxiety at all, but in everything, by prayer and petition, with thanksgiving, make your requests known to God. Then the peace of God that surpasses all understanding will guard your hearts and minds in Christ Jesus.

The Word of the Lord

All: Thanks be to God.

Intercessions

(After each petition is read, the children will put a flower, one for the beatitude mentioned, into the vase.)

All: *(Response to each petition)* Stay with us, Lord, and be our joy.

Leaders of Prayer: That we may become poor in spirit and be happy to share with others . . . ℟

That we may try to help those who are sorrowing . . . ℟

That we may become gentle and more willing to serve others . . . ℟

That we may become holy by loving God with all our hearts . . . ℟

That we may be forgiving and show mercy to those in need . . . ℟

That we may be clean of heart by loving God and others . . . ℟

That we may become peacemakers for God and for others . . . ℟

That we may be strong enough to suffer for what is right . . . ℟

Leader: In the Beatitudes, Jesus teaches us that we can have joy if we love and serve God and others. Paul tells us about having a glad heart.

Second Reading adapted from 2 Corinthians 9:6–7

Reader 2: A reading from a letter of Saint Paul

Whoever plants a few seeds will have a small crop. Whoever plants many seeds will have a large crop. Be generous, then, when you give. Do not give sadly or grudgingly. Give with a glad heart, because God loves a cheerful giver.

The Word of the Lord

All: Thanks be to God.

Silent Prayer

What makes you happy? What does Jesus say will make you happy? Ask Jesus to help you be a cheerful and generous giver.

Leader: Jesus tells us about the happiness of heaven. Let us listen.

Third Reading adapted from Revelation 22: 4–14

Reader 3: A reading from the Book of Revelation

Jesus says, "I am coming soon. Happy are they who keep my words. I will reward each one for what he or she has done. Happy are they who have the life of grace. To them, the Holy Spirit will say, 'Come.' They will be able to come through the city gates."

The Word of the Lord

All: Thanks be to God.

Psalm Prayer

Side A: All you people, clap your hands, shout to God with cries of gladness,

Side B: For the LORD, the Most High, is the great king over all the earth.

Side A: For king of all the earth is God; let the trumpets blast with joy,

Side B: Sing praise to God, sing praise; sing praise to our king.

adapted from
Psalm 47:2,3,8,6,7

Leader: Jesus showed us in the eight Beatitudes how to live in hope and in love. He has blessed us with happiness in this celebration. Let us thank Jesus and tell him we will try to live lives pleasing to him.

All: We offer our prayer in the name of the Father and of the Son and of the Holy Spirit. Amen.

Closing Song

Looking Back at Unit 5

You learned in this unit that Jesus gave us the Beatitudes as a guide to Christian living and as a means to reach happiness, both in this life and in the one to come. Living the Beatitudes with courage and love, we follow the example of Jesus, Mary, and the saints.

When we are poor in spirit, sorrowing, meek, merciful, and clean of heart—when we hunger and thirst for righteousness, try to be peacemakers, and are persecuted for what is right—we are living the fullness of the Christian life.

Living the Message

Check (✓) each sentence that describes you.

❑ 1. I know the meaning of the Beatitudes.

❑ 2. I am not selfish but try to share what I have.

❑ 3. I try to do what is right even when it is hard.

❑ 4. I try to be kind and gentle.

❑ 5. I pray to become a good, loving Christian.

Word to Know

martyr

Planning Ahead

Draw a picture of something you will do for someone at home and in your neighborhood to show your love for Jesus. Write on the lines what you will do.

At Home	In My Neighborhood
I will _____ .	I will _____ .

Gather and Go Forth

Know and Proclaim

We study our Catholic faith so we have the knowledge to live the message of Christ through our words and deeds.

We Know Our Faith	We Proclaim Our Faith
Christians are called to imitate the saints and become living witnesses to Christ.	As Catholics, we study the lives of the saints for examples of how to live our faith fully. We follow their example when we love God as Jesus did, even when it is not easy.
Our Blessed Mother Mary loved and suffered as Jesus did. She is the Queen of Martyrs.	We venerate Mother Mary with different prayers, such as the *Angelus*, the *Memorare*, and the Act of Consecration to Mary.
Jesus teaches us in the Beatitudes that those who are persecuted for the sake of righteousness will find happiness in heaven.	Catholics accept suffering and remain hopeful because Jesus asks us to love others as he did and not to be afraid. Those who suffer and die for Jesus are martyrs.

The Lord has given us great gifts. How can we not be filled with joy and tell the world of the blessings we have received?

"It is impossible for us not to speak about what we have seen and heard."

Acts of the Apostles 4:20

Test Your Catholic Knowledge

Fill in the circle that best answers the question.

Which of the following best describes what it means to be persecuted for the sake of righteousness?

- ○ always being right and never making mistakes
- ○ becoming a saint
- ○ being rejected by the world for following Jesus' teachings
- ○ helping those who cannot help themselves

A Catholic to Know

From the time Ignatius was a teenager in Spain, he was a soldier. His life was filled with adventure, and he paid little attention to his faith. Ignatius used his talents only for his own glory. However, when his leg was shattered during battle in 1521, he spent his time reading about Christ and the lives of the saints while he healed. Ignatius realized he had been living a selfish life and decided to dedicate himself to serving God and God's people. Ignatius gathered people who felt the same way and founded the Society of Jesus, or the Jesuits, to teach about Jesus and serve others. Saint Ignatius was brave enough to change. We can pray to him to intercede for us and ask the Holy Spirit for the strength to follow a path to God.

Saint Ignatius of Loyola

Witness and Share

These sentences describe what Catholics believe. Listen carefully as they are read. Ask yourself, "How strong are my Catholic beliefs?"

My Way to Faith

- Like Saint Ignatius, I seek to live an unselfish life.

- I pray to Mary because she will help me stay close to her Son, Jesus.

- I follow God's laws of love by practicing the Beatitudes.

- I accept times when I'm made fun of for doing what is right.

Share Your Faith

List ways below that you can live joyfully and show others the happiness you feel as a child of God. Invite your family to add to your list and join you in putting these ideas into action.

_____

_____

_____

_____

Let There Be Peace

The paper crane has become an international symbol for peace. It started with a young girl from Japan who died as a result of the effects of war. Sadako Sasaki was just two years old at the end of World War II when an atomic bomb was dropped on Hiroshima, a town near her home. At the age of 11 she was diagnosed with leukemia as a result of exposure to radiation from the bomb nine years earlier.

Sadako's best friend told her of the Japanese legend that said that anyone who makes a thousand paper cranes would be granted a wish. Sadako began the intricate work of folding the cranes, and she created hundreds of them before she died. Inspired by her courage, Sadako's friends committed to make the rest of the cranes so that she could be buried with the thousand cranes. Her story spread among the children of Japan, who donated money for a statue to honor Sadako and all the children who died as a result of the war. The inscription at the monument in Hiroshima's Peace Park reads

Children's Peace Monument, Hiroshima, Japan.

"This is our cry. This is our prayer. Peace in the world."

Even today, the story of the paper cranes continues to spread, giving children a way to express their hopes for peace in the world. To learn how to make a paper crane, go to **www.christourlife.com/paper-cranes-of-peace.htm**.

Family Feature

Raise a Toast to Peace

Origami is the traditional Japanese art of paper folding. With patience, attention, and skill, those who practice origami can make many beautiful objects. Here is a simple origami exercise you can try at home. When you are finished folding your paper drinking cups, you can decorate them with signs of peace. Then use the cups to toast peace and harmony in your home and in the world.

Visit **www.christourlife.com** for more family resources.

How to Make a Paper Drinking Cup

1. Take an eight-inch square of paper and fold it diagonally into a triangle.

2. Next fold the left corner up to meet the right edge of the paper.

3. Fold the right corner up to meet the left edge of the paper.

4. Fold down the front flap toward you and the back flap away from you.

5. Squeeze the sides of the bottom, and the cup will open.

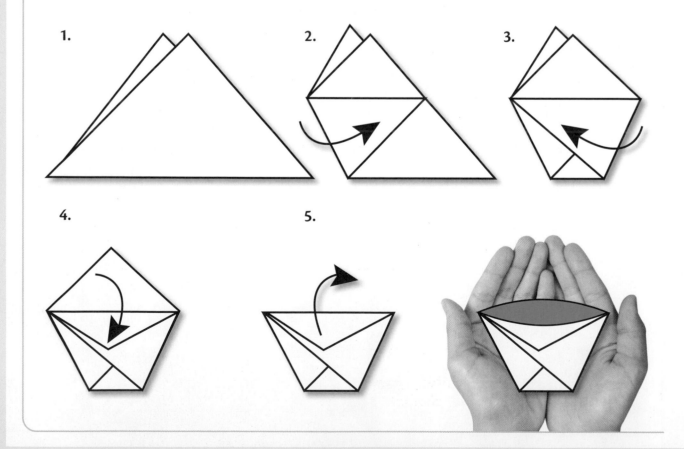

Prescription for Peace and Happiness

The Beatitudes (Matthew 5:1–10) are Jesus' prescription for true happiness and peace. Like all profound religious concepts, they involve paradoxes—the meek will inherit, those who hunger will be satisfied. The Beatitudes present a challenge that all serious believers must grow into over the course of their lives. Read them often and be open to the truths they contain.

Spelling Fun

On the lines below see how many words you can make out of the letters in the word *beatitude.*

_____   _____

_____   _____

_____   _____

_____   _____

_____   _____

_____   _____

_____   _____

_____   _____

_____   _____

_____   _____

Ten words is good. Fifteen words is great. Twenty or more, you're a real champ!

From Sorrow to Joy

Follow the directions and you will find out what "Beatitude people" receive.

HARDSHIP

Remove the third and fourth letters.

Add an *N* to the end.

Change the *S* to a *V.*

Change the *HIP* to an *E.*

Insert an E between the *H* and *A.*

_____

Family Feature

Bee-attitudes

In the Sermon on the Mount, Jesus gave us the Beatitudes (Matthew 5:1–10) as ways that we can find peace and happiness in life. What are some of the "bee-attitudes" (the attitudes that shape the way you are) that you need to have peace and happiness in your home? In each of the bees below, join with family members to write down the attitudes that make for peace and joy.

Possible answers: honesty, forgiveness, respectfulness, understanding, sense of humor, prayer time, kindness

Special Seasons and Lessons

The Year in Our Church

Ordinary Time

Christmas · Ordinary Time · Lent

Holy Week · Easter

Advent

Ash Wednesday

Epiphany

Christmas

Palm Sunday
Holy Thursday
Good Friday
Holy Saturday
Easter Sunday

First Sunday
of Advent

All Souls Day
All Saints Day

Winter
Spring
Fall
Summer

Ascension
Pentecost

Ordinary Time

Liturgical Calendar

The liturgical calendar highlights the feast
days and seasons of the Church year. Various
colors symbolize the different seasons.

1|Feast of All Saints

Jesus taught us what it means to be happy in the Kingdom of God. We call this teaching the Beatitudes. *Beatitudes* means "deep happiness or blessing."

This is what Jesus taught.

Happy are the poor in spirit,
    for theirs is the kingdom of heaven.
Happy are they who mourn,
    for they will be comforted.
Happy are the meek,
    for they will inherit the land.
Happy are they who hunger and thirst for
        righteousness,
    for they will be satisfied.
Happy are the merciful,
    for they will be shown mercy.
Happy are the clean of heart,
    for they will see God.
Happy are the peacemakers,
    for they will be called children of God.
Happy are they who are persecuted for
        the sake of righteousness,
    for theirs is the kingdom of heaven.

adapted from Matthew 5:3–10

The saints are those who have lived the Beatitudes and who now enjoy eternal happiness. They are now with God in heaven.

On Feast of All Saints, November 1, we hear the Beatitudes proclaimed in the Gospel. Jesus' words describe God's promise of eternal happiness. They also describe the path to holiness. The Beatitudes explain what it means to live as a disciple of Christ.

Saints Living Beatitudes

Choose one of the Beatitudes and identify a saint who has lived this Beatitude. Then write how you can also live this Beatitude today. An example is provided.

Beatitude: Happy are the poor in spirit, for theirs is the kingdom of heaven.

Saint: St. Francis of Assisi, who lived simply and shared all that he had with the poor.

Living this Beatitude today: We can share with others. We can be thankful for the things that we have and not desire things we do not need. We can live simply.

Beatitude: _____

_____

_____

_____

Saint: _____

Living this Beatitude today: _____

_____

_____

_____

_____

2 | Advent

During Advent, we prepare a straight highway for the Lord. We ask God to help us make low the mountains created by our sin and selfishness. We try to raise the valleys by filling them with our love, prayer, and good deeds. How will you prepare a straight highway for the Lord?

Preparing the Way

Write some things that you want to change during Advent so that you can make low the mountains of sin and selfishness.

Write some good deeds that you will do for Jesus to raise the valleys.

Advent is a time when we can tear down what keeps us from sharing with others. We can put love, prayers, and good deeds in the empty spaces of our hearts.

Time for Advent

Complete the words in the sentences below.

Advent is a time when we l __ __ __ for Jesus' coming.

Advent is a time when we p __ __ __ __ __ __ for Jesus' coming into our hearts.

3 | Christmas

We Celebrate Christmas as a Season

Christmas is the day we remember the Nativity of the Lord, December 25. And, like Advent, Christmas is also a season. The Christmas Season begins on Christmas Eve and ends on the Feast of the Baptism of the Lord. Within the season of Christmas are several important feasts, including the Feast of Epiphany. On Epiphany, we remember the Magi who followed the light of a new star that led them to Jesus, the Light of the World, a Light to all the Nations.

Match the Season

How is the season of Advent different from the season of Christmas? Match the season in the space provided. Write the letter C for Christmas or A for Advent.

_____ white (feast)

_____ waiting and preparing

_____ Christmas tree

_____ star

_____ preparation for the Messiah

_____ Nativity

_____ purple

_____ welcoming

_____ Advent wreath

_____ stories about Jesus' birth

We Welcome Christ

Opening Song
(O Come, All Ye Faithful)

Opening Prayer

Leader: Christ our Light, open our hearts to welcome you with love during this Christmas season.

All: Amen.

Gospel (John 1:1–14):

A reading from the holy Gospel according to John.

In the beginning was the Word,
    and the Word was with God,
and the Word was God.
He was in the beginning with God.

All things came to be
    through him,
and without him
    nothing came to be.

What came to be through
    him was life,
and this life was the
    light of the human
    race;

the light shines in the
    darkness,
and the darkness has
    not overcome it.

And the Word became flesh
and made his dwelling
    among us,
and we saw his glory,
the glory as of the
    Father's only Son,
full of grace and truth.

The Gospel of the Lord.

All: Praise to you, Lord Jesus Christ.

Quiet Prayer Response

In the quiet of your heart, tell Jesus how you will welcome him into your heart this Christmas season.

Closing Prayer

May the light of Christ continue to enlighten our hearts that we will see and serve Christ in others. Amen.

4│Lent

At the Easter Vigil, we bless and light the Paschal Candle (also called the Easter Candle). We place the Alpha and the Omega on the candle. Alpha and Omega are symbols for Christ. The Alpha symbol tells us that Christ is the beginning of all things, and the Omega symbol tells us that he is the end of all things.

At Easter we celebrate Jesus' passing over from Death to new life. We call this the Paschal Mystery. Our Baptism is a participation in Jesus' Dying and rising to new life.

During Lent, we prepare to live more faithfully the Paschal Mystery. We do this through prayer, fasting, and almsgiving. Through these Lenten practices we find ways to move away from selfishness and sin so that we can share in the new life Jesus gives to us.

Write ways you will participate in these Lenten practices:

Prayer:_____

_____

Fasting:_____

_____

Almsgiving:_____

_____

Complete the Words

Fill in the missing letters to show what you have learned.

The mystery of Christ's suffering, Death, and Resurrection:

__ __ S __ __ __ L   __ Y __ __ __ __ Y

We participate in the Paschal Mystery through our

__ __ P __ __ __ M

The great feast on which we celebrate Christ's Paschal Mystery:

__ __ S __ __ R

The season during which we prepare to live the Paschal Mystery more faithfully:

__ E __ __

5|Holy Week

All during Lent we have been getting ready for Easter, the holiest day of the year. During the week before Easter, we make our final preparations. This week is called Holy Week. During Holy Week, we remember the events that led to Jesus' sacrifice on the Cross for our salvation.

Passion (Palm) Sunday

The last Sunday of Lent is called Passion Sunday and is sometimes also called Palm Sunday. We remember that the crowds waved palms and called Jesus king as he rode into Jerusalem. They shouted, "Hosanna to the Son of David" (Matthew 21:9).

Before Mass the priest blesses palm branches. We then walk in procession with them. We hear the Gospel story of Jesus' Death on the Cross. After Mass, we take the palms home. Each time we look at a palm, it reminds us to love and praise Jesus every day. We can pray, "Praise and honor to you, Lord Jesus Christ, King of endless glory."

The Easter Triduum

During Holy Week, we celebrate the Easter Triduum. The word *Triduum* means "three days." We celebrate the Easter Triduum on three days as we remember the Paschal Mystery.

On Holy Thursday night, we remember Jesus' Last Supper. We remember how Jesus showed his love for his friends by washing their feet. We remember Jesus' gift of himself in the Eucharist. At church the priest washes the feet of twelve people to remind us that we are all to serve others as Jesus did. We honor the Blessed Sacrament in a procession.

On Good Friday, we remember that Jesus died for us. We listen to the Gospel of Jesus' passion and Death. We venerate the Cross because it is the way to salvation.

On Holy Saturday evening, we remember that Jesus was buried in the tomb. We wait in hope for Easter, remembering all the great things God has done to save us. On this night we will celebrate the Easter Vigil, the high point of the Easter Triduum, which then ends on Easter Sunday.

The Stations of the Cross

Throughout the year, and especially during Lent and Holy Week, we pray the Stations of the Cross, also known as the Way of the Cross. The fourteen stations of the Stations of the Cross tell what happened on Good Friday, the day after Jesus' Last Supper. They tell the story of how Jesus suffered and died because he loved us so much. At each station, we think about the event shown and we say a prayer. We thank Jesus for his great love.

Recognize a Station

For each situation, write the number of the station from Jesus' "Way of the Cross" booklet that can tell you how to follow Jesus.

1. I'm with some friends who start looking at a book with bad pictures. I'm afraid to say that I don't want to see the pictures.

_____

2. No matter how hard I try, I make lots of spelling mistakes in my writing. I feel like giving up.

_____

3. My friend is really sick. I want to visit him in the hospital, but I am afraid it will make me sad.

_____

4. I practiced a lot and wanted to win the swim meet, but a friend won it instead.

_____

5. My friend is working really hard to do his math problems, but he still doesn't get the right answers. I'm pretty good at math.

_____

6 | Easter

What might have been the thoughts and feelings of the disciples of Jesus on that first Easter morning, when they discovered that his tomb was empty?

Imagine what it was like: Jesus, your friend, was arrested and sentenced to Death. He was beaten and made to carry a cross. Then he was crucified. Sad and scared, some friends buried him in the tomb. The tomb was sealed with a large stone.

Now, three days later, some of your friends are reporting amazing experiences. Some have been to the tomb and found that the stone has been rolled away. Jesus' body is not inside. Not only that, Mary of Magdala says that she saw two angels in the tomb and that she met Jesus in the garden near the tomb. She said that she didn't recognize him at first; she thought he was the gardener. But then Jesus spoke to her, and she knew him at once.

adapted from John 20:1–18

What would you have thought? What would you have done?

The disciples of Jesus were sad, confused, and fearful on that first Easter day. They stayed together because they were afraid. But then things became clearer:

On the evening of that first day of the week, when the doors were locked, where the disciples were, for fear of the Jews, Jesus came and stood in their midst and said to them, "Peace be with you." When he had said this, he showed them his hands and his side. The disciples rejoiced when they saw the Lord. [Jesus] said to them again, "Peace be with you. As the Father has sent me, so I send you." And when he had said this, he breathed on them and said to them, "Receive the holy Spirit. Whose sins you forgive are forgiven them, and whose sins you retain are retained.

John 20:19–23

Easter and the Gift of Peace

When the risen Lord appeared to his disciples, the first thing he said to them is "Peace be with you." He knew what his friends needed most. They needed to know that everything was now okay. They needed to see that the figure before them was really Jesus raised from the dead. They needed to know that Jesus forgave them. They needed courage and strength to face the days ahead. They needed to know that Jesus had not abandoned them and that he was going to be with them always in his gift of the Holy Spirit.

Jesus' greeting communicated all of these things to his disciples . . . and to us. Jesus says to us, "Peace be with you." Jesus knows that we need his peace, too.

Peace Prayer

Write a prayer to Jesus telling him what you most need his gift of peace to do for you. Use the letters in the word "peace" to start each line of your prayer.

P_____

E_____

A_____

C_____

E_____

Amen

7 | Pentecost

Fifty days after Easter, we celebrate the Feast of Pentecost. We remember how the disciples received the gift of the Holy Spirit, just as Jesus had promised. We celebrate the gift of the Holy Spirit at work in our Church and in our lives.

The apostles had all gathered together in Jerusalem as Jesus had told them to do. While they waited for the Holy Spirit, they prayed. Suddenly there was the sound of a loud wind. Something like tongues of fire rested on the heads of those who were there. The Holy Spirit had come! The apostles began to speak in different languages to people who had arrived from different nations.

adapted from Acts of the Apostles 2:1–11

How is the appearance of the Holy Spirit described in this reading?

_____

What do the disciples do after receiving the gift of the Holy Spirit?

_____

We cannot see the Holy Spirit. However, we can see the effects of the Holy Spirit in our lives. Saint Paul wrote about this in a letter to early Christians:

. . . the fruit of the Spirit is love, joy, peace, patience, kindness, generosity, faithfulness, gentleness, self-control. . . . If we live in the Spirit, let us also follow the Spirit.

Galatians 5:22–23, 25

We call these the Fruits of the Holy Spirit. In addition to the nine Fruits of the Holy Spirit named by Saint Paul, the Church has identified three more: goodness, modesty, and chastity. When we see these qualities, we know the Holy Spirit is working in our lives.

Pentecost Prayer Service

Opening Song

First Reading from The Acts of the Apostles 2:1–11

Intercessions

> The response is: "Into our hearts, O Spirit, come!"

Leader: We thank you, heavenly Father, for giving us Jesus and for sending the Spirit in his name . . . ℟

We pray that the Spirit enlightens the minds and hearts of our Holy Father, all bishops, priests, deacons, and all of the faithful . . . ℟

We pray that our hearts be filled with the love of God, as the apostles' hearts were filled on the first Pentecost . . . ℟

We ask the Holy Spirit to come to each person's heart today and make all Christians living temples of God . . . ℟

We ask that the Holy Spirit will comfort the sick, the dying, and all those who suffer because of a lack of love . . . ℟

Second Reading from Romans 8:26–27

Response to the Second Reading: Song

Closing Prayer

All: Breathe in me, O Holy Spirit,
That my thoughts
May be all holy.
Act in me, O Holy Spirit,
That my work, too,
May be holy.
Draw my heart, O Holy Spirit,
That I love
Only what is holy.
Strengthen me, Holy Spirit,
That I may defend all that is holy.
Guard me then, O Holy Spirit,
That I always
May be holy.

What Catholics Should Know

(continued on next page)

(continued from previous page)

Prayer and How We Pray

God is always with us. He wants us to talk to him and listen to him. We can do this because through the Holy Spirit, God teaches us how to pray.

We Pray in Many Ways

The Church teaches us to pray often and in many different ways. In a prayer for a blessing, we call on God's power and care for a person, place, or thing. When we adore God, we worship him above all else. In a prayer of petition, we ask something for ourselves. We can pray for others in a prayer of intercession. We express sorrow for our sins in a prayer of contrition and thank God in a prayer of thanksgiving. Finally, we praise God in a prayer of praise. We can pray alone or with others, silently or out loud.

We Meditate and Contemplate

To meditate is to think about God. We try to keep our attention and focus on God using Scripture, prayer books, or religious images to help us and to spark our imagination.

To contemplate means that we rest quietly in God's presence.

We Get Ready to Pray

We live in a busy, noisy, and fast-paced world. Because of this, we can have difficulty concentrating. In order to meditate or reflect, we need to prepare ourselves. We can get ready for meditation by moving our bodies into a comfortable position, sitting with our backs straight and both feet on the floor. We can close our eyes, fold our hands in front of us, take a deep breath, and then slowly let it out. We can establish a rhythm by slowly counting to three while breathing in and slowly counting to three while breathing out. Concentrating on our breathing helps us quiet our thoughts.

We Avoid Distractions

If we become distracted by thinking about something such as the day at school or a sporting event, we can just go back to thinking about our breathing. After a little practice, we will be able to avoid distractions, pray with our imagination, and spend time with God or Jesus in our hearts.

Prayers We Pray as Catholics

We can pray with any words that come to mind. Sometimes when we find that choosing our own words is difficult, we can use traditional prayers. Memorizing traditional prayers such as the following can be very helpful. When we memorize prayers, we take them to heart, meaning that we not only learn the words but also try to understand and live them. See the inside front and back covers of your book for the most frequently used prayers.

Angelus

Verse. The Angel of the Lord declared unto Mary.
Response. And she conceived of the Holy Spirit.

Hail Mary, full of grace, the Lord is with thee.
Blessed art thou among women,
and blessed is the fruit of thy womb, Jesus.
Holy Mary, Mother of God,
pray for us sinners,
now and at the hour of our death.
Amen.

Verse. Behold the handmaid of the Lord.
Response. Be it done unto me according to thy word.
Hail Mary.

Verse. And the Word was made flesh.
Response. And dwelt among us.
Hail Mary.

Verse. Pray for us, O holy Mother of God.
Response. That we may be made worthy of the promises of Christ.

Let us pray,
Pour forth, we beseech thee, O Lord, thy grace into our hearts; that we, to whom the Incarnation of Christ, thy Son, was made known by the message of an angel, may by his Passion and Cross be brought to the glory of his Resurrection. Through the same Christ, our Lord.
Amen.

Nicene Creed

I believe in one God,
the Father almighty,
maker of heaven and earth,
of all things visible and invisible.

I believe in one Lord Jesus Christ,
the Only Begotten Son of God,
born of the Father before all ages.
God from God, Light from Light,
true God from true God,
begotten, not made, consubstantial with
    the Father;
through him all things were made.
for us men and for our salvation
he came down from heaven,
and by the Holy Spirit was incarnate of
    the Virgin Mary,
and became man.

For our sake he was crucified under
    Pontius Pilate,
he suffered death and was buried,
and rose again on the third day
in accordance with the Scriptures.

He ascended into heaven
and is seated at the right hand of the
    Father.
He will come again in glory
to judge the living and the dead
and his kingdom will have no end.

I believe in the Holy Spirit, the Lord, the
    giver of life,
who proceeds from the Father and the
    Son,
who with the Father and the Son is
    adored and glorified,
who has spoken through the prophets.

I believe in one, holy, catholic and
    apostolic Church.
I confess one Baptism for the forgiveness
    of sins
and I look forward to the resurrection of
    the dead
and the life of the world to come.
Amen.

Hail Holy Queen (*Salve Regina*)

Hail, Holy Queen, Mother of Mercy,
our life, our sweetness and our hope.
To you do we cry,
poor banished children of Eve.
To you do we send up our sighs,
mourning and weeping in this valley
   of tears.
Turn then, most gracious advocate,
your eyes of mercy toward us,
and after this exile
show unto us the blessed fruit of thy
   womb,
Jesus.
O clement, O loving,
O sweet Virgin Mary.

Act of Contrition

O my God, I am heartily sorry for having offended Thee, and I detest all my sins because of thy just punishments, but most of all because they offend Thee, my God, who art all good and deserving of all my love. I firmly resolve with the help of Thy grace to sin no more and to avoid the near occasion of sin.
Amen.

Act of Contrition (Prayer of the Penitent)

My God,
I am sorry for my sins with all my heart.
In choosing to do wrong
and failing to do good,
I have sinned against you
whom I should love above all things.
I firmly intend, with your help,
to do penance,
to sin no more,
and to avoid whatever leads me to sin.
Our Savior Jesus Christ
suffered and died for us.
In his name, my God, have mercy.
Amen.

Certain prayers that are shared by the universal Church can be learned in Latin and prayed as a sign of the universal nature of the Church. The English versions of the following prayers appear on the inside front and back covers.

Signum Crucis (Sign of the Cross)

In nomine Patris
et Filii
et Spiritus Sancti.
Amen.

Gloria Patri (Glory Be to the Father)

Gloria Patri
et Filio
et Spiritui Sancto.
Sicut erat in principio,
et nunc et semper
et in sae cula saeculorum.
Amen.

Pater Noster (Our Father)

Pater noster, qui es in caelis:
sanctificetur Nomen Tuum;
adveniat Regnum Tuum;
fiat voluntas Tua,
sicut in caelo, et in terra.
Panem nostrum
cotidianum da nobis hodie;
et dimitte nobis debita nostra,
sicut et nos dimittimus
debitoribus nostris;
et ne nos inducas in tentationem;
sed libera nos a Malo.
Amen.

Ave, Maria (Hail Mary)

Ave, Maria, gratia plena,
Dominus tecum.
Benedicta tu in mulieribus,
et benedictus fructus ventris tui, Iesus.
Sancta Maria, Mater Dei,
ora pro nobis peccatoribus,
nunc et in hora mortis nostrae.
Amen.

Upon entering a church, a boy makes the Sign of the Cross after dipping his fingers in holy water. Catholics make the Sign of the Cross during Mass and at other times as well.

The Rosary

The Rosary helps us pray to Jesus through Mary. When we pray the Rosary, we think about the special events, or mysteries, in the lives of Jesus and Mary.

The Rosary is made up of a string of beads and a crucifix. We hold the crucifix in our hands as we pray the Sign of the Cross. Then we pray the Apostles' Creed. Next to the crucifix, there is a single bead followed by a set of three beads and another single bead. We pray the Lord's Prayer as we hold the first single bead and a Hail Mary at each bead in the set of three that follows. Then we pray the Glory Be to the Father. On the next single bead, we think about the first mystery and pray the Lord's Prayer.

There are five sets of 10 beads; each set is called a decade. We pray a Hail Mary on each bead of a decade as we reflect on a particular mystery in the lives of Jesus and Mary. The Glory Be to the Father is prayed at the end of each set. Between sets is a single bead on which we think about one of the mysteries and pray the Lord's Prayer. In some places, people pray the Hail Holy

Our Lady of the Rosary, stained glass, Correze, France.

Queen after the last decade. See page 239. We end by holding the crucifix in our hands as we pray the Sign of the Cross.

PRAYING THE ROSARY

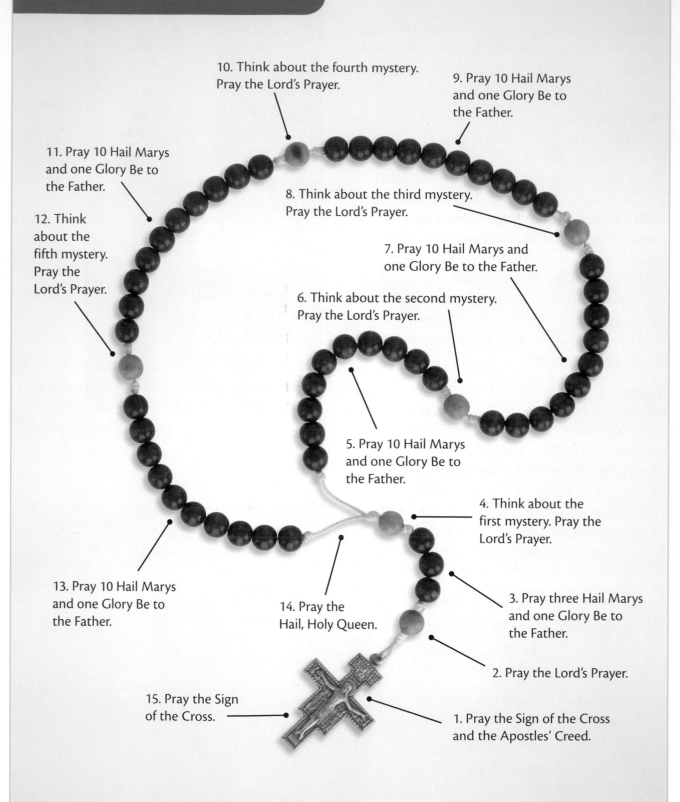

10. Think about the fourth mystery. Pray the Lord's Prayer.

9. Pray 10 Hail Marys and one Glory Be to the Father.

11. Pray 10 Hail Marys and one Glory Be to the Father.

8. Think about the third mystery. Pray the Lord's Prayer.

12. Think about the fifth mystery. Pray the Lord's Prayer.

7. Pray 10 Hail Marys and one Glory Be to the Father.

6. Think about the second mystery. Pray the Lord's Prayer.

5. Pray 10 Hail Marys and one Glory Be to the Father.

4. Think about the first mystery. Pray the Lord's Prayer.

13. Pray 10 Hail Marys and one Glory Be to the Father.

14. Pray the Hail, Holy Queen.

3. Pray three Hail Marys and one Glory Be to the Father.

2. Pray the Lord's Prayer.

15. Pray the Sign of the Cross.

1. Pray the Sign of the Cross and the Apostles' Creed.

Mysteries of the Rosary

The Church had three sets of mysteries for many centuries. In 2002, Pope John Paul II proposed a fourth set of mysteries—the Mysteries of Light, or the Luminous Mysteries. According to his suggestion, the four sets of mysteries might be prayed on the following days: the Joyful Mysteries on Monday and Saturday, the Sorrowful Mysteries on Tuesday and Friday, the Glorious Mysteries on Wednesday and Sunday, and the Luminous Mysteries on Thursday.

St. John Paul II.

The Joyful Mysteries

1. *The Annunciation.* Mary learns she has been chosen to be the mother of Jesus.

2. *The Visitation.* Mary visits Elizabeth, who tells her that she will always be remembered.

3. *The Nativity.* Jesus is born in a stable in Bethlehem.

4. *The Presentation.* Mary and Joseph take the infant Jesus to the Temple to present him to God.

5. *The Finding of Jesus in the Temple.* Jesus is found in the Temple, discussing his faith with the teachers.

The Luminous Mysteries

1. *The Baptism of Jesus in the River Jordan.* God proclaims that Jesus is his beloved Son.

2. *The Wedding Feast at Cana.* At Mary's request, Jesus performs his first miracle.

3. *The Proclamation of the Kingdom of God.* Jesus calls all to conversion and service to the kingdom.

4. *The Transfiguration of Jesus.* Jesus is revealed in glory to Peter, James, and John.

5. *The Institution of the Eucharist.* Jesus gives us his Body and Blood at the Last Supper.

The Sorrowful Mysteries

1. *The Agony in the Garden.* Jesus prays in the garden of Gethsemane on the night before he dies.

2. *The Scourging at the Pillar.* Jesus is beaten with whips.

3. *The Crowning with Thorns.* Jesus is mocked and crowned with thorns.

4. *The Carrying of the Cross.* Jesus carries the Cross on which he will be crucified.

5. *The Crucifixion.* Jesus is nailed to the Cross and dies.

The Glorious Mysteries

1. *The Resurrection.* God the Father raises Jesus from the dead.

2. *The Ascension.* Jesus returns to his Father in heaven.

3. *The Coming of the Holy Spirit.* The Holy Spirit comes to bring new life to the disciples.

4. *The Assumption of Mary.* At the end of her life on earth, Mary is taken body and soul into heaven.

5. *The Coronation of Mary.* Mary is crowned as queen of heaven and earth.

Stations of the Cross

The 14 Stations of the Cross represent events from Jesus' passion and Death. At each station, we use our senses and our imagination to reflect prayerfully on Jesus' suffering, Death, and Resurrection.

1. Jesus Is Condemned to Death.
Pontius Pilate condemns Jesus to Death.

2. Jesus Takes Up His Cross.
Jesus willingly accepts and patiently bears his Cross.

3. Jesus Falls the First Time.
Weakened by torments and loss of blood, Jesus falls beneath his Cross.

4. Jesus Meets His Sorrowful Mother.
Jesus meets his mother, Mary, who is filled with grief.

5. Simon of Cyrene Helps Jesus Carry the Cross.
Soldiers force Simon of Cyrene to carry the Cross.

6. Veronica Wipes the Face of Jesus.
Veronica steps through the crowd to wipe the face of Jesus.

7. Jesus Falls a Second Time.
Jesus falls beneath the weight of the Cross a second time.

8. Jesus Meets the Women of Jerusalem.
Jesus tells the women to weep not for him, but for themselves and for their children.

9. Jesus Falls the Third Time.
Weakened almost to the point of Death, Jesus falls a third time.

10. Jesus Is Stripped of His Garments.
The soldiers strip Jesus of his garments, treating him as a common criminal.

11. Jesus Is Nailed to the Cross.
Jesus' hands and feet are nailed to the Cross.

12. Jesus Dies on the Cross.
After suffering greatly on the Cross, Jesus bows his head and dies.

13. Jesus Is Taken Down from the Cross.
The lifeless body of Jesus is tenderly placed in the arms of Mary, his mother.

14. Jesus Is Laid in the Tomb.
Jesus' disciples place his body in the tomb.

The closing prayer—sometimes included as a 15th station—reflects on the Resurrection of Jesus.

Celebrating and Living Our Catholic Faith

The Seven Sacraments

Jesus touches our lives through the sacraments. Our celebrations of the sacraments are signs of Jesus' presence in our lives and a means for receiving his grace. The Church celebrates seven sacraments, which are divided into three categories.

Sacraments of Initiation

These sacraments lay the foundation of every Christian life.

Baptism

In Baptism we receive new life in Christ. Baptism takes away Original Sin and gives us new birth in the Holy Spirit. Its sign is the pouring of water.

Confirmation

Confirmation seals our life of faith in Jesus. Its signs are the laying on of hands on a person's head, most often by a bishop, and the anointing with chrism. Like Baptism, Confirmation is received only once.

Eucharist

The Eucharist nourishes our life of faith. We receive the Body and Blood of Christ under the appearances of bread and wine.

Sacraments of Healing

These sacraments celebrate the healing power of Jesus.

Penance and Reconciliation

Through this sacrament we receive God's forgiveness. Forgiveness requires being sorry for our sins. In Reconciliation we receive Jesus' healing grace through absolution by the priest. The signs of this sacrament are the confession of sins and the words of absolution.

Anointing of the Sick

This sacrament unites a sick person's suffering with that of Jesus and brings forgiveness of sins. Oil, a symbol of strength, is the sign of this sacrament. A person is anointed with oil of the sick and receives the laying on of hands from a priest.

Oil used during the Sacrament of Anointing of the Sick.

Sacraments at the Service of Communion

These sacraments help members serve the community.

Holy Orders

In Holy Orders, men are ordained as priests, deacons, or bishops. Priests serve as leaders of their communities, and deacons serve to remind us of our baptismal call to help others. Bishops carry on the teachings of the apostles. The signs of this sacrament are the laying on of hands and the anointing with chrism by a bishop.

Matrimony

In Matrimony a baptized man and a woman are united with each other as a sign of the unity between Jesus and his Church. Matrimony requires the consent of the husband and the wife as expressed in the marriage vows. The husband and the wife and their wedding rings are the signs of this sacrament.

The Order of Mass

Sunday is the day on which we celebrate the Resurrection of Jesus. Sunday is the Lord's Day. We gather for Mass, rest

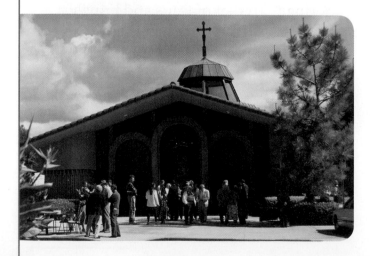

from work, and perform works of mercy. People all over the world gather at God's eucharistic table as brothers and sisters.

The Mass is the high point of the Christian life, and it follows a set order.

Introductory Rites—preparing to celebrate the Eucharist

- *Entrance Chant*—We gather as a community and praise God in song.

- *Greeting*—We pray the Sign of the Cross. The priest welcomes us.

- *Penitential Act*—We remember our sins and ask God for mercy.

- Gloria—We praise God in song.

- *Collect*—We ask God to hear our prayers.

Liturgy of the Word—hearing God's plan of salvation

- *First Reading*—We listen to God's Word, usually from the Old Testament.

- *Responsorial Psalm*—We respond to God's Word in song.

- *Second Reading*—We listen to God's Word from the New Testament.

- *Gospel Acclamation*—We sing "Alleluia!" (except during Lent) to praise God for the Good News.

- *Gospel Reading*—We stand and listen to the Gospel of the Lord.

- *Homily*—The priest or deacon explains God's Word.

- *Profession of Faith*—We proclaim our faith through the Nicene Creed.

- *Prayer of the Faithful*—We pray for our needs and the needs of others.

Liturgy of the Eucharist—celebrating Jesus' presence in the Eucharist

- *Presentation and Preparation of the Gifts*— We bring gifts of bread and wine to the altar.
- *Prayer over the Offerings*—The priest prays that God will accept our sacrifice.
- *Eucharistic Prayer*—This prayer of thanksgiving is the center and high point of the entire celebration.
  - *Preface*—We give thanks and praise to God.
  - *Holy, Holy, Holy*—We sing an acclamation of praise.
  - *Consecration*—The bread and wine are transformed into the Body and Blood of Jesus Christ, our Risen Lord.
  - *The Mystery of Faith*—We proclaim the mystery of our faith.
  - *Amen*—We affirm the words and actions of the Eucharistic Prayer.

Communion Rite—preparing to receive the Body and Blood of Jesus Christ

- *The Lord's Prayer*—We pray the Lord's Prayer.
- *Sign of Peace*—We offer one another Christ's peace.
- *Lamb of God*—We pray for forgiveness, mercy, and peace.

- *Communion*—We receive the Body and Blood of Jesus Christ.
- *Prayer after Communion*—We pray that the Eucharist will strengthen us to live as Jesus did.

Concluding Rites—going forth to glorify the Lord by our lives

- *Final Blessing*—We receive God's blessing.
- *Dismissal*—We go forth to announce the Gospel of the Lord to others through our words and actions.

Holy Days of Obligation

Holy days of obligation are the days other than Sundays on which we celebrate the great things that God has done for us through Jesus and the saints. On holy days of obligation, Catholics gather for Mass.

Six holy days of obligation are celebrated in the United States.

January 1—Mary, Mother of God

40 days after Easter—Ascension (In many U.S. dioceses, it is the Seventh Sunday of Easter.)

August 15—Assumption of the Blessed Virgin Mary

November 1—All Saints

December 8—Immaculate Conception

December 25—Nativity of Our Lord Jesus Christ

Ascension.

Precepts of the Church

The Precepts of the Church describe the minimum effort we must make in prayer and in living a moral life. All Catholics are called to move beyond the minimum by growing in love of God and love of neighbor. The Precepts are as follows:

1. To keep holy the day of the Lord's Resurrection. To worship God by participating in Mass every Sunday and on holy days of obligation. To avoid those activities (like needless work) that would hinder worship, joy, or relaxation.

2. To confess one's sins once a year so as to prepare to receive the Eucharist and to continue a life of conversion.

3. To lead a sacramental life. To receive Holy Communion at least during the Easter season.

4. To do penance, including abstaining from meat and fasting from food on the appointed days.

5. To strengthen and support the Church—to assist with the material needs of the Church according to one's ability.

Living Our Faith

The Ten Commandments

As believers in Jesus Christ, we are called to a new life and are asked to make moral choices that keep us unified with God. With the help and grace of the Holy Spirit, we can choose ways to act that keep us close to God, help other people, and be witnesses to Jesus in the world.

The Ten Commandments guide us in making choices that help us live as God wants us to live. The first three commandments tell us how to love God; the other seven tell us how to love our neighbor.

Moses with the Ten Commandments.

1. I am the Lord your God: you shall not have strange gods before me.

2. You shall not take the name of the Lord your God in vain.

3. Remember to keep holy the Lord's Day.

4. Honor your father and your mother.

5. You shall not kill.

6. You shall not commit adultery.

7. You shall not steal.

8. You shall not bear false witness against your neighbor.

9. You shall not covet your neighbor's wife.

10. You shall not covet your neighbor's goods.

The Great Commandment

The Ten Commandments are fulfilled in Jesus' Great Commandment: "You shall love God with all your heart, with all your soul, with all your mind, and with all your strength.

You shall love your neighbor as yourself." (adapted from Mark 12:30–31)

The New Commandment

Before his Death on the cross, Jesus gave his disciples a new commandment: "Love one another. As I have loved you, so you also should love one another." (John 13:34)

The Church of the Beatitudes, overlooking the Sea of Galilee, Israel.

The Beatitudes

The Beatitudes are the teachings of Jesus in the Sermon on the Mount, described in Matthew 5:1–10. The Beatitudes fulfill God's promises made to Abraham and to his descendants and describe the rewards that will be ours as loyal followers of Christ.

Blessed are the poor in spirit,
for theirs is the kingdom of heaven.

Blessed are they who mourn,
for they will be comforted.

Blessed are the meek,
for they will inherit the land.

Blessed are they who hunger and thirst
for righteousness,
for they will be satisfied.

Blessed are the merciful,
for they will be shown mercy.

Blessed are the clean of heart,
for they will see God.

Blessed are the peacemakers,
for they will be called children of God.

Blessed are they who are persecuted
for the sake of righteousness,
for theirs is the kingdom of heaven.

Making Good Choices

Our conscience is the inner voice that helps us know the law God has placed in our hearts. Our conscience helps us to judge the moral qualities of our own actions. It guides us to do good and avoid evil.

The Holy Spirit can help us form a good conscience. We form our conscience by studying the teachings of the Church and following the guidance of our parents and pastoral leaders.

God has given every human being freedom of choice. This does not mean that we have the right to do whatever we please. We can live in true freedom with the Holy Spirit, who gives us the virtue of prudence. This virtue helps us recognize what is good in every situation and to make correct choices. The Holy Spirit gives us the gifts of wisdom and understanding to help us make the right choices in life in relationship to God and others. The gift of counsel helps us reflect on making correct choices in life.

The Ten Commandments help us make moral choices

that are pleasing to God. We have the grace of the sacraments, the teachings of the Church, and the good example of saints and fellow Christians to help us make good choices.

Making moral choices involves the following steps:

1. Ask the Holy Spirit for help.

2. Think about God's law and the teachings of the Church.

3. Think about what will happen as a result of your choice.

4. Seek advice from someone you respect, and remember that Jesus is with you.

5. Ask yourself how your choice will affect your relationships with God and others.

Making moral choices takes into consideration the object of the choice, our intention in making the choice, and the circumstances in which the choice is made. It is never right to make an evil choice in the hope of gaining something good.

An Examination of Conscience

An examination of conscience is the act of reflecting on how we have hurt our relationships with God and others. The questions below help us in our examination of conscience.

My Relationship with God

What steps am I taking to help me grow closer to God and to others?

Do I participate at Mass with attention and devotion on Sundays and holy days?

Do I pray often and read the Bible?

Do I use God's name and the names of Jesus, Mary, and the saints with love and reverence?

My Relationships with Family, Friends, and Neighbors

Have I set a bad example by my words or actions? Have I treated others fairly? Have I spread stories that hurt other people?

Am I loving toward those in my family? Am I respectful of my neighbors, my friends, and those in authority?

Do I show respect for my body and for the bodies of others? Do I keep away from forms of entertainment that do not respect God's gift of sexuality?

Have I taken or damaged anything that did not belong to me? Have I cheated, copied homework, or lied?

Do I quarrel with others just so I can get my own way? Do I insult others to try to make them think they are less than I am? Do I hold grudges and try to hurt people who I think have hurt me?

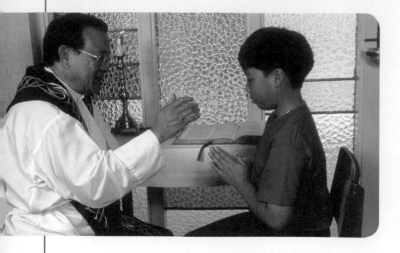

How to Make a Good Confession

An examination of conscience is an important part of preparing for the Sacrament of Reconciliation. The Sacrament of Reconciliation includes the following steps:

- The priest greets us, and we pray the Sign of the Cross. He invites us to trust in God. He may read God's Word with us.

- We confess our sins. The priest may help and counsel us.

- The priest gives us a penance to perform. Penance is an act of kindness, prayers to pray, or both.

- The priest asks us to express our sorrow, usually by reciting the Act of Contrition.

- We receive absolution. The priest says, "I absolve you from your sins in the name of the Father, and of the Son, and of the Holy Spirit." We respond, "Amen."

- The priest dismisses us by saying, "Go in peace." We go forth to perform the act of penance he has given us.

Virtues

Virtues are gifts from God that lead us to live in a close relationship with him. Virtues are like habits. They need to be practiced; they can be lost if they are neglected. The three most important virtues are called the *theological virtues* because they come from God and lead to God. The *cardinal virtues* are human virtues acquired by education and good actions. *Cardinal* comes from *cardo,* the Latin word for *hinge,* meaning "that on which other things depend."

Theological Virtues
faith   hope   charity

Cardinal Virtues
prudence   fortitude
justice   temperance

Gifts of the Holy Spirit

The Holy Spirit makes it possible for us to do what God asks by giving us these gifts.

wisdom	understanding
counsel	fortitude
knowledge	fear of the Lord
piety	

Fruits of the Holy Spirit
The Fruits of the Holy Spirit are signs of the Holy Spirit's action in our lives.

love	kindness	faithfulness
joy	goodness	modesty
peace	generosity	self-control
patience	gentleness	chastity

Works of Mercy

The Corporal and Spiritual Works of Mercy are actions we can perform that extend God's compassion and mercy to those in need.

Corporal Works of Mercy

The Corporal Works of Mercy are the kind acts by which we help our neighbors with their material and physical needs:

- Feed the hungry
- Give drink to the thirsty.
- Clothe the naked.
- Shelter the homeless.
- Visit the sick.
- Visit the imprisoned.
- Bury the dead.

Spiritual Works of Mercy

The Spiritual Works of Mercy are acts of compassion by which we help our neighbors with their emotional and spiritual needs:

- Counsel the doubtful.
- Instruct the ignorant.
- Admonish sinners.
- Comfort the afflicted.
- Forgive offenses.
- Bear wrongs patiently.
- Pray for the living and the dead.

The Bible and You

God speaks to us in many ways. One way that God speaks to us is through the Bible. The Bible is the most important book in Christian life because it is God's message, or revelation. The Bible is the story of God's promise to care for us, especially through his Son, Jesus. At Mass we hear stories from the Bible. We can also read the Bible on our own.

The Bible is not just one book; it is a collection of many books. The writings in the Bible were inspired by the Holy Spirit and written by different authors using different styles.

The Bible is made up of two parts. The Old Testament contains 46 books that tell stories about the Jewish people and their faith in God before Jesus was born. It also contains the Ten Commandments, which guide us to live as God wants us to live.

The New Testament contains 27 books that tell the story of Jesus' life, Death, and Resurrection, and the experience of the early Christians. For Christians the most important books of the New Testament are the four Gospels—Matthew, Mark, Luke, and John. Many of the 27 books are letters written by Saint Paul.

How Do You Find a Passage in the Bible?

Bible passages are identified by book, chapter, and verse—for example, Gn 1:28. The name of the book comes first. It is often abbreviated. Your Bible's table of contents will help you find out what the abbreviation means. In our example, *Gn* stands for the Book of Genesis. After the name of the book, there are two or more numbers. The first number identifies the chapter, which in our example is chapter 1. The chapter number is followed by a colon. The second number or numbers identify the verses. Our example shows verse 28.

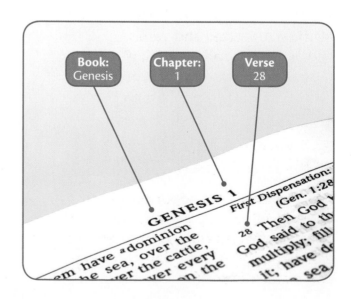

Showing Our Love for the World

Through the themes of Catholic Social Teaching, the Church encourages us to participate in the following areas of social action.

Life and Dignity of the Human Person

All human life is sacred, and all people must be respected and valued over material goods. We are called to ask whether our actions as a society respect or threaten the life and dignity of the human person.

Call to Family, Community, and Participation

Families must be supported so that people can participate in society, build a community spirit, and promote the well-being of all, especially the poor and vulnerable.

Rights and Responsibilities

Every person has a right to life as well as a right to those things required for human decency. As Catholics, we have a responsibility to protect these basic human rights in order to achieve a healthy society.

Option for the Poor and Vulnerable

In our world, many people are rich, while others are extremely poor. As Catholics, we are called to pay special attention to the needs of the poor by defending and promoting their dignity and by meeting their immediate material needs.

The Dignity of Work and the Rights of Workers

The basic rights of workers must be respected: the right to productive work, fair wages, and private property; and the right to organize, join unions, and pursue economic opportunity. Catholics believe that the economy is meant to serve people and that work is not merely a way to make a living but an important way in which we participate in God's creation.

Solidarity

Because God is our Father, we are all brothers and sisters with the responsibility to care for one another. Solidarity is the attitude that leads Christians to share spiritual and material goods. Solidarity unites rich and poor, weak and strong, and helps create a society that recognizes that we depend on one another.

Care for God's Creation

God is the creator of all people and all things, and he wants us to enjoy his creation. The responsibility to care for all that God has made is a requirement of our faith.

Glossary

A

Abba an informal word for *Father* in the language Jesus spoke. Jesus called God the Father "Abba."

absolution the forgiveness God offers us in the Sacrament of Penance and Reconciliation. After we say that we are sorry for our sins, we receive God's absolution from the priest.

adore to worship God above all else because he is our Creator. The First Commandment tells us to adore God.

adultery being unfaithful to one's husband or wife. A person who commits adultery breaks his or her. marriage promises.

altar the table in the church on which the priest celebrates Mass, during which the sacrifice of Christ on the Cross is made present in the Sacrament of the Eucharist. The altar represents two aspects of the mystery of the Eucharist. First, it is where Jesus Christ offers himself for our sins. Second, it is where he gives us himself as our food for eternal life.

ambo a raised stand from which a person reads the Word of God during Mass

angel a spiritual creature who brings a message from God

Angelus a prayer honoring the Incarnation of Jesus. The Angelus is prayed in the morning, at noon, and in the evening.

Annunciation the announcement to Mary by the angel Gabriel that God had chosen her to be the mother of Jesus

Anointing of the Sick a sacrament of healing that unites a sick person's suffering with that of Christ and brings comfort, forgiveness of sins, and, if God wills, physical healing. The signs of the sacrament are holy oil, called chrism, and the priest's laying on of hands.

Stained glass image of the **Annunciation.**

apostle one of twelve special men who accompanied Jesus in his ministry and were witnesses to the Resurrection

Apostles' Creed a statement of Christian belief. The Apostles' Creed, developed out of a creed used in Baptism in Rome, lists simple statements of belief in God the Father, Jesus Christ the Son, and the Holy Spirit. The profession of faith used in Baptism today is based on the Apostles' Creed.

Ascension the return of Jesus to heaven. In the Acts of the Apostles, it is written that Jesus, after his Resurrection, spent 40 days on earth, instructing his followers. He then returned to his Father in heaven.

Assumption Mary's being taken to heaven, body and soul, by God at the end of her life. The feast of the Assumption is celebrated on August 15.

B

Baptism the first of the three sacraments by which we become members of the Church. Baptism frees us from Original Sin and gives us new life in Jesus Christ through the Holy Spirit.

Beatitudes the eight ways we can behave to live a blessed life. Jesus teaches us that if we live according to the Beatitudes, we will live a happy Christian life.

benediction a prayer service in which we honor Jesus in the Blessed Sacrament and receive his blessing

Bible a collection of books that tell the history of God's promise to care for us and his call for us to be faithful to him. God asked that people be faithful first through the beliefs of the Jewish people and then through belief in the life, Death, and Resurrection of Jesus Christ.

bishop a man who has received the fullness of Holy Orders. He has inherited his duties from the original apostles. He cares for the Church today and is a principal teacher in the Church.

Blessed Sacrament the Body of Christ. The consecrated hosts are kept in the tabernacle to adore and to be taken to the sick.

blessing a prayer that calls for God's power and care upon some person, place, thing, or special activity

Body and Blood of Christ following the prayer of consecration by the priest, the Body and Blood of Jesus Christ under the appearances of bread and wine. It still looks like bread and wine, but it is truly the Body and Blood of Jesus Christ.

C

catholic one of the four Marks of the Church. The Church is catholic because Jesus is fully present in it and because Jesus has given the Church to the whole world.

charity a virtue given to us by God. Charity helps us love God above all things and our neighbor as ourselves.

Christ a title that means "anointed with oil." It is from a Greek word that means the same thing as the Hebrew word *Messiah,* or "anointed." It is the name given to Jesus after the Resurrection.

Christian the name given to all those who have been anointed through the gift of the Holy Spirit in Baptism and have become followers of Jesus Christ

Christmas the day on which we celebrate the birth of Jesus (December 25)

Church the name given to all the followers of Christ throughout the world. It is also the name of the building where we gather to pray to God and the name of our community as we gather to praise God.

commandment a standard, or rule, for living as God wants us to live. Jesus summarized all the commandments into two: love God and love your neighbor.

Communion of Saints the union of all who have been saved in Jesus Christ, both those who are alive and those who have died

confession the act of telling our sins to a priest in the Sacrament of Penance and Reconciliation. The sacrament itself is sometimes referred to as "confession."

Confirmation the sacrament that completes the grace we receive in Baptism. Confirmation seals, or confirms, this grace through the seven Gifts of the Holy Spirit that we receive as part of Confirmation. This sacrament also unites us more closely in Jesus Christ.

conscience the inner voice that helps each of us know the law that God has placed in our hearts. It guides us to do good and avoid evil.

contrition the sorrow we feel when we know that we have sinned, followed by the decision not to sin again. Contrition is the most important part of our celebration of the Sacrament of Penance and Reconciliation.

Corporal Works of Mercy kind acts by which we help our neighbors with their everyday, material needs. Corporal Works of Mercy include feeding the hungry, giving drink to the thirsty, clothing the naked, sheltering the homeless, visiting the sick and the imprisoned, and burying the dead.

covenant a solemn agreement between people or between people and God. God made covenants with humanity through agreements with Noah, Abraham, and Moses. These covenants offered salvation. God's new and final covenant was established through Jesus' life, Death, and Resurrection.

Creation God's act of making everything that exists outside himself. Creation is everything that exists. God said that all creation is good.

Creator God, who made everything that is and whom we can come to know through everything he created

creed a brief summary of what people believe. The Apostles' Creed is a summary of Christian beliefs.

D

deacon a man ordained through the Sacrament of Holy Orders to help the bishop and priests in the work of the Church

devil a spirit created good by God who became evil because of disobedience. The devil tempted Jesus in the desert.

disciple a person who has accepted Jesus' message and tries to live as he did

E

Easter the celebration of the bodily raising of Jesus Christ from the dead. Easter is the most important Christian feast.

Emmanuel a name from the Old Testament that means "God with us." Because Jesus is always with us, we often call him by the name *Emmanuel.*

Celebrating the **Eucharist** at Mass.

epistle a letter written by Saint Paul or another leader to a group of Christians in the early Church. Twenty-one of the 27 books of the New Testament are epistles.

Eucharist the sacrament in which we give thanks to God for giving us Jesus Christ. The Body and Blood of Christ, which we receive at Mass, brings us into union with Jesus' saving Death and Resurrection.

Evangelist one of the writers of the four Gospels: Matthew, Mark, Luke, and John. The term *evangelist* is also used to describe anyone engaged in spreading the Gospel.

evangelization the sharing of the good news, by word or example, of the salvation we have received in Jesus Christ. Jesus commissioned his disciples to go forth into the world and tell the good news. Evangelization is the responsibility of every Christian. The New Evangelization calls believers to a deeper faith and invites those who have heard the Gospel but not been transformed by it to have a true encounter with Christ.

A sculpture of the **Holy Family.**

examination of conscience the act of prayerfully thinking about what we have said or done that may have hurt our relationship with God or others. An examination of conscience is an important part of preparing to celebrate the Sacrament of Penance and Reconciliation.

F

faith a gift of God that helps us believe in him and live as he wants us to live. We express our faith in the words of the Apostles' Creed.

fasting limiting the amount we eat for a period of time, to express sorrow for sin and to make ourselves more aware of God's action in our lives

free will our ability to choose to do good because God has made us like him

G

Gospel the good news of God's mercy and love. We experience this news in the story of Jesus' life, Death, and Resurrection. The story is presented to us in four books in the New Testament: the Gospels of Matthew, Mark, Luke, and John.

grace the gift of God given to us without our deserving it. Sanctifying grace fills us with his life and enables us to always be his friends. Grace also helps us live as God wants us to.

Great Commandment Jesus' essential teaching that we are to love God and to love our neighbor as we love ourselves

H

heaven the life with God that is full of happiness and never ends

Hebrews the descendants of Abraham, Isaac, and Jacob, who were enslaved in Egypt. God helped Moses lead the Hebrew people out of slavery.

holy one of the four Marks of the Church. It is the kind of life we live when we share in the life of God, who is all holiness. The Church is holy because of its union with Jesus Christ.

Holy Communion the reception of the Body and Blood of Christ during Holy Mass. It brings us into union with Jesus Christ and his saving Death and Resurrection.

Holy Family the family made up of Jesus; his mother, Mary; and his foster father, Joseph

Holy Matrimony a sacrament that unites a baptized man and woman with each other for life as a sign of the unity between Jesus and his Church

Holy Orders a sacrament that ordains men to serve the Church as priests, deacons, or bishops

Holy Spirit the third Person of the Trinity, who is sent to us as our helper and, through Baptism and Confirmation, fills us with God's life.

homily an explanation of God's Word. A homily explains the words of God that we hear in the Bible readings at church.

hope the trust that God will always be with us. We also trust that he will make us happy now and help us live in a way that keeps us with him forever.

I

Incarnation the Son of God, Jesus, being born as a full human being in order to save us. The Incarnation is one of the main mysteries of our faith.

inspired influenced by the Holy Spirit. The human authors of Scripture were influenced by the Holy Spirit. The creative inspiration of the Holy Spirit makes sure that the Scripture is taught according to the truth God wants us to know for our salvation.

Israelites the descendants of Abraham, Isaac, and Jacob. God changed Jacob's name to "Israel," and Jacob's 12 sons and their children became the leaders of the 12 tribes of Israel. (*See* Hebrews.)

J

Jesus the Son of God, who was born of the Virgin Mary and who died and was raised from the dead so that we can live with God forever. His name means "God saves."

Joseph the foster father of Jesus, who was engaged to Mary when the angel announced that Mary would have a child through the power of the Holy Spirit

justice the strong, firm desire to give to God and others what is due them. Justice is one of the four central human virtues, called the cardinal virtues, by which we guide our Christian life.

K

Kingdom of God God's rule over us. We experience the Kingdom of God in part now, and we will experience it fully in heaven. The Kingdom of God was announced in the Gospel and is present in the Eucharist.

L

Last Supper the last meal Jesus ate with his disciples on the night before he died. At the Last Supper, Jesus took bread and wine, blessed them, and said that they were his Body and Blood. Every Mass is a remembrance of this last meal.

Lectionary for Mass the book that contains all the Bible stories we read at Mass

Liturgy of the Eucharist the second half of the Mass, in which the bread and wine are transformed into the Body and Blood of Jesus Christ, which we then receive in Holy Communion.

Liturgy of the Word the first half of the Mass, in which we listen to God's Word from the Bible and consider what it means for us today.

(At right) Stained glass image of the **Last Supper,** Abbey Notre Dame, Beaugency, France.

Lord the name for God that was used in place of the name he revealed to Moses, *Yahweh*, which was considered too sacred to pronounce. The New Testament also uses the title Lord for Jesus, recognizing him as God himself.

Lord's Day Sunday is the day Christians set aside for special worship of God. Each Sunday Mass commemorates the Resurrection of Jesus on Easter Sunday. Besides telling us to offer God worship we all owe him, the Third Commandment says Sunday is a day to relax the mind and body and to perform works of mercy.

M

martyrs those who have given their lives for the faith. It comes from the Greek word for "witness." A martyr is the supreme witness to the truth of the faith and to Christ to whom he or she is united. The seventh chapter of the Acts of the Apostles recounts the death of the first martyr, the deacon Stephen.

Mary the mother of Jesus. She is called blessed and "full of grace" because God chose her to be the mother of the Son of God.

Mass the most important sacramental celebration of the Church. The celebration of the Mass was established by Jesus at the Last Supper as a remembrance of his Death and Resurrection. At Mass we listen to God's Word from the Bible and receive the Body and Blood of Christ in Holy Communion.

Messiah a title that means "anointed with oil." It is from a Hebrew word that means the same as the Greek word *Christ*, the name given to Jesus after the Resurrection.

miracle act of wonder that cannot be explained by natural causes but is a work of God. In the Gospels, Jesus works miracles as a sign that the Kingdom of God is present in his ministry.

mission the work of Jesus Christ that is continued in the Church through the Holy Spirit. The mission of the Church is to proclaim salvation through Jesus' life, Death, and Resurrection.

moral choice a choice to do what is right. We make moral choices because they are what we believe God wants. We can make them because we have the freedom to choose what is right and avoid what is wrong.

moral law a rule for living that has been established by God and people in authority who are concerned about the good of all people. Moral laws are based on God's direction to us to do what is right and to avoid what is wrong.

mortal sin a serious decision to turn away from God by doing something that we know is wrong and so cuts us off from God's life

mystery a truth revealed by God that we cannot completely understand. The truth that the Son of God became man is a mystery of our faith.

❮ The Bible contains both the **Old Testament** and the **New Testament.**

Painting of **Pentecost,** St. Maron's Church, Minneapolis, Minnesota.

N

New Testament the 27 books of the second part of the Bible, which tell of the teaching, ministry, and saving events of the life of Jesus. The four Gospels present Jesus' life, Death, and Resurrection. The Acts of the Apostles tells the story of the message of salvation as it spreads through the growth of the Church. Various letters instruct us on how to live as followers of Jesus Christ. The Book of Revelation offers encouragement to Christians living through persecution.

O

obedience the act of willingly following what God asks us to do for our salvation. The Fourth Commandment requires children to obey their parents, and all people are required to obey civil authority when it acts for the good of all.

Old Testament the first 46 books of the Bible, which tell of God's covenant with the people of Israel and his plan for the salvation of all people. The first five books are known as the Torah. The Old Testament is fulfilled in the New Testament, but God's covenant presented in the Old Testament has permanent value and has never been revoked, or set aside.

Ordinary Time the part of the liturgical year outside of the seasons of feasts and the preparation for them. Ordinary means not common, but counted time, as in ordinal numbers. It is devoted to growth in understanding the mystery of Christ in its fullness. The color of Ordinary Time is green to symbolize growth.

Original Sin the result of the sin by which the first human beings disobeyed God and chose to follow their own will rather than God's will. Because of this act, all human beings lost the original blessing that God intended, and they became subject to sin and death. In Baptism we are restored to life with God through Jesus Christ.

P

parable one of the simple stories that Jesus told to show us what the Kingdom of God is like. Parables present images, or scenes, drawn from everyday life. These images show us the radical, or serious, choice we make when we respond to the invitation to enter the Kingdom of God.

John the Baptist was a **prophet.**

parish a community of believers in Jesus Christ who meet regularly in a specific area to worship God under the leadership of a pastor

Paschal Mystery the work of salvation accomplished by Jesus Christ through his passion, Death, Resurrection, and Ascension. The Paschal Mystery is celebrated in the liturgy of the Church. Its saving effects are experienced by us in the sacraments.

Passover the Jewish festival that commemorates the delivery of the Hebrew people from slavery in Egypt. In the Eucharist we celebrate our passover from death to life through Jesus' Death and Resurrection.

penance the turning away from sin because we want to live as God wants us to live (*See* Sacrament of Penance and Reconciliation.)

Pentecost the 50th day after Jesus was raised from the dead. On this day the Holy Spirit was sent from heaven, and the Church was born.

personal sin a sin we choose to commit, whether serious (mortal) or less serious (venial). Although the result of Original Sin is to leave us with a tendency to sin, God's grace, especially through the sacraments, helps us choose good over sin.

pope the Bishop of Rome, successor of Saint Peter, and leader of the Roman Catholic Church. Because he has the authority to act in the name of Christ, the pope is called the Vicar of Christ. The pope and all the bishops together make up the living, teaching office of the Church.

prayer the raising of our hearts and minds to God. We are able to speak to and listen to God in prayer because he teaches us how to do so.

prayer of petition a request of God asking him to fulfill a need. When we share in God's saving love, we understand that every need is one that we can ask God to help us with through petition.

precepts of the Church those positive requirements that the pastoral authority of the Church has determined as necessary. These requirements describe the minimum effort we must make in prayer and the moral life. The Precepts of the Church ensure that all Catholics move beyond the minimum by growing in love of God and love of neighbor.

priest a man who has accepted God's special call to serve the Church by guiding it and building it up through the celebration of the sacraments

prophet a person called by God to speak to the people for him. John the Baptist was a great prophet.

psalm a prayer in the form of a poem. Psalms were written to be sung in public worship. Each psalm expresses an aspect, or feature, of the depth of human prayer. Over several centuries 150 psalms were gathered to form the Book of Psalms, used in worship in Old Testament times.

purgatory a state of final cleansing after death of all our human imperfections to prepare us to enter into the joy of God's presence in heaven

R

reconciliation the renewal of friendship after that friendship has been broken by some action or lack of action. In the Sacrament of Penance and Reconciliation, through God's mercy and forgiveness, we are reconciled with God, the Church, and others.

Redeemer Jesus Christ, whose life, Death on the Cross, and Resurrection from the dead set us free from sin and bring us redemption.

Resurrection the bodily raising of Jesus Christ from the dead on the third day after his Death on the Cross. The Resurrection is the crowning truth of our faith.

Revelation God's communication of himself to us through the words and deeds he has used throughout history. Revelation shows us the mystery of his plan for our salvation in his Son, Jesus Christ.

Rosary a prayer in honor of the Blessed Virgin Mary. When we pray the Rosary, we meditate on the mysteries of Jesus Christ's life while praying the Hail Mary on five sets of 10 beads and the Lord's Prayer on the beads in between.

S

Sabbath the seventh day, when God rested after finishing the work of creation. The Third Commandment requires us to keep the Sabbath holy. For Christians Sunday became the Sabbath because it was the day Jesus rose from the dead and the new creation in Jesus Christ began.

sacrament one of seven ways through which God's life enters our lives through the work of the Holy Spirit. Jesus gave us three sacraments that bring us into the Church: Baptism, Confirmation, and the Eucharist. He gave us two sacraments that bring us healing: Penance and Anointing of the Sick. He also gave us two sacraments that help members serve the community: Matrimony and Holy Orders.

Sacrament of Penance and Reconciliation the sacrament in which we celebrate God's forgiveness of our sins and our reconciliation with God and the Church. Reconciliation includes sorrow for the sins we have committed, confession of sins, absolution by the priest, and doing the penance that shows our sorrow.

sacramental an object, a prayer, or a blessing given by the Church to help us grow in our spiritual life

sacrifice a gift given to God to give him thanks. Jesus' sacrifice on the Cross was the greatest sacrifice.

Sacrifice of the Mass the sacrifice of Jesus on the Cross, which is remembered and made present in the Eucharist

(At right) Baptism is a **sacrament.**

saint a holy person who has died and is united with God. The Church has said that this person is now with God forever in heaven.

salvation the gift of forgiveness of sin and the restoration of friendship with God. God alone can give us salvation.

Satan the leader of the evil spirits. His name means "adversary." God allows Satan to tempt us.

Savior Jesus, the Son of God, who became human to forgive our sins and restore our friendship with God. *Jesus* means "God saves."

Scripture the holy writings of Jews and Christians collected in the Old and New Testaments of the Bible

Sermon on the Mount the words of Jesus, written in chapters 5 through 7 of the Gospel of Matthew, in which Jesus reveals how he has fulfilled God's law given to Moses. The Sermon on the Mount begins with the eight Beatitudes and includes the Lord's Prayer.

sin a choice we make on purpose that offends God and hurts our relationships with other people. Some sin is mortal and needs to be confessed in the Sacrament of Penance and Reconciliation. Other sin is venial, or less serious.

Son of God the title revealed by Jesus that indicates his unique relationship to God the Father

soul the part of us that makes us human and an image of God. Body and soul together form one unique human nature. The soul is responsible for our consciousness and our freedom.

Spiritual Works of Mercy the kind acts through which we help our neighbors meet the needs that are more than material. The Spiritual Works of Mercy include counseling the doubtful, instructing the ignorant, admonishing sinners, comforting the afflicted, forgiving offenses, bearing wrongs patiently, and praying for the living and the dead.

synagogue the Jewish place of assembly for prayer, instruction, and study of the Law. Jesus attended the synagogue regularly to pray and to teach.

T

tabernacle a container in which the Blessed Sacrament is kept so that Holy Communion can be taken to the sick and the dying.

Temple the center of Jewish worship in Jerusalem where sacrifices were offered to God

temptation an attraction, from outside us or from inside us, that can lead us to not follow God's commands

Ten Commandments the 10 rules that God gave to Moses on Mount Sinai that sum up God's law and show us what is required to love God and our neighbor

Trinity the mystery of one God existing in three Persons: the Father, the Son, and the Holy Spirit.

V

venial sin a choice we make that weakens our relationship with God or other people. It wounds and diminishes the divine life in us.

W

witness the passing on to others, by our words and actions, the faith that we have been given. Every Christian has the duty to give witness to the good news about Jesus Christ that he or she has come to know.

worship the adoration and honor given to God in public prayer

Y

Yahweh the name of God in Hebrew, which God told Moses from the burning bush. *Yahweh* means "I am who am." Out of respect for God's name, Jews never say this name but replace it with other names.

Index

Son of God, 266
Sorrowful Mysteries, 243. *See also*
    Rosary
soul, 266
Spiritual Works of Mercy, 200, 205, 266
Stations of the Cross, 185, 228, 244
storytelling, family, 78a, 79b
suffering, comfort for those, 183, 184
synagogue, 266. *See also* Temple

T

tabernacle, 266
talent, 131
Temple, 92, 266
temptation, 266
Ten Commandments, 62, 63, 64, 65, 266.
    See also Commandments, Ten *for*
    specific commandments
Teresa of Ávila, Saint, 88
Teresa of Calcutta, Blessed, 58
Thanksgiving, 78d
Thérèse of Lisieux, Saint, 34a, 68, 195
Thomas, Saint, 6
Thomas Aquinas, Saint, 190
Triduum, 227. *See also* Easter
Trinity, 3, 266
truth
    Jesus suffers for, 158
    speaking, 157

V

venial sin, 48, 266
Veronica, 185, 244
virtue, 34d

W

witness, 266
Word of God, 113, 163
worship, 59, 266
    Eucharist, 53
    love, offered in, 54
    prayer as, 53
    service as, 53

Y

Yahweh, 266

Scripture Index

Art Credits

Page positions are abbreviated as follows: (t) top, (c) center, (b) bottom, (l) left, (r) right.

FRONT MATTER:
i Lori Lohstoeter. **iii**(t) © iStockphoto.com/keeweeboy; (c) Stockbyte/Getty Images; (bl) © iStockphoto.com/alohaspirit; (br) The Crosiers/Gene Plaisted, OSC. **iv**(t) Bronwyn Kidd/Digital Vision/Getty Images; (b) © iStockphoto.com/duncan1890. **v**(b) © iStockphoto.com/ManoAfrica. **vi**(c) Kraig Scarbinsky/Photodisc/Getty Images; (b) Digital Vision/Photodisc/Getty Images.

UNIT 1:
1–2 Mel Yates/Digital Vision/Getty Images. **3**(t) The Crosiers/Gene Plaisted, OSC; (b) Nancy R. Cohen/Digital Vision/Getty Images. **5** The Crosiers/Gene Plaisted, OSC. **6**(t) The Crosiers/Gene Plaisted, OSC; (b) © iStockphoto.com/Blacqbook. **7**(b) Kathryn Seckman Kirsch. **8** Siede Preis/Photodisc/Getty Images. **11**(t) The Crosiers/Gene Plaisted, OSC. **12–13** Dick Mlodock. **14**(b) The Crosiers/Gene Plaisted, OSC. **15** Stockbyte/Getty Images. **17** ColorBlind/Photodisc/Getty Images. **18** The Crosiers/Gene Plaisted, OSC. **19**(t) Digital Vision/Getty Images; (b) Gary Yeowell/The Image Bank/Getty Images. **20**(tl) The Crosiers/Gene Plaisted, OSC; (r) Media Color's/Alamy; (bl) Bill Wittman. **21**(t) The Crosiers/Gene Plaisted, OSC; (b) © iStockphoto.com/rarpia. **22** © iStockphoto.com/MattiaATH. **23** The Crosiers/Gene Plaisted, OSC. **24** Phil Martin Photography. **25** © iStockphoto.com/GlobalStock. **27**(b) The Crosiers/Gene Plaisted, OSC. **28**(t) C Squared Studios/Photodisc; (br) C Squared Studios/Photodisc. **29**(t) AgnusImages.com. **30–31** © iStockphoto.com/duncan1890. **33** © iStockphoto.com/fotoVoyager. **34** The Crosiers/Gene Plaisted, OSC. **34a**(t) Stockbyte/Getty; (b) The Crosiers/Gene Plaisted, OSC. **34b** The Crosiers/Gene Plaisted, OSC; Loyola Press Photography. **34d**(t) Ryan McVay/Photodisc/Getty Images; (ct) © iStockphoto.com/Gewitterkind; (cb) Dennis MacDonald/Alamy; (b) © iStockphoto.com/Renphoto.

UNIT 2:
35–36 Alistair Berg/Digital Vision/Getty Images. **37**(t) Digital Vision/Getty Images; (b) The Crosiers/Gene Plaisted, OSC. **38** Wiliam Gorman. **39**(t, b) Wiliam Gorman. **40** SW Productions/Photodisc/Getty Images. **42** © iStockphoto.com/Kameel. **43** Jupiterimages. **44** The Crosiers/Gene Plaisted, OSC. **45**(t) © iStockphoto.com/Fotogma; (b) William Gorman. **46**(c) Kathryn Seckman Kirsch; (b) The Crosiers/Gene Plaisted, OSC. **47** Phil Martin Photography. **48**(t) The Crosiers/Gene Plaisted, OSC; (b) Digital Vision/Veer. **49** (*Left top to bottom, Right top to bottom*) © iStockphoto.com/PhotoInc; © iStockphoto.com/bonniej; © iStockphoto.com/diane39, Ryan McVay/Photodisc/Getty Images. © iStockphoto.com/Pixlmaker; © iStockphoto.com/MsDancy; Royalty-free image; © iStockphoto.com/ronen; Digital Vision/Getty Images; Daniel Pangbourne/Digital Vision/Getty Images. **51** Dmitriy Shironosov/Alamy. **52** The Crosiers/Gene Plaisted, OSC. **53**(t, b) Bill Wittman. **54** Kathryn Seckman Kirsch. **55**(c) © iStockphoto.com/tzara; (b) Alloy Photography/Veer. **56**(bl) Kathryn Seckman Kirsch; (br) Daniel Allan/Digital Vision/Getty Images. **57**(tl) Digital Vision/Getty Images; (tc) Photos.com; (tr) © iStockphoto.com/JynMeyerDesign; (bl) © iStockphoto.com/delirium; (br) © iStockphoto.com/Kativ. **58** JP Laffont/Sygma/Corbis. **59** Phil Martin Photography. **60** The Crosiers/Gene Plaisted, OSC. **61**(t) The Crosiers/Gene Plaisted, OSC; (b) Stockbyte/Getty Images. **62** © iStockphoto.com/wrangel. **63** Dick Mlodock. **64**(t, b) The Crosiers/Gene Plaisted, OSC. **65** © iStockphoto.com/hdoddema. **66**(t) Kathryn Seckman Kirsch; (b) © iStockphoto.com/RBFried. **68** The Crosiers/Gene Plaisted, OSC. **69**(t) The Crosiers/Gene Plaisted, OSC; (b) Douglas Klauba. **70** The Crosiers/Gene Plaisted, OSC. **71**(t) DeAgostini/SuperStock. **72**(b) © iStockphoto.com/jane. **73**(t) © iStockphoto.com/Kativ; (c) Phil Martin Photography; (b) © iStockphoto.com/video1. **74–75** © iStockphoto.com/fotoVoyager. **76** Kathryn Seckman Kirsch. **77** Jupiterimages/Stockbyte/Thinkstock. **78** The Crosiers/Gene Plaisted, OSC. **78a**(t) Stockbyte/Getty Images; (b) Len Ebert/PC&F Inc. **78b** © iStockphoto.com/Skashkin. **78c** Kathryn Seckman Kirsch. **78d**(t) Purestock/Getty Images; (b) Kathryn Seckman Kirsch.

UNIT 3:
79–80 Blend Images/Veer. **81**(t) © iStockphoto.com/Maica; (b) Stockbyte/Getty. **82** fStop/Veer. **83**(tcl) © iStockphoto.com/Creativestock; (tcr) © iStockphoto.com/stocksnapper; (tr) © iStockphoto.com/arekmalang; (b) Fancy Photography/Veer. **84(t, c, bl)** The Crosiers/Gene Plaisted, OSC; Rafael Lopez. **85**(tl) Stockbyte/Getty Images; (tr) Bill Wittman; (bl) Bill Wittman; (br) Photos.com. **86** Stockbyte/Getty Images. **88** The Crosiers/Gene Plaisted, OSC. **89**(t) © iStockphoto.com/mandygodbehear; (b) The Crosiers/Gene Plaisted, OSC. **90**(b) © iStockphoto.com/barsik. **91** Robert Korta. **92**(t) Robert Korta. **93** Kathryn Seckman Kirsch. **94** © iStockphoto.com/stevenallan. **95** © iStockphoto.com/ideabug. **96** The Crosiers/Gene Plaisted, OSC. **97**(t) Bill Wittman; (b) The Crosiers/Gene Plaisted, OSC. **98**(t) © iStockphoto.com/Smileyjoanne; (b) Digital Vision/Getty Images. **99**(t) The Crosiers/Gene Plaisted, OSC; (b) © iStockphoto.com/jacomstephens. **100**(t, b) The Crosiers/Gene Plaisted, OSC. **101** Kathryn Seckman Kirsch. **104** The Crosiers/Gene Plaisted, OSC. **105**(t) © iStockphoto.com/Hallgerd; (c) © iStockphoto.com/alohaspirit; (b) Robert Korta. **106**(tl) © iStockphoto.com/tstajduhar; (tr) © iStockphoto.com/heniadis; (bl) © iStockphoto.com/donald_gruener; (cr) © iStockphoto.com/DwightLyman; (br) © iStockphoto.com/bobherbert. **107**(t) Photodisc/Getty Images; (b) © iStockphoto.com/PhotoEuphoria. **108** Karen Kouf. **109** Don Farrall/Photodisc/Getty Images. **110–111** © iStockphoto.com/alexsl. **112** Kathryn Seckman Kirsch. **113** Fancy Photography/Veer. **114** The Crosiers/Gene Plaisted, OSC. **114a** Photos.com. **114b** Kevin Peschke and Mia Basile McGloin. **114c** Per Magnus Persson/Veer. **114d** © iStockphoto.com/dsteller.

UNIT 4:
115–116 Stockbyte/Getty Images. **117**(t) The Crosiers/Gene Plaisted, OSC. **118**(t) Kathryn Seckman Kirsch and Robert Voights; (b) The Crosiers/Gene Plaisted, OSC. **119** Robert Korta. **120**(t) © iStockphoto.com/RonTech2000; (b) Kathryn Seckman Kirsch. **121** © iStockphoto.com/RonTech2000. **123** Wavebreakmedia Ltd/Thinkstock. **124** The Crosiers/Gene Plaisted, OSC. **125**(t) Bill Wittman; (cl) Bronwyn Kidd/Digital Vision/Getty Images; (cr) © iStockphoto.com; (bl) Photodisc/Getty Images; (br) © iStockphoto.com. **126**(t) Stockbyte/Getty Images; (b) © iStockphoto.com/digitalpretzel. **127**(t) Dick Mlodock; (b) Kathryn Seckman Kirsch. **128**(b) Dick Mlodock. **129**(tl) © iStockphoto.com; (tr) Ryan McVay/Photodisc/Getty Images; (c) Buccina Studios/Photodisc/Getty Images; (b) © iStockphoto.com/RUSSELLTATEdotCOM. **130** © iStockphoto.com/RichVintage. **131** Topic Photo Agency/Corbis. **132** The Crosiers/Gene Plaisted, OSC. **133**(t) © iStockphoto.com/Grafissimo; (b) The Crosiers/Gene Plaisted, OSC. **134**(t) The Crosiers/Gene Plaisted, OSC; (b) Bill Wittman. **135**(t) Ryan McVay/Photodisc/Getty Images; (b) © iStockphoto.com/Paigefalk. **136**(t) © iStockphoto.com. **137** Stuart O'Sullivan/Stone/Getty Images. **138** © iStockphoto.com. **139** Catalin Petolea/Alamy. **140** The Crosiers/Gene Plaisted, OSC. **141**(t) The Crosiers/Gene Plaisted, OSC. **142**(t) © iStockphoto.com/bonniej. **143** © iStockphoto.com/macrofocus. **144**(t) Getty Images/Handout/Archive Photos/Getty Images; (b) © iStockphoto.com/alexsl. **147** Warling Studios. **148** Zvonimir Atletic/Shutterstock. **149**(t) The Crosiers/Gene Plaisted, OSC; (b) © iStockphoto.com/caracterdesign. **150**(t) The Crosiers/Gene Plaisted, OSC; (b) © iStockphoto.com/Elenathewise. **151** © iStockphoto.com/samgrandy. **152**(t) © iStockphoto.com/highhorse; (b) The Crosiers/Gene Plaisted, OSC. **153** The Barron Prize. **155** Push Pictures/Corbis. **156** Courtesy of Institute of the Brothers of the Christian Schools. **157**(t) © iStockphoto.com/mammamaart; (b) Bill Wittman. **158** Robert Korta. **159**(t) Dick Mlodock. **160**(r) © iStockphoto.com. **161** Lois Axeman. **163** Fuse/Thinkstock. **164** The Crosiers/Gene Plaisted, OSC. **165**(t) © iStockphoto.com/pjjones;

(b) The Crosiers/Gene Plaisted, OSC. **166** Robert Voights and Kathryn Seckman Kirsch. **170** Phil Martin Photography. **171** Jose Luis Pelaez, Inc./Blend Images/Corbis. **172** The Crosiers/Gene Plaisted, OSC. **172b**(t) © iStockphoto.com/FrankyDeMeyer; (c) The Crosiers/Gene Plaisted, OSC. **172c**(t) © iStockphoto.com/gabyjalbert; (ct) Photos.com; (c) © iStockphoto.com/rainyk; (cb) © iStockphoto.com/djeecee; (b) Digital Vision/Getty Images. **172d**(tl) © iStockphoto.com; (tr) © iStockphoto.com/sonyae; (c) The Crosiers/Gene Plaisted, OSC; (b) © iStockphoto.com/duckycards.

UNIT 5:

173–174 Ocean Photography/Veer. **175**(t) © iStockphoto.com; (b) Dick Mlodock. **176**(t) The Crosiers/Gene Plaisted, OSC; (cl) Jeff Greenberg/PhotoEdit; (r, bl) Bill Wittman. **177** William Gorman. **178** The Crosiers/Gene Plaisted, OSC. **179** © iStockphoto.com/kenpix. **181** © iStockphoto.com/Alina555. **182** The Crosiers/Gene Plaisted, OSC. **183**(t, b) The Crosiers/Gene Plaisted, OSC. **184**(t) Dick Mlodock; (b) © iStockphoto.com/spfoto. **185**(t) © iStockphoto.com/cobalt; (b) The Crosiers/Gene Plaisted, OSC. **186** The Crosiers/Gene Plaisted, OSC. **187** Kathryn Seckman Kirsch. **190** The Crosiers/Gene Plaisted, OSC. **191**(t, b) The Crosiers/Gene Plaisted, OSC. **192** William Gorman. **193**(l) Mary Wilshire; (r) Stockbyte/Getty Images. **194** Dick Mlodock. **195**(t, c, b) The Crosiers/Gene Plaisted, OSC. **196** The Crosiers/Gene Plaisted, OSC. **198** Rafael Lopez. **199**(t) The Crosiers/Gene Plaisted, OSC; (b) © iStockphoto.com/ALSOMUS. **200** The Crosiers/Gene Plaisted, OSC. **201**(t) Bill Wittman; (b) The Crosiers/Gene Plaisted, OSC. **202**(t) John Howard/Getty Images; (b) © iStockphoto.com/Graffizone. **203** Robert Voights. **204** The Crosiers/Gene Plaisted, OSC. **205** © iStockphoto.com/GlobalStock. **206** The Crosiers/Gene Plaisted, OSC. **207**(t) Digital Vision/Getty Images; (c) The Crosiers/Gene Plaisted, OSC; (b) © iStockphoto.com/philberndt. **208** Mike Watson. **210**(l) © iStockphoto.com/theboone; (r) © iStockphoto.com. **211–213** © iStockphoto.com/pianoman. **215** Apollofoto/Shutterstock. **216** Warling Studios. **216a** Yoshikazu Tsuno/AFP/Getty Images; © iStockphoto.com/iamagoo. **216b**(t) Kathryn Seckman Kirsch and George Hamblin/Steve Edsey & Sons; (br) © iStockphoto.com/paulaphoto. **216c** Digital Vision/Getty Images. **216d** Kathryn Seckman Kirsch.

SPECIAL SEASONS AND LESSONS:

217(t) © iStockphoto.com/klikk; (c) The Crosiers/Gene Plaisted, OSC. **218** Susan Tolonen. **219** The Crosiers/Gene Plaisted, OSC. **220** The Crosiers/Gene Plaisted, OSC. **221**(l, r) Kathryn Seckman Kirsch. **223** The Crosiers/Gene Plaisted, OSC. **224** © iStockphoto.com. **225** Kathryn Seckman Kirsch. **226** © iStockphoto.com. **227**(t) © iStockphoto.com/klikk; (b) The Crosiers/Gene Plaisted, OSC. **228**(tl) Digital Vision/Getty Images; (tc) © iStockphoto.com/bonniej; (tr) Ryan McVay/Photodisc/Getty Images; (bl) © iStockphoto.com/rayna; (bc) Ryan McVay/Photodisc/Getty Images; (br) © iStockphoto.com/keeweeboy. **229**(t) The Crosiers/Gene Plaisted, OSC. **230**(t) Bill Wittman; (b) © iStockphoto.com. **231**(t) The Crosiers/Gene Plaisted, OSC.

WHAT CATHOLICS SHOULD KNOW:

233 © iStockphoto.com/abalcazar. **234**(t) © iStockphoto.com/colevineyard; (b) PhotoEdit.com. **235**(t) Stockbyte/Getty Images; (b) Lon C. Diehl/PhotoEdit. **236**(t) Stockbyte/Getty Images; (b) The Crosiers/Gene Plaisted, OSC. **238**(b) © iStockphoto.com/Pixlmaker. **239** The Crosiers/Gene Plaisted, OSC. **240**(t) vario images GmbH & Co.KG/Alamy; (b) Myrleen Pearson/PhotoEdit. **241**(t) The Crosiers/Gene Plaisted, OSC; (b) Design Pics/Fotosearch. **242** Greg Kuepfer. **243**(t) CSI Productions/Alamy. **244** From Fourteen Mosaic Stations of the Cross © Our Lady of the Angels Monastery Inc., Hanceville Alabama. All Rights Reserved. **245**(t) © iStockphoto.com/TerryHealy; (b) Greg Kuepfer. **247**(t) Myrleen Pearson/PhotoEdit; (b) The Crosiers/Gene Plaisted, OSC. **248**(l) Stockbyte/Getty Images; (tr) Myrleen Pearson/PhotoEdit; (br) AgnusImages.com. **249** Stock Montage, Inc/Alamy. **250**(t) Richard T. Nowitz/Corbis; (b) The Crosiers/Gene Plaisted, OSC. **252** Myrleen Pearson/PhotoEdit. **253**(b) Myrleen Pearson/PhotoEdit. **255** Jeff Greenberg/PhotoEdit.

GLOSSARY:

257 The Crosiers/Gene Plaisted, OSC. **259** JLP/Deimos/Corbis. **261** The Crosiers/Gene Plaisted, OSC. **263** The Crosiers/Gene Plaisted, OSC. **264** The Crosiers/Gene Plaisted, OSC. **265** Digital Vision/Getty Images.

LESSON CUTOUTS AND PULLOUTS:

275(t) Kathryn Seckman Kirsch; (c) The Crosiers/Gene Plaisted, OSC; (b) Kathryn Seckman Kirsch.
Way of the Cross Booklet (stations): Nan Brooks.
Reconciliation Booklet (3): The Crosiers/Gene Plaisted, OSC; © iStockphoto.com/KosherDiva; Kathryn Seckman Kirsch.
Walking with Jesus Booklet: (cover) The Crosiers/Gene Plaisted, OSC;© iStockphoto.com/caracterdesign; © iStockphoto.com/Marti157900.
Walking with Jesus Booklet: Kathryn Seckman Kirsch; © iStockphoto.com/jamesmacallister; © iStockphoto.com/rzdeb; © iStockphoto.comLPETTET. Kathryn Seckman Kirsch; Con Tanasiuk/Design Pics/Corbis.
Along the Way of Holiness: Kathryn Seckman Kirsch.
Advent Calendar: Kathryn Seckman Kirsch.

Lesson Cutouts and Pullouts

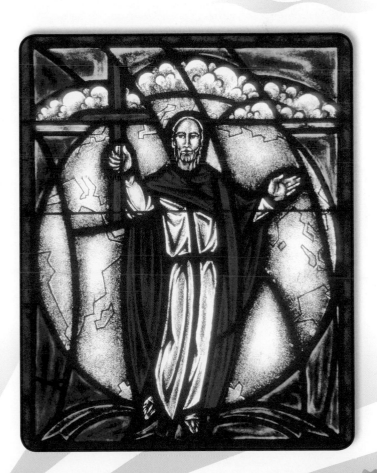

- Act of Faith Card

- Jesus Card

- VIP Shield

- Christ Candle

- My Way of the Cross Booklet

- I Celebrate the Sacrament of Reconciliation Booklet

- Walking with Jesus Booklet

- Along the Way of Holiness

- Advent Calendar

Act of Faith

O my God, I firmly believe

that you are one God in three divine Persons,

Father, Son, and Holy Spirit.

I believe that your divine Son became man

and died for our sins and that he will come

to judge the living and the dead.

I believe these and all the truths

which the Holy Catholic Church teaches

because you have revealed them

who are eternal truth and wisdom,

who can neither deceive nor be deceived.

In this faith I intend to live and die.

Amen

Chapter 1

Fold back.

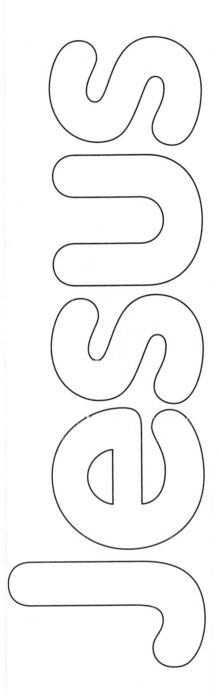

Chapter 11

Cut.

Chapter 13

Cut along candle to fold line.

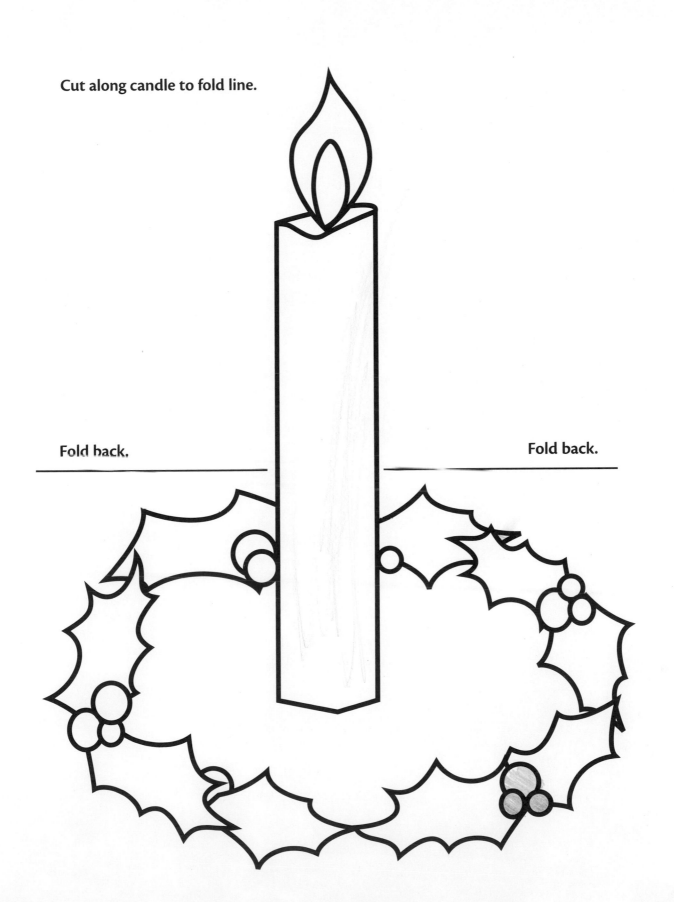

Fold back.   Fold back.

Christmas

Jesus Rises from the Dead

Jesus is our Savior. His death destroyed the power of sin and death. His Resurrection gave us new life— a never-ending life of glory with God.

Think. Do my words and actions tell others that I am a child of God?

Pray. Heavenly Father, help me to do everything to bring others to you. Let me grow each day in the new life Jesus offers me.

My Way of the Cross Booklet

God, our Father, you sent Jesus, your Son, to bring us to eternal life with you. Jesus loves you, and he loves me so much that he was willing to suffer and die. Help me to love you and all people as Jesus does, and to follow him on the Way of the Cross. Amen.

This booklet belongs to

Thirteenth Station

Jesus Is Taken Down from the Cross

Friends of Jesus gently took his lifeless body from the cross. They laid it in the arms of Mary, his Mother.

Think. Do I respect the bodies of others as temples of God?

Pray. Dear Jesus, show me how to be kind and gentle. Teach me how to care for others.

Second Station

Jesus Is Made to Carry His Cross

Jesus did not complain when the heavy cross was laid upon his shoulders.

Think. Do I love God and others enough to do what is good, even when I do not feel like doing it?

Pray. I want to follow you, Jesus. Help me to carry my cross.

First Station

Jesus Is Condemned to Death

Jesus had done nothing wrong but was condemned to death. Pilate knew that Jesus was innocent, but he thought the crowds would turn against him if he set Jesus free.

Think. When others do wrong, do I join them?

Pray. Help me, Jesus, to be fair and to do what is right.

2

Fourteenth Station

Jesus Is Placed in the Tomb

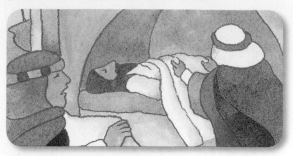

A friend of Jesus' offered to bury his body in the tomb prepared for his own death.

Think. What am I willing to share with others today?

Pray. Dear Jesus, help me to follow you faithfully, even when I am frightened and lonely.

15

Third Station

Jesus Falls the First Time

Jesus was weak and tired. The cross was heavy, and he fell. Soldiers shouted at him to get up, but no one came to help him.

Think. Who needs my help in carrying a cross today?

Pray. Dear Jesus, help me to be kind to those in need.

4

Twelfth Station

Jesus Dies on the Cross

Jesus suffered for three long hours on the cross. He forgave those who hurt him, and he gave us his Mother to care for us.

Think. Am I willing to forgive others, even those who have hurt me?

Pray. I adore you, O Christ, and I bless you, because by your holy cross, you have redeemed the world.

13

Eleventh Station

Jesus Is Nailed to the Cross

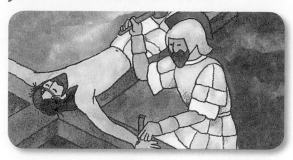

Jesus' hands and feet were nailed to the cross. How greatly he suffered to free us from sin! But he did not cry out in pain.

Think. Do I control myself when I am angry?

Pray. Dear Jesus, help me when I am treated unfairly.

12

Fourth Station

Jesus Meets His Mother

It was hard for Mary to see her Son suffering, but she followed Jesus all the way to Calvary. She was willing to suffer with him.

Think. How can I help my parents today?

Pray. Mary, Mother of Sorrows, pray for my family. Help us to love Jesus more each day.

5

Ninth Station

Jesus Falls the Third Time

A third time Jesus fell beneath the heavy cross. He was worn out, but he struggled back to his feet to free us from the power of sin.

Think. Does my example help others to do the right thing?

Pray. Dear Jesus, give everyone who is tired and discouraged the strength to follow you.

10

Sixth Station

Veronica Wipes the Face of Jesus

The holy woman Veronica wanted to help Jesus. She pushed her way past the soldiers to wipe the face of Jesus.

Think. Who might need my kindness today?

Pray. Dear Jesus, help me choose to help others, even when I must stand alone.

7

Fifth Station

Simon Helps Jesus Carry His Cross

Simon of Cyrene was forced to help Jesus carry his cross. When Simon took up the cross, Jesus' pain was a little less.

Think. How can I help someone today?

Pray. Jesus, I could not help you carry your cross, but whatever I do to others I do to you. Help me to be kind and helpful.

Tenth Station

Jesus Is Stripped of His Clothes

The soldiers roughly tore the clothes from Jesus' body. They did not care how they made Jesus feel.

Think. Do I treat people with respect?

Pray. Dear Jesus, help me to be respectful to others in all I think, do, and say.

Seventh Station

Jesus Falls the Second Time

Jesus fell a second time under his heavy cross, but he did not give up. Again he lifted the cross and continued on his way.

Think. When something is difficult, do I just give up?

Pray. Dear Jesus, help me when I am discouraged and feel weak. I want to follow you in everything I do.

Eighth Station

Jesus Meets the Women of Jerusalem

Some women wept when they saw Jesus suffering as he carried his cross. Jesus looked at the women kindly and asked them not to cry for him. Even in his suffering, Jesus thought of others.

Think. How can I help people when they are sad?

Pray. Dear Jesus, help me comfort those who are sad. Teach me what to say.

How Much Have I Loved Others?

- Have I obeyed my parents and others who take their place? How have I shown them my love by my words and actions?

- How have I cared for the gifts of life? Have I been kind to everyone in my family? to others? Have I hurt anyone by something I have said or done?

- Have I shown respect for my body and those of others? Have my thoughts, words, and actions been pure?

- How well have I cared for all that God has given me? Have I been careful with or damaged the things of others?

- Have I been honest? Have I returned what I borrowed? Have I taken something that was not mine?

- Have I spoken the truth? Have I kept private information of others to myself? Have I kept all my promises?

6

Jesus and the Sinful Woman

One day Jesus was invited out for a meal. While Jesus and the other guests were eating, a sinful woman came to tell Jesus she was sorry.

The sinful woman went to Jesus and wept. Her tears fell on his feet, and she wiped them away with her long hair. Jesus looked at her with love. He knew how sorry she was and how much she loved him.

3

5. Confess Your Sins to the Priest

- Greet the priest when he welcomes you.
- Make the Sign of the Cross.
- The priest may read God's Word with you.
- Listen while the priest asks God to help you make a good confession.
- Confess your sins. You may begin by saying how long it has been since your last confession.
- Listen to the penance the priest gives you. Pray an Act of Contrition.
- Say "Amen" after the priest prays the words of absolution.

6. Thank God for His Forgiving Love

Priest: Give thanks to the Lord, for he is good.

You: His mercy endures forever.

Do the penance you were given as soon as you can.

8

I Celebrate the Sacrament of Reconciliation

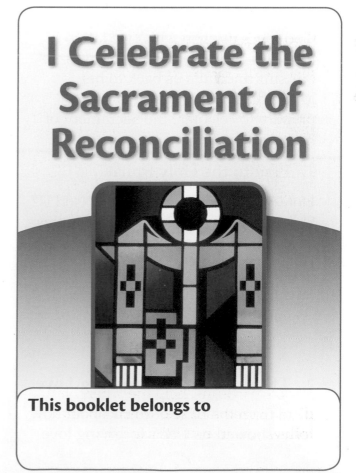

This booklet belongs to

Jesus said, "Her many sins have been forgiven, so she has shown great love."

Then Jesus spoke to the woman and said, "Your sins are forgiven. Your faith has saved you. Go in peace."

adapted from Luke 7:47–50

The woman's heart was filled with peace and joy.

If we confess our sins, then God, who is faithful and just, will forgive them. He will cleanse us from every wrongdoing.

adapted from 1 John 1:9

3. Examine Your Conscience

We examine our consciences to find out how we have loved God and others. We ask ourselves how we have kept God's commandments.

How Much Have I Loved God?

- Have I remembered to speak to God in prayer each morning and evening? How well have I prayed?
- Have I always used God's name with love and respect?
- Have I celebrated the Eucharist on Sunday (or Saturday evening) and holy days? How well have I prayed and sung during Mass? Have I been on time?
- Have I thanked God for his goodness?
- Have I told God I was sorry when I have sinned?
- Have I often asked God to help me?

God loves us even when we fail to love him and others. God forgives our sins and calls us back to his love. This booklet will help you prepare to celebrate the Sacrament of Reconciliation.

1. Pray to the Holy Spirit

Holy Spirit, show me how good God is. Show me how I can love God and others as Jesus did. Show me how I have failed. Help me to be sorry for my sins.

> *Verse.* Come, Holy Spirit, fill the hearts of your faithful.
> *Response.* And kindle in them the fire of your love.

2. Think of God's Forgiving Love

Read from the Bible or think about how Jesus showed us God's forgiving love.

4. Pray an Act of Contrition

We tell God that we are sorry for our sins when we pray an Act of Contrition.

O my God, I am heartily sorry for having offended Thee, and I detest all my sins because of thy just punishments, but most of all because they offend Thee, my God, who art all good and deserving of all my love. I firmly resolve with the help of Thy grace to sin no more and to avoid the near occasion of sin. Amen.

Ask God to help you think of some way to show that you are really sorry.

A Final Scripture Story

The collectors of the temple tax came to Peter and said, "Doesn't Jesus pay the temple tax?"

"Yes," Peter said.

When Peter came into the house, before he had time to speak, Jesus asked him: "What is your opinion? From whom do the kings take taxes? From their subjects or from foreigners?"

Peter said, "From foreigners."

Jesus said, "Then the subjects need not pay. But so that we may not offend them, go to the sea, drop in a hook, and take the first fish that comes up. Open its mouth and you will find a coin worth twice the temple tax. Give that to them for me and for you."

adapted from Matthew 17:24–27

Did Jesus have to pay the temple tax? Why did he pay it? Why do you think Jesus sent Peter to fish for the tax?

What does this story tell us about Jesus? What does it tell us about Peter?

Talk to Jesus about obeying your parents and others who care for you.

12

Walking with Jesus

A Scripture Prayer Booklet

This booklet belongs to

*Blessed are the peacemakers,
for they will be called
children of God.*

Matthew 5:9

Read. Let us then pursue what leads to peace and to building up one another. (Romans 14:19)

Think. Saint Paul tells us to pursue, or "go after," what leads to peace. What will lead to peace when somebody calls me a name? when a bully tries to pick a fight with me? when my brother or sister and I argue about doing some chore?

Pray. Jesus, King of Peace, fill me with your peace. Help me to be at peace and to spread your peace to others. [Add your own words. Speak to Jesus.]

Act. How can I be a peacemaker at school? at home? in my neighborhood?

Your turn! Would you like to present another beatitude as these two have been? Try it!

11

At Baptism, you received a special invitation to heaven. But how do you get there? Saint Thomas asked that question at the Last Supper: "How can we know the way?" Jesus' answer was also meant for us.

I am the way and the truth and the life. No one comes to the Father except through me.

John 14:6

Who is our way to the Father? _____

Through Scripture activities in this booklet, you will learn how to walk with Jesus.

Fill in the missing words in this poem-prayer:

Dear Jesus,

If you walk with me,

Happy will I _____!

I'll try to be like you

In everything I _____.

Love, _____

2

Along the Beatitude Way

Read the "footprints" and follow the directions. Each time you do what you decided, color a flower petal.

Blessed are the poor in spirit, for theirs is the kingdom of heaven.

Matthew 5:3

PEACE

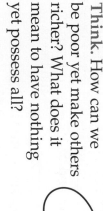

Read. We are treated as . . . poor yet enriching many; as having nothing and yet possessing all things. (2 Corinthians 6:8–10)

Think. How can we be poor yet make others richer? What does it mean to have nothing yet possess all?

Pray. Jesus, make me poor in spirit, that I may want heavenly instead of earthly things. [Add your own words. Talk to Jesus.]

Act. What can I give someone today that won't cost me anything but will enrich that person? [A smile?]

Along the Way of God's Word

Let the word of Christ dwell in you richly . . .

Colossians 3:16

Choose a verse here and let it dwell in you. Think about it, pray about it, and learn it by heart. Then color the heart near that verse.

♡ Your love for me is great . . .
Psalm 86:13

♡ Envy and anger shorten one's life . . . .
Sirach 30:24

♡ Happy are those . . . who seek the Lord with all their heart.
Psalm 119:2

♡ You are the salt of the earth.
Matthew 5:13

♡ This I command you: love one another.
John 15:17

♡ For the wages of sin is death, but the gift of God is eternal life in Christ Jesus our Lord.
Romans 6:23

♡ Cast all your worries upon him because he cares for you.
1 Peter 5:7

♡ Do not be conquered by evil but conquer evil with good.
Romans 12:21

♡ Rejoice in the Lord always.
Philippians 4:4

♡ Do you not realize that Jesus Christ is in you?
2 Corinthians 13:5

Read. "The second is like it: You shall love your neighbor as yourself." (Matthew 22:39)

Think. The second greatest commandment includes the Fourth through Tenth Commandments. Finish the summaries of these commandments:

Fourth: O _____, love, and respect your parents.

Fifth: Respect l _____, your own and that of others.

Sixth and Ninth: Be faithful and p _____ in thought, word, and action; respect your b _____ and others'.

Eighth: Be t _____ in what you say and do; respect the t _____.

Seventh and Tenth: Be fair and h _____ in dealing with others; respect your p _____ and theirs.

What word appears in every summary? _____

Pray. Dear Lord, thank you for making me and giving me so many gifts. [Name some.] Thank you for my family and friends, and all of their gifts. Help me to respect myself and others. [Add your own words. Talk to Jesus.]

Act. What do I need to do to show more respect for myself? How can I show more respect for my family? What can I do to show more respect for friends, classmates, and others (maybe someone I have not treated kindly)?

Along the Way of Forgiveness

"What woman having ten coins and losing one would not light a lamp and sweep the house, searching carefully until she finds it? And when she does find it, she calls together her friends and neighbors and says to them, 'Rejoice with me because I have found the coin that I lost.' In just the same way, I tell you, there will be rejoicing among the angels of God over one sinner who repents."

Luke 15:8–10

God looks for sinners the way the woman looked for her lost coin.

Did you ever lose something? How did you feel?

How do you think Jesus feels when a person he loves, and even died for, turns away from him?

Talk to God about his love for sinners like you. Ask for the grace to forgive sinners as God forgives them.

Plan to celebrate the Sacrament of Reconciliation soon.

Along the Way of the Commandments

Read. You shall love the Lord, your God, with all your heart, with all your soul, and with all your mind. This is the greatest and the first commandment.

Matthew 22:37–38

Think. The first and greatest commandment Jesus gave us combines the first three of the Ten Commandments. Do you recall what these are? This little verse will help you.

First: I must honor God;
Second: honor his name;
Third: keep the Lord's Day holy—
That will be my aim!

Pray. Loving Jesus, help me to show my love for you, your Father, and the Holy Spirit by honoring you and God's name and by worshiping and praying to you. [Add your own words. Speak to Jesus.]

Act. Decide on a special way to show your love for God—in prayer, by honoring God's name, and through worship.

Along the Way of the Eucharist

. . . the Lord Jesus, on the night he was handed over, took bread, and after he had given thanks, broke it and said, "This is my body that is for you. Do this in remembrance of me."

1 Corinthians 11:23–24

Think about the wonderful gift of the Eucharist. God feeds us at Mass with his Word and with himself. Pay close attention to the readings for two Sundays. Then answer these questions.

Sunday 1
What was one important idea in the readings?
_____

What was one good thought you heard in the Homily?
_____

Sunday 2
What message in the readings did you hear?
_____

What new idea did you hear in the Homily?
_____

Try to form the habit of reading Scripture at least five minutes every Sunday to celebrate the Lord's Day!

Along the Way of Holiness

Use this calendar for a month to help you live out the Word of God.
Ask someone to help you find the passage for the day. When you
have read it and have done what is suggested, put a star in the circle.

Sunday	Monday	Tuesday	Wednesday	Thursday	Friday	Saturday
○ Try to remember one good thought from the readings at Sunday Mass.	○ *Eph 1:1–2* Be kind to everyone you meet today.	○ *Col 3:15* Thank your parents or teacher for something.	○ *Mt 5:44* Forgive someone who has hurt you. Say a prayer for that person.	○ *Sir 6:14* Tell your best friend what makes him or her special.	○ *Phil 4:4* Smile at everyone you meet.	○ *1 Thes 5:18* List things that happened to you lately and thank God for them.
○ Tell someone about the readings or the Homily from the Sunday Mass.	○ *Jas 2:15–17* Give your allowance to a group that helps those who are needy.	○ *Eph 4:25* Decide always to tell the truth. Ask God to help you.	○ *Ps 139:13–14* Thank God for the gift of life.	○ *Col 3:17* Do your homework extra well for the Lord.	○ *Phil 4:6* Pray about something that is worrying you.	○ *Pro 15:1* Answer politely your parents and others who care for you.
○ Discuss the Homily with someone.	○ *Jn 3:16* Memorize this verse and thank God for his love.	○ *Mt 5:16* Help with dinner, set the table, or wash the dishes.	○ *Ps 98:1* Sing a song for the Lord or write your own psalm.	○ *Ti 3:1* Obey all the rules, even the little ones.	○ *Heb 13:2* Invite someone to your home or to do something with you.	○ *Mt 6:6* Spend an extra five minutes in quiet prayer in your room.
○ Memorize a verse or two from the Sunday readings.	○ *Mt 25:40* Help a friend with a chore or with homework.	○ *Col 3:12* Say nice things about other people.	○ *Ps 136:1* List good things that God has given you. Thank God.	○ *Rom 12:17* Ask God to help you love as God loves us.	○ *1 Thes 5:11* Put a thank-you note to a family member where he or she will find it.	○ *Lk 6:38* Make a bookmark with God is good on it and give it to someone.

Advent Calendar

	Monday	Tuesday	Wednesday	Thursday	Friday	Saturday
First Week of Advent **Prayer:** *To you, my God, I lift my soul. I trust in you.*	Mary and Joseph lived happily in Nazareth, doing their daily work with joy. *I will do my daily work well today, and with joy—for God.*	Joseph received the order from the Roman ruler to go to Bethlehem and register. *I will respect my parents, teachers, and others in authority.*	Mary and Joseph got their house ready and packed what they would need for the trip. *I will not complain today, even if I must do things I do not like.*	Mary and Joseph traveled by donkey. *I will be satisfied with the things I have and not ask for things that I do not need.*	Mary and Joseph ate the same food that the poor people ate on their journey. *I will eat healthful foods today rather than those that are not good for me. I will thank God for the food I have and pray for those who are hungry.*	After traveling all day, Mary and Joseph shared a meal and found a place to rest. *I will do something special to bring joy to my parents and family today.*
Second Week of Advent **Prayer:** *Come, Lord Jesus, and save all the nations.*	Mary and Joseph traveled with many different people on their way to Bethlehem. *I will be kind to all I meet today—and in a special way to someone I do not like.*	Mary and Joseph were very tired at the end of the day because travel was uncomfortable and hard. *I will help my parents with some chores to give them time to relax after a long day's work.*	When Mary and Joseph reached Bethlehem, they were pushed and pressed by the crowd. They tried to stay calm. *I will keep calm and not lose my temper when I am pushed or treated rudely.*	Joseph and Mary looked for a clean, comfortable place to stay. *I will honor Mary in a special way today by being cheerful. I will pray the Joyful Mysteries of the Rosary.*	Joseph and Mary went from door to door, but in every place they heard "No room!" *I will make room in my heart for others and will try to show special love for someone who seems lonely or unhappy.*	Mary and Joseph tried not to be discouraged when told there was no room. Many people would have liked to help. *I will ask Mary to help me make room for Jesus in my heart by doing what he wants me to do.*

O Come, Jesus

Third Week of Advent

Prayer: *I will be happy, O Lord, for you are near!*

Monday	**Tuesday**	**Wednesday**	**Thursday**	**Friday**	**Saturday**	
Mary and Joseph were offered only a stable to stay in. They accepted gratefully.	The animals helped to warm the stable by being there.	Joseph cleaned the stable for Mary and for Jesus, who would soon be born.	Joseph and Mary put fresh straw in the manger to make a bed for the Christ Child.	Joseph and Mary tried to make the stable clothes that would keep the baby Jesus warm.	Mary unpacked the swaddling clothes that would keep the baby Jesus warm.	
I will show gratitude for the kindness shown to me today.	*I will share the warmth of my friendship with others, especially with someone I do not like.*	*I will keep my heart pure today by thinking, doing, and speaking only kind things.*	*I will brighten the day for others by smiling and showing how happy I am that Jesus is coming.*	*I will secretly do a kind act for someone who is not very friendly toward me.*	*I will warm my heart with love for Jesus by doing a kind act for everyone in my family.*	

Fourth Week of Advent

Prayer: *Come, Emmanuel; come, O ransom captive Israel!*

Monday	**Tuesday**	**Wednesday**	**Thursday**	**Friday/ Saturday**	**Christmas Day**
Mary and Joseph waited patiently for the coming of Jesus.	Mary and Joseph thanked God for a safe trip and for the stable to stay in.	Mary and Joseph were at peace because they trusted God to care for them.	A beautiful, very bright star shone in the night sky over the stable.	Mary and Joseph prepared for the coming of Jesus.	Mary and Joseph welcomed Jesus with great love!
I will try to be patient today, especially when others keep me waiting or do things that bother me.	*I will thank God for all he gives me. I will show my parents I am grateful for all they do for me.*	*I will trust God to help me today to be a peacemaker in school and at home.*	*I will bring the brightness of joy to everyone I meet today.*	*I will be helpful at home on these last days before Jesus' birthday.*	*I will also welcome Jesus with great love and offer him all my good acts and prayers during the weeks of Advent.*